Safe Spaces

Creating a Psychosocially Safe Workplace

Lisa McAdams

Cover and design layout by: Eled Cernik

Table of Contents

Dedication

To my children Lucy and Matthew
for being my WHY however tough the how.
I am so proud of who you are becoming.

Acknowledgements

A sincere thank you to **Victoria Butt** from Parity Consulting for your invaluable advice and thoughtful feedback over the years. Your insights have been instrumental in shaping this journey, and your unwavering support has made a lasting impact. I am deeply grateful for your wisdom and guidance, which have helped bring this book to life. Thank you also for holding the event to launch this book—your belief in this project and the work I do means more than words can express.

With deep gratitude, I thank you **Simone Allan** for your generous support and sponsorship, making it possible to bring this book to life and share it with the world. I am honoured to serve as an ambassador for the Women's Resilience Centre and proud to align with its mission of empowering and uplifting women.

Meeting **Rob Caslick** and becoming an ambassador for Two Good Co. has been a truly life-changing experience. Your incredible sponsorship and unwavering support over the last nine years have made this journey possible. Your belief in this mission has been invaluable, and your dedication to social impact continues to inspire me. I am deeply grateful for our partnership and honoured to walk alongside you in creating safer, more inclusive workplaces.

A special thank you to **Suzie Barnett** from Two Good Co. for being an incredible mentor, a trusted guide, and a constant source of wisdom throughout this journey. Your unwavering support has been invaluable, and I am deeply grateful for your thoughtful review of this book. Your insights, encouragement, and belief in my work have made a profound difference. Thank you for standing by me every step of the way.

Thank you to **Maureen Kyne** Upward Bullying Expert for your thoughtful review and your generosity in sharing your professional knowledge over the past decade. Your insights and expertise have been instrumental in my growth, both personally and professionally. The confidence of knowing your advice was just a phone call away has been invaluable, allowing me to build my business and expand my knowledge with assurance. Your mentorship has made a lasting impact, and I am truly grateful for your unwavering support throughout this journey.

A sincere thank you to **Alison Flemming** for her thoughtful review and her unwavering belief in the work I do. Your support and encouragement have been invaluable, and your faith in this mission has inspired me to continue pushing forward. I am deeply grateful for your contribution to this journey.

About Safe Space Workplace

Safe Space Workplace was founded by Lisa McAdams with a clear and compelling mission: to transform workplaces into environments where every individual feels safe, valued, and supported. As an industry leader in creating psychosocially safe workplaces, Safe Space Workplace is dedicated to eradicating toxic work environments and fostering cultures of respect, diversity, equity, inclusion and empathy.

Our work centres around implementing comprehensive strategies that address the root causes of workplace toxicity, including domestic and family violence (DFV), mental health challenges, and difficult interpersonal dynamics. Through tailored training programs, robust policy development, and ongoing support, Safe Space Workplace empowers organisations to take proactive steps toward enhancing employee well-being, reducing risk, and improving overall performance.

At Safe Space Workplace, we believe that a healthy work environment is not just a nice-to-have, but a fundamental right. Our commitment is to work closely with organisations to ensure that they not only comply with legal and ethical standards but also thrive by embracing the principles of psychosocial safety. By partnering with Safe Space Workplace, companies are investing in their most valuable asset—their people—and paving the way for a brighter, more sustainable future.

About Lisa McAdams

Lisa McAdams is a visionary leader and dedicated advocate for creating psychosocially safe workplaces. As the founder and director of Safe Space Workplace, Lisa has committed her career to fostering environments where employees can thrive free from the detrimental effects of toxic behaviours and unsafe conditions.

Lisa's journey began with a deep-seated passion for DFV support and well-being. Her extensive background in working in corporate finance provided her with a unique perspective on the challenges that workplaces face regarding employee safety and well-being. Recognising the pervasive issues of DFV and the critical need for mental health initiatives, Lisa established Safe Space Workplace in 2015 with a mission to address these challenges head-on.

Under Lisa's leadership, Safe Space Workplace has become a beacon of hope and change for organisations striving to improve their work environments. Her approach is holistic, focusing not only on identifying and mitigating psychosocial hazards but also on building a culture of empathy, understanding, and support. Lisa's expertise in psychosocial safety, combined with her dedication to advocacy and education, has enabled her to develop comprehensive programs and strategies tailored to the unique needs of each organisation.

One of the cornerstones of Lisa's work is her commitment to education and empowerment. She believes that knowledge is the key to change and has designed a range of training programs to equip leaders, managers, and employees with the skills and understanding necessary to create and maintain safe workplaces.

Her training sessions are known for their engaging, interactive approach, ensuring that participants leave with actionable insights and a renewed commitment to fostering a safe and supportive environment.

Lisa's influence extends beyond the walls of Safe Space Workplace. She is a sought-after speaker, author, and consultant, frequently sharing her insights and expertise at conferences, workshops, and in the media. Her book, *Domestic Violence: Changing Culture, Saving Lives – A Workplace Guide for Developing a Culture of Empathy and Understanding*, has been widely acclaimed for its practical advice and compassionate approach.

Lisa's dedication to her cause is unwavering. She continues to work tirelessly to raise awareness, advocate for change, and support organisations in their journey toward creating psychosocially safe workplaces. Her vision is a future where every workplace is a safe space, in which employees are respected, valued, and supported in their professional and personal lives.

At Safe Space Workplace, Lisa McAdams leads by example, inspiring others to join her in the pursuit of safer, healthier and more inclusive work environments. Her work is not just about compliance or ticking boxes; it's about making a real, lasting difference in the lives of employees and the overall success of organisations.

A Note from the Author

I believe with a big enough why we can take on any how.

When people ask why I'm so deeply committed to creating psychosocially safe workplaces, my why comes from a personal place. My journey towards this mission began not just in adulthood but much earlier, shaped by a childhood filled with neglect and abuse. For many years, I had no positive role models to look up to, and it was only when I entered the workforce and found a good mentor that my life began to shift.

Growing up in a difficult home environment meant I was constantly searching for stability and safety. The lack of positive role models during my formative years left a void that I struggled to fill on my own. The workplace became a crucial space for me, one where I began to find structure and, ultimately, mentorship.

Workplaces, I've learned, are neutral ground. They have the potential to either improve our circumstances or worsen them, especially when we bring personal baggage into professional settings, which most of us do. When I found my first positive mentor in the workplace, it was life changing. For the first time, I had someone to guide me, believe in my potential, and model the behaviours and values I had never been exposed to. This experience cemented my belief that workplaces are more than just places of employment; they can also be places of healing and growth if designed with care and thought.

I've seen firsthand how a toxic workplace can exacerbate the emotional scars someone brings with them. A manager who engages in bullying, or a workplace culture that fosters high levels of stress and burnout, can deepen existing wounds. On the other hand, a workplace that prioritises psychosocial safety—

where mental health and well-being are protected—can have the opposite effect. It can become a place where individuals feel supported, valued, and encouraged to grow.

Psychosocial safety in the workplace isn't just about preventing harm; it's about creating environments where people can flourish, no matter what they've experienced outside of work. It's about breaking cycles of harm and giving people the tools and support they need to thrive. This is why I'm so passionate about this mission—it's deeply personal and rooted in my own life story.

Coming from a financial background, I've also seen the hard numbers behind the benefits of creating psychosocially safe workplaces. It's not just an ethical or moral imperative—it makes solid financial sense. A workplace that values mental health and well-being sees fewer cases of burnout, lower turnover rates, and higher employee engagement.

Studies show that poor mental health costs Australian businesses billions of dollars each year in absenteeism, presenteeism, and compensation claims. When employees are supported, their productivity increases, and their loyalty to the company deepens, which translates into better financial outcomes. It's an investment in people that pays off in both the short and long term.

In essence, psychosocial safety is not just a **"nice to have"**—it's a business imperative. By reducing risks associated with poor mental health, employers can mitigate legal liabilities, improve workplace morale, and boost their bottom line.

My personal experiences have shaped every aspect of my professional mission. I understand, on a visceral level, how vital a psychosocially safe workplace can be because I've experienced both ends of the spectrum. As a business leader, a coach, and an expert, I work every day to help organisations build cultures of safety, empathy, and trust—spaces where people can bring their full selves without fear of harm.

For me, this isn't just a job. It's a calling that stems from my past, my passion for change, and my belief that we can all create better workplaces that not only enhance business outcomes but also transform lives.

If you know your why at Safe Space Workplace, we have created the how!

Lisa McAdams

Foreword

Creating a workplace where people feel safe, respected, and empowered is no longer just a nice-to-have—it's critical to the success, reputation, and longevity of any organisation. As the world evolves and employees demand environments that prioritise their mental health and well-being, leaders face a critical moment. A commitment to psychosocial safety ensures that workplaces don't just avoid harm but actively foster trust, inclusion, and resilience.

In *Safe Spaces: Creating Psychosocially Safe Workplaces*, Lisa McAdams provides a comprehensive guide to creating environments where people can thrive. This book equips leaders, managers, and employees with practical strategies to cultivate meaningful cultural change—offering a path to healthier, more productive workplaces.

Lisa McAdams brings both lived experience and professional expertise to this work. Drawing on her background in finance and corporate leadership, as well as her personal journey, she has developed a holistic approach to workplace safety. This is a book born out of real-world experience, six years in the making, with solutions grounded in practice. What sets *Safe Spaces* apart is its focus on both prevention and intervention. It challenges organisations to not only manage risks but to proactively build cultures of psychosocial safety that reduce financial and reputational risks.

The Shifting Focus of Workplace Safety

Historically, workplace safety has centred on preventing physical harm. However, the concept of safety has evolved to recognise that psychological well-being is just as essential. Psychological safety, as defined by Professor Amy Edmondson, refers to an environment where individuals feel safe to speak up, express their ideas, and admit mistakes without fear of retribution (Edmondson, 1999). It is the foundation of trust, innovation, and engagement—three critical elements of any thriving organisation.

Organisations that embrace psychosocial safety don't just comply with regulations; they foster environments where employees feel valued and heard. Studies by Safe Work Australia (2021) have shown that workplaces with high psychosocial safety enjoy lower turnover, higher engagement, and better productivity. This book explores these benefits in detail, making a compelling case for why companies need to invest in safety beyond physical measures.

A New Lens on Domestic Family Violence (DFV) and Workplace Responsibility

One of the most significant contributions of *Safe Spaces* is its focus on the intersection between workplaces and domestic family violence (DFV). Traditionally, DFV has been considered a personal issue confined to the home, but Lisa challenges this assumption. She highlights how DFV inevitably spills into the workplace, affecting performance, attendance, and mental health. The book provides practical tools for organisations to support employees impacted by DFV, promote awareness, and integrate these efforts with Employee Assistance Programs (EAPs).

The statistics speak volumes—more than one-third of employees who experience DFV report that it impacts their work performance (Australian Institute of Health and Welfare, 2022). Workplaces that ignore this reality risk not only reputational damage but also lost productivity and higher absenteeism. Lisa emphasises that supporting employees impacted by DFV is both a moral and business imperative, and she outlines strategies for leaders to embed DFV support into workplace policies.

Addressing Coercive Behaviours and Unresolved Trauma

Lisa does not shy away from difficult topics. She delves into how unresolved trauma—both in employees and leaders—affects workplace culture. Leaders with unresolved trauma can perpetuate toxic behaviours, undermining the very culture they are responsible for nurturing. *Safe Spaces* explores how organisations can address these challenges by fostering trauma-informed leadership and providing tools for managing difficult personalities.

The book also tackles coercive behaviours such as exclusion, manipulation, and upward bullying. These behaviours erode trust and disrupt team dynamics, yet they are often difficult to detect. Lisa provides practical guidance on how to recognise and address these behaviours, empowering employees to move from being passive bystanders to proactive upstanders. This section is particularly insightful, offering real-world case studies that illustrate the transformative impact of upstander behaviour on workplace culture.

The Role of Leadership and Top-Down Culture Change

Leadership plays a pivotal role in embedding psychosocial safety. As Lisa demonstrates throughout *Safe Spaces*, cultural change must begin at the top. Leaders set the tone for workplace behaviour, and their actions directly impact the organisation's values and culture. This book offers a blueprint for leaders to model the behaviours they wish to see and create an environment where accountability, respect, and inclusion thrive.

However, leadership buy-in is only the first step. Lisa emphasises that building a safe workplace requires sustained effort, continuous learning, and regular reinforcement. Organisations must align their policies and practices with their values, ensuring that psychosocial safety becomes part of their operational DNA. This long-term commitment is crucial for fostering resilience and adaptability in the face of change.

Why This Book Is Essential Now

The release of *Safe Spaces* on the first day of the 16 Days of Activism underscores its importance in the current social and business climate. This global campaign to end gender-based violence serves as a reminder that workplaces have a critical role to play in addressing broader social issues. Lisa's book offers organisations the tools they need to engage meaningfully with these issues and become leaders in psychosocial safety and gender equity.

With increasing awareness of mental health and well-being, there is no better time for organisations to embrace the principles outlined in *Safe Spaces*. Companies that take proactive steps to create safe, inclusive environments will not only reduce risks but also enhance their reputation as employers of choice. As Lisa points out, psychosocial safety is not just about compliance—it is about building workplaces where people want to work, contribute, and grow.

Practical Tools and Resources for Lasting Impact

One of the most valuable aspects of *Safe Spaces* is its practicality. The book includes assessments, toolkits, sample policies, and case studies, making it a practical resource for organisations at any stage of their journey toward psychosocial safety. Whether you are a leader looking to transform your workplace or an employee seeking to make a difference, this book offers the tools and guidance needed to create meaningful change.

Lisa's experience in consulting with organisations of all sizes is reflected in the book's structure, which allows readers to tailor the content to their specific needs. The Safe Space Workplace model begins with a **comprehensive needs assessment**, identifying gaps in policies, procedures, and workplace culture. This proven process ensures tailored strategies that align with the specific goals and challenges of each organisation. By evaluating employee well-being, psychosocial safety, and leadership engagement, the assessment provides a clear roadmap for sustainable improvement.

With this personalised approach, organisations address immediate concerns while embedding lasting cultural change. The process ensures that businesses—regardless of size or sector—develop safe, supportive environments that foster productivity, trust, and employee well-being, creating a positive and resilient workplace for the future.

A Call to Action

"Safe Spaces is more than just a book—it is a call to action to make workplaces psychosocially safe, for the benefit of all."

List of Abbreviations

AHRC	Australian Human Rights Commission
AMA	American Management Association
ANAO	Australian National Audit Office
ANROWS	Australian National Research Organisation for Women's Safety
APA	American Psychological Association
APS	Australian Public Service
ATO	Australian Taxation Office
CAEPV	Corporate Alliance to End Partner Violence
CDC	Centers for Disease Control and Prevention
CIPD	Chartered Institute of Personnel and Development
DE&I	Diversity, equity, and inclusion
DFV	Domestic and family violence
EAP	Employee Assistance Programs
EAPA	Employee Assistance Professionals Association
EI	Emotional intelligence
ERGs	Employee resource groups
HCI	Human Capital Institute
HR	Human Resources
HSE	Health and Safety Executive
ICF	International Coach Federation
ICISF	International Critical Incident Stress Foundation
ILO	International Labour Organization
ISO	Organization for Standardization

JAN	Job Accommodation Network
KPIs	Key performance indicators
MHCC	Mental Health Commission of Canada
MHFA	Mental Health First Aid
NAMI	National Alliance on Mental Illness
NHS	National Health Service
NIOSH	National Institute for Occupational Safety and Health
OHS	Occupational health and safety
OSHA	Occupational Safety and Health Administration
PSC	Psychosocial safety climate
PTSD	Post-traumatic stress disorder
PwC	PricewaterhouseCoopers
SAMHSA	Substance Abuse and Mental Health Services Administration
SHRM	ociety for Human Resource Management
WBI	Workplace Bullying Institute
WHO	World Health Organization
WHS	Work Health and Safety

Introduction

The Importance of Psychosocial Safety

In today's fast-paced, competitive business environment, the well-being of employees often takes a back seat to productivity and profit margins. However, the true success of any organisation is deeply rooted in the health and safety of its workforce. Psychosocial safety, an often overlooked aspect of workplace safety, is critical in fostering a supportive and productive work environment.

Psychosocial safety refers to the prevention and management of workplace risks to the mental health and well-being of employees. These risks can include stress, harassment, bullying, and other forms of psychological harm. Ensuring a psychosocially safe workplace not only protects employees from harm but also enhances their overall job satisfaction and engagement.

Organisations that prioritise psychosocial safety experience numerous benefits. Employees in such environments are more likely to be motivated, loyal, and productive. They are less likely to experience burnout, depression, or anxiety, which in turn reduces absenteeism and turnover rates. By promoting a culture of respect, trust, and support, organisations can foster a more positive and collaborative work atmosphere, leading to improved performance and innovation.

Moreover, the importance of psychosocial safety extends beyond individual well-being to encompass organisational resilience and sustainability. In a psychosocially safe workplace, employees are encouraged to speak up about their concerns and challenges without fear of retaliation. This open communication enables organisations to identify and address issues promptly, preventing them from escalating into more significant problems. It also helps in building a strong sense of community and belonging among employees, which is essential for navigating times of change and crisis.

As we delve into the intricacies of creating a psychosocially safe workplace, it is essential to recognise that this is not merely a compliance requirement. Rather, it is a strategic investment in the future of your organisation. The following chapters will provide a comprehensive guide on how to assess, develop, implement, and sustain psychosocial safety measures tailored to the unique needs and goals of your organisation. Together, we can create a work environment where every employee feels valued, supported, and empowered to thrive.

Understanding Psychosocial Hazards

In the pursuit of creating a safe and thriving workplace, it's crucial to understand the nature of psychosocial hazards. Unlike physical hazards, which are often visible and tangible, psychosocial hazards are less obvious. However, they are equally detrimental to the well-being of employees and the overall health of an organisation.

Psychosocial hazards refer to aspects of work design, organisation, and management that pose risks to the mental and emotional health of employees. These hazards can manifest in various forms, such as excessive workloads, lack of support from management, unclear job roles, workplace bullying, and discrimination. They can lead to stress, anxiety, depression, and a host of other mental health issues if not adequately addressed.

One of the key challenges in managing psychosocial hazards is their subjective nature. What may be a significant stressor for one employee might be a minor inconvenience for another. Therefore, it's essential to foster an environment where employees feel comfortable voicing their concerns and experiences. By actively listening to and addressing these concerns, organisations can identify potential psychosocial hazards and take proactive steps to mitigate them.

The impact of psychosocial hazards extends beyond individual employees to affect the entire organisation. High levels of stress and poor mental health among employees can lead to decreased productivity, increased absenteeism, and higher turnover rates. Furthermore, a workplace plagued by psychosocial hazards is likely to experience a decline in morale and engagement, which can stifle innovation and collaboration.

Understanding psychosocial hazards is the first step in creating a psychosocially safe workplace. It requires a holistic approach that considers the various factors contributing to employees' mental and emotional well-being. In the following chapters, we will explore practical strategies for identifying, assessing, and managing psychosocial hazards within your organisation. By doing so, we can pave the way for a healthier, more supportive, and ultimately more successful workplace.

The Benefits of a Psychosocially Safe Workplace

Creating a psychosocially safe workplace is essential not only for the well-being of employees but also for the overall success and sustainability of an organisation. The importance of such an environment cannot be overstated, as the benefits extend far beyond mere compliance with health and safety regulations.

A psychosocially safe workplace fosters an atmosphere where employees can thrive, which in turn propels the organisation toward greater achievements. Let's explore the key benefits of prioritising psychosocial safety.

First and foremost, a psychosocially safe workplace significantly enhances employee well-being. When employees feel secure and supported, their stress levels decrease, leading to better mental and emotional health. This positive impact on well-being reduces absenteeism and presenteeism, ensuring that employees are engaged and productive. Employees who are not weighed down by mental health issues can focus better on their tasks, leading to increased efficiency and output.

Moreover, creating a supportive environment results in higher employee retention rates. Organisations that prioritise psychosocial safety are more likely to retain their top talent. High turnover rates, often a symptom of an unhealthy work environment, can be costly and disruptive. By fostering a culture of support and well-being, organisations can save on the costs associated with hiring and training new employees, while also maintaining a stable and experienced workforce.

Additionally, a psychosocially safe workplace enhances team collaboration and innovation. When employees feel safe, they are more comfortable sharing ideas and collaborating with colleagues. This openness leads to greater innovation as employees are not afraid to take risks and propose new solutions. Trust and respect among team members foster teamwork and collective problem-solving, driving the organisation forward.

A commitment to psychosocial safety also improves an organisation's reputation. Companies known for their dedication to employee well-being are viewed more favourably by potential employees, clients, and partners. This positive reputation can attract top talent and build strong relationships with clients and stakeholders, providing a significant competitive advantage.

From a legal and financial perspective, implementing psychosocial safety measures helps organisations comply with health and safety regulations, reducing the risk of legal issues and associated costs. Furthermore, healthier employees contribute to lower healthcare costs and fewer disability claims, offering financial benefits to the organisation.

Finally, a psychosocially safe workplace cultivates a positive organisational culture where respect, empathy, and support are the norms. This culture not only enhances the work experience for employees but also drives organisational success. A positive culture is a powerful driver of employee engagement, satisfaction, and loyalty, all of which are crucial for long-term success.

The benefits of a psychosocially safe workplace are manifold and far-reaching. By investing in psychosocial safety, organisations can create an environment that supports the well-being of their employees and drives long-term success. Read on to explore the strategies and practices necessary to implement and maintain a psychosocially safe workplace, ensuring a thriving, productive, and harmonious work environment.

PART 1

Foundations of Psychosocial Safety

CHAPTER 1
Defining Psychosocial Safety

Psychosocial safety in the workplace refers to an environment where employees feel secure, supported, and free from psychological and social risks that can harm their mental health and overall well-being. This concept goes beyond physical safety to encompass the emotional and psychological aspects of the workplace. A psychosocially safe workplace is one where employees are protected from bullying, harassment, discrimination, and other forms of harmful behaviour.

The foundation of psychosocial safety lies in creating a culture where respect, inclusivity, and support are paramount. This includes fostering open communication, promoting work-life balance, and ensuring employees have access to the resources and support they need to thrive personally and professionally. By prioritising psychosocial safety, organisations can create a more positive, productive, and healthy work environment.

What is Psychosocial Safety?

Psychosocial safety is a core element of workplace well-being, recognised in legislation such as Australia's **Work Health and Safety Act 2011**, which mandates employers to manage both physical and psychological risks. It involves the proactive management of workplace stressors, including workload, interpersonal conflict, job insecurity, and discrimination. Safe Work Australia defines psychosocial safety as the practice of ensuring that work environments support employees' mental health, reducing the risk of stress-related harm (Safe Work Australia, 2021).

Psychosocial safety aligns closely with the principles of **psychological safety**, which Edmondson described as the shared belief that team members feel safe to take risks and express their thoughts or concerns without fear of being judged or punished. This concept underpins the shift from workplaces focused purely on productivity to those that prioritise human connection, collaboration, and resilience (Edmondson, 1999).

Key Concepts and Terminology

To effectively implement and maintain psychosocial safety in the workplace, it is essential to understand the key concepts and terminology associated with this field. These include:

- *Psychosocial Hazards:* Aspects of the work environment and job tasks that can cause psychological or social harm. Examples include excessive workload, lack of control over work, poor support from supervisors and colleagues, and exposure to violence or harassment.

- *Psychosocial Safety Climate (PSC):* The shared perceptions among employees about the policies, practices, and procedures in place to protect their psychological health and safety. A positive PSC is characterised by a strong organisational commitment to mental health, supportive leadership, and effective communication channels.

- *Workplace Bullying:* Repeated, unreasonable actions directed toward an employee or group of employees that create a risk to health and safety. Bullying can include verbal abuse, social exclusion, and other forms of psychological aggression.

- **Work-Life Balance:** The equilibrium between personal life and work life. Maintaining a healthy work-life balance is crucial for preventing burnout and ensuring long-term well-being.

- **Mental Health Stigma:** Negative attitudes and beliefs that lead to discrimination against people with mental health conditions. Reducing stigma is essential for encouraging employees to seek help and support.

- **Employee Assistance Programs (EAPs):** Work-based intervention programs designed to assist employees in resolving personal problems that may be affecting their performance. EAPs can offer counselling, referrals, and other support services.

Legal and Ethical Considerations

Creating a psychosocially safe workplace is not only a moral imperative but also a legal requirement in many jurisdictions. Organisations must comply with occupational health and safety (OHS) laws and regulations that mandate the protection of employees from psychological harm. Failure to do so can result in legal consequences, financial penalties, and damage to the organisation's reputation.

In Australia, for instance, the *Work Health and Safety Act 2011* requires employers to ensure the health and safety of their workers, which includes psychological health. Similar regulations exist in other countries, such as the *Health and Safety at Work Act 1974* in the UK and the *Occupational Safety and Health Act 1970* in the US. These laws highlight the importance of identifying, assessing, and controlling psychosocial risks in the workplace.

Psychosocial safety became part of Australian legislation on April 1, 2023. This marked a significant development as amendments were made to the Work Health and Safety (WHS) regulations to explicitly address psychosocial hazards. The changes require employers to manage and mitigate risks related to mental health in the workplace, including factors like excessive workloads, bullying, harassment, and poor organisational culture. These regulations were introduced to ensure that employers take proactive steps to create mentally healthy work environments, in line with the duty of care already required under WHS laws.

Ethically, organisations have a responsibility to provide a safe and supportive environment for their employees. This includes taking proactive measures to prevent psychosocial hazards and addressing any issues that arise promptly and effectively. Ethical leadership and a commitment to employee well-being are fundamental to fostering a culture of trust and respect.

Research and Best Practices

Research in the field of occupational health and psychology has provided valuable insights into the impact of psychosocial safety on employee well-being and organisational performance. Studies have shown that a positive PSC is associated with lower levels of stress, anxiety, and depression among employees. It also correlates with higher job satisfaction, engagement, and productivity.

For example, a study published in the *Journal of Occupational Health Psychology* found that organisations with high PSC had employees who reported better mental health and higher levels of job satisfaction. Another study in the *International Journal of Environmental Research and Public Health* highlighted the role of supportive leadership in enhancing psychosocial safety and reducing burnout.

Implementing best practices for psychosocial safety involves a multi-faceted approach. Key strategies include:

- *Leadership Commitment:* Demonstrate a genuine commitment to psychosocial safety through leaders who prioritise mental health, promote open communication, and lead by example.

- *Comprehensive Policies:* Develop and implement policies that address psychosocial risks, such as anti-bullying and harassment policies, mental health support programs, and work-life balance initiatives.

- *Employee Training:* Provide regular training on topics related to psychosocial safety, including stress management, conflict resolution, and mental health awareness.

- *Support Systems:* Establish support systems such as EAPs, peer support networks, and mental health champions to provide employees with the resources and assistance they need.

- *Regular Assessments:* Conduct regular assessments and audits to identify psychosocial hazards, evaluate the effectiveness of existing measures, and make necessary improvements.

- *Employee Involvement:* Involve employees in the development and implementation of psychosocial safety initiatives to ensure that their needs and concerns are addressed.

Core Components of Psychosocial Safety

1. **Open Communication:** Encouraging employees to speak openly without fear of retribution or judgement promotes better problem-solving and innovation (Edmondson, 2018).

2. **Respect and Inclusion:** Embracing diversity and addressing discriminatory behaviour strengthens trust and cohesion within teams (Australian Human Rights Commission, 2014).

3. **Support for Mental Health:** Providing access to Employee Assistance Programs (EAPs) and mental health resources ensures that employees feel supported during difficult times (Black Dog Institute, 2021).

4. **Clear Policies and Accountability:** Establishing clear behavioural expectations through policies ensures consistency in maintaining a safe work environment (Safe Work Australia, 2021).

The Role of Leadership in Psychosocial Safety

Leadership plays a pivotal role in establishing and maintaining a psychosocially safe workplace. Leaders set the tone for organisational culture and have a significant influence on the attitudes and behaviours of their employees. Effective leadership in the context of psychosocial safety involves several key components:

- *Vision and Commitment:* Leaders must articulate a clear vision for psychosocial safety and demonstrate a strong commitment to achieving it. This includes allocating resources, setting measurable goals, and holding themselves accountable for progress.

TechCorp

TechCorp, a leading technology company, recognised the importance of psychosocial safety in fostering innovation and productivity. The company implemented a comprehensive mental health program that included regular stress management workshops, access to counselling services, and flexible work arrangements. As a result, employee satisfaction and retention rates improved significantly, and the company reported a notable increase in productivity.

HealthCarePlus

HealthCarePlus, a healthcare provider, faced high levels of burnout and stress among its employees. To address this, the organisation launched a psychosocial safety initiative that included training for managers on recognising and addressing psychosocial hazards, peer support networks, and a robust EAP. The initiative led to a reduction in absenteeism and turnover, and employees reported feeling more supported and valued.

EduCo

EduCo, an educational institution, focused on creating a positive PSC by involving employees in the development of its policies and programs. The organisation conducted regular surveys to gather employee feedback and used the insights to inform its initiatives. This collaborative approach resulted in a more engaged and motivated workforce, with improved mental health outcomes and overall job satisfaction.

Key Takeaways

Understanding the foundations of psychosocial safety is crucial for creating a workplace that prioritises its employees' mental health and well-being. By defining key concepts, adhering to legal and ethical standards, and implementing best practices, organisations can foster a culture of respect, support, and safety. This not only benefits employees but also contributes to the overall success and sustainability of the organisation. Through commitment and collaboration, we can build workplaces where everyone can thrive, free from the psychological and social risks that would undermine their well-being.

The role of leadership in establishing and maintaining a psychosocially safe workplace cannot be overstated. Effective leaders set the tone for organisational culture, model desired behaviours, and provide the support and resources needed to ensure employee well-being. By continuously assessing and improving their initiatives, leaders can create an environment where psychosocial safety is embedded in the fabric of the organisation.

The journey toward creating a psychosocially safe workplace is an ongoing process that requires dedication, collaboration, and a commitment to continuous improvement. By prioritising psychosocial safety, organisations can create a positive and supportive work environment that benefits both employees and the organisation as a whole. Through the collective efforts of leaders, employees, and other stakeholders, we can build workplaces that promote mental health, well-being, and success for everyone.

References:

Edmondson, A. C. (1999). Psychological safety and learning behavior in work teams. *Administrative Science Quarterly, 44*(2), 350-383.

Safe Work Australia. (2021). *Work-related psychological health and safety: A systematic approach to meeting your duties.* Retrieved from https://www.safeworkaustralia.gov.au

World Health Organization. (2019). *Mental health in the workplace.* Retrieved from https://www.who.int

Black Dog Institute. (2021). *Workplace mental health toolkit.* Retrieved from https://www.blackdoginstitute.org.au

Australian Human Rights Commission. (2014). *Workplace discrimination, harassment, and bullying.* Retrieved from https://humanrights.gov.au

Duhigg, C. (2016). *What Google learned from its quest to build the perfect team. The New York Times.* Retrieved from https://www.nytimes.com

CHAPTER 2

The Impact of Psychosocial Safety on Organisations

Improved Employee Well-Being

The well-being of employees is a critical factor in the overall success of any organisation. Research consistently shows that a positive psychosocial work environment significantly enhances employee well-being. When employees feel psychologically safe, they are less likely to experience stress, anxiety, and burnout. This, in turn, leads to better mental and physical health, increased job satisfaction, and higher morale.

A study published in the *Journal of Occupational Health Psychology* found that organisations with high levels of psychosocial safety climate (PSC) had employees who reported lower levels of stress and higher levels of well-being. The study highlighted that employees who perceive their workplace as supportive of their psychological health are more likely to engage in healthy behaviours, seek help when needed, and maintain a positive outlook on their work and life (Dollard & Bakker, 2010).

Moreover, the World Health Organization (WHO) emphasises that promoting mental health in the workplace is crucial for the overall health of employees. The WHO's guidelines on mental health at work suggest that organisations should create a psychosocially safe environment to prevent mental health issues and promote well-being. This includes addressing psychosocial risks, providing support, and fostering a culture of openness and understanding (WHO, 2021).

Enhanced Productivity and Performance

A psychosocially safe workplace not only benefits employees' well-being but also positively impacts productivity and performance. When employees feel supported and valued, they are more likely to be engaged and motivated, leading to higher levels of productivity. Additionally, a positive work environment fosters creativity, innovation, and collaboration, which are essential for organisational success.

Research published in the *Harvard Business Review* indicates that employees who feel psychologically safe are more likely to contribute new ideas and take initiative. This is because they are not afraid of being judged or penalised for making mistakes or expressing unconventional thoughts. As a result, organisations that prioritise psychosocial safety often see improvements in innovation and overall performance (Edmondson, 1999).

Furthermore, a study by the American Psychological Association (APA) found that workplaces that support employees' mental health have higher levels of productivity. The study revealed that employees in supportive environments were more focused, less likely to take sick leave, and more committed to their work. This underscores the importance of creating a psychosocially safe workplace to enhance overall organisational performance (APA, 2019).

Reducing Turnover and Absenteeism

High turnover and absenteeism rates can be detrimental to an organisation, leading to increased costs and disruptions in operations. A psychosocially safe workplace can significantly reduce these issues by fostering a supportive and positive environment where employees feel valued and motivated to stay.

Research shows that employees are more likely to remain with an organisation that prioritises their well-being and provides a supportive work environment. A study published in the *Journal of Applied Psychology* found that organisations with high PSC experienced lower turnover rates. Employees were more likely to stay because they felt their psychological health was supported and their contributions were valued (Tuckey, Dollard, & Bakker, 2012).

Additionally, the Chartered Institute of Personnel and Development (CIPD) highlights that reducing workplace stress and promoting mental health can decrease absenteeism. When employees feel psychologically safe and supported, they are less likely to take sick leave due to stress-related issues. This not only reduces absenteeism but also improves overall productivity and morale (CIPD, 2020).

Practical Steps for Enhancing Psychosocial Safety

Implementing and maintaining a psychosocially safe workplace requires a strategic approach and commitment from leadership. Here are some practical steps organisations can take to enhance psychosocial safety:

1. *Leadership Commitment:* Demonstrate a genuine commitment to psychosocial safety by ensuring leaders prioritise mental health, promote open communication, and lead by example. This includes leaders allocating resources, setting measurable goals, and holding themselves accountable for progress.

2. *Comprehensive Policies:* Develop and implement policies that address psychosocial risks, such as anti-bullying and harassment policies, mental health support

programs, and work-life balance initiatives. Ensure these policies are communicated effectively to all employees.

3. *Employee Training:* Provide regular training on topics related to psychosocial safety, including stress management, conflict resolution, and mental health awareness. Training should be tailored to different levels within the organisation, including leaders, managers, and employees.

4. *Support Systems:* Establish support systems such as Employee Assistance Programs (EAPs), peer support networks, and mental health champions to provide employees with the resources and assistance they need. Ensure these systems are easily accessible and well-publicised.

5. *Regular Assessments:* Conduct regular assessments and audits to identify psychosocial hazards, evaluate the effectiveness of existing measures, and make necessary improvements. Use surveys, focus groups, and feedback mechanisms to gather insights from employees.

6. *Employee Involvement:* Involve employees in the development and implementation of psychosocial safety initiatives to ensure that their needs and concerns are addressed. Encourage employees to participate in decision-making processes and provide feedback.

7. *Promoting Work-Life Balance:* Implement policies and practices that promote work-life balance, such as flexible working hours, remote work options, and opportunities for personal and professional development. Encourage employees to take breaks and prioritise their well-being.

8. *Creating a Supportive Culture:* Foster a culture of respect, inclusivity, and support. Recognise and celebrate achievements, encourage collaboration, and provide opportunities for social interactions and team-building activities.

Real-World Examples

Examining real-world examples of organisations that have successfully implemented psychosocial safety initiatives can provide valuable insights and inspiration. Here are a few examples:

Google

Google is renowned for its innovative and supportive workplace culture. The company has implemented several initiatives to promote psychosocial safety, including flexible work arrangements, mental health support programs, and a strong emphasis on work-life balance. Google's approach to employee well-being has resulted in high levels of job satisfaction, low turnover rates, and increased productivity. A study by the *Harvard Business Review* highlighted that Google's supportive culture fosters innovation and creativity, leading to the development of groundbreaking products and services (Duhigg, 2016).

Salesforce

Salesforce, a leading cloud-based software company, prioritises employee well-being through its comprehensive mental health programs and supportive workplace culture. The company offers regular stress management workshops, access to counselling services, and initiatives to promote work-life balance. Salesforce's commitment to psychosocial safety has resulted in high employee satisfaction, reduced turnover, and improved performance. The company's efforts have been recognised by numerous awards, including being named one of the best places to work by *Fortune* magazine (Salesforce, 2020).

Australian Taxation Office (ATO)

The Australian Taxation Office (ATO) has made significant strides in promoting psychosocial safety among its employees. The organisation implemented a comprehensive mental health strategy that includes training for managers on recognising and addressing psychosocial risks, peer support networks, and access to mental health resources. As a result, the ATO has seen a reduction in absenteeism, improved employee well-being, and enhanced productivity. The ATO's approach serves as a model for other public sector organisations looking to create a supportive and safe work environment (ATO, 2018).

Key Takeaways

The impact of psychosocial safety on organisations is profound and far-reaching. By prioritising psychosocial safety, organisations can improve employee well-being, enhance productivity and performance, and reduce turnover and absenteeism. Real-world examples from companies like Google, Salesforce, and the Australian Taxation Office demonstrate the tangible benefits of creating a psychosocially safe work environment.

To achieve these benefits, organisations must take a strategic, long-term, and committed approach. This includes demonstrating leadership commitment, developing comprehensive policies, providing employee training, establishing support systems, conducting regular assessments, involving employees in decision-making, promoting work-life balance, and fostering a supportive culture.

Ultimately, creating a psychosocially safe workplace is not only a moral and legal imperative but also a key driver of organisational success. By investing in the mental health and well-being of employees, organisations can build a positive, productive, and resilient workforce that is well-equipped to navigate the challenges of the modern workplace.

References:

- American Psychological Association (APA). (2019). Workplace well-being linked to productivity. Retrieved from https://www.apa.org/news/press/releases/stress/2019/stress-workplace-productivity

- Australian Government Department of Employment and Workplace Relations. Retrieved from https://www.dewr.gov.au/

- Australian Taxation Office (ATO). (2018). Mental health and wellbeing strategy. Retrieved from https://www.ato.gov.au/About-ATO/Access,-accountability-and-reporting/Our-commitment-to-the-community/Mental-health-and-wellbeing-strategy/

- Chartered Institute of Personnel and Development (CIPD). (2020). Health and well-being at work survey. Retrieved from https://www.cipd.co.uk/knowledge/culture/well-being/health-well-being-work

- Dollard, M. F., & Bakker, A. B. (2010). Psychosocial safety climate as a precursor to conducive work environments, psychological health problems, and employee engagement. *Journal of Occupational Health Psychology, 15*(3), 273-289.

⊙ Duhigg, C. (2016). What Google learned from its quest to build the perfect team. *The New York Times*. Retrieved from https://www.nytimes.com/2016/02/28/magazine/what-google-learned-from-its-quest-to-build-the-perfect-team.html

⊙ Edmondson, A. C. (1999). Psychological safety and learning behaviour in work teams. *Administrative Science Quarterly, 44*(2), 350-383.

⊙ Salesforce. (2020). Salesforce ranks among the best places to work. Retrieved from https://www.salesforce.com/company/news-press/stories/2020/01/01212020/

⊙ Safe Work Australia. 2022. Psychosocial hazards. Retrieved from https://www.safeworkaustralia.gov.au/

PART 2

Assessing Your Workplace

CHAPTER 3

Conducting a Psychosocial Safety Audit

A psychosocial safety audit is a crucial first step in assessing the current state of your workplace's psychosocial environment. This process involves systematically evaluating existing policies, practices, and workplace culture to identify strengths and areas for improvement. An effective audit can help uncover hidden risks, highlight successful strategies, and provide a roadmap for creating a safer and more supportive work environment.

A comprehensive psychosocial safety audit typically includes several key components:

1. *Reviewing Policies and Procedures:* This involves examining current policies and procedures related to mental health, domestic and family violence (DFV), workplace safety, and employee well-being. Key documents to review might include employee handbooks, safety manuals, toolkits, and human resources (HR) policies on issues such as harassment, bullying, DFV, and mental health support. The goal is to ensure that these policies are up-to-date, comprehensive, and effectively communicated to all employees.

2. *Conducting Surveys and Interviews:* Employee surveys and interviews are invaluable tools for gathering insights into the workplace culture and identifying psychosocial hazards. Surveys should be anonymous to encourage honest feedback and cover topics such as job satisfaction, stress levels, and perceptions of safe-

ty and support. Interviews can provide deeper insights and help to clarify any issues identified in the surveys.

3. *Observing Workplace Dynamics:* Observing interactions and behaviours in the workplace can provide additional context and help identify areas where psychosocial safety might be compromised. This might involve shadowing employees, attending meetings, and observing the general atmosphere in different departments.

4. *Analysing Incident Reports:* Reviewing records of past incidents, such as reports of bullying, harassment, or mental health issues, can help identify patterns and areas of concern. This analysis can highlight specific departments or teams that may require additional support or intervention.

The Australian National Audit Office (ANAO) emphasises the importance of a thorough and systematic approach to auditing workplace safety. Their guidelines suggest that organisations should use a combination of quantitative and qualitative data to get a comprehensive understanding of their psychosocial safety climate (PSC) (ANAO, 2020).

Identifying Existing Policies and Practices

Once the audit is complete, the next step is to identify and evaluate the existing policies and practices in place to support psychosocial safety. This involves assessing the effectiveness of current measures and identifying gaps or areas for improvement.

Key Areas to Evaluate:

1. *Mental Health Policies: These* should cover a range of topics, including stress management, support for men-

tal health conditions, and procedures for handling mental health crises. Policies should be clearly communicated to all employees and regularly reviewed to ensure they remain relevant and effective.

2. *Anti-Bullying and Harassment Policies:* Effective anti-bullying and harassment policies are essential for creating a safe and supportive work environment. These policies should outline clear procedures for reporting and addressing incidents, as well as consequences for perpetrators.

3. *Work-Life Balance Initiatives:* Policies that promote work-life balance, such as flexible working arrangements, parental leave, and support for caregiving responsibilities, can significantly impact employee well-being. Assessing the availability and uptake of these initiatives can help identify areas for improvement.

4. *Employee Assistance Programs (EAPs):* EAPs provide confidential support and resources for employees dealing with personal or work-related issues. Evaluating the usage and effectiveness of EAPs can offer insights into their impact on employee well-being.

5. *Training and Development Programs:* Ongoing training on topics such as mental health awareness, stress management, DFV support and conflict resolution is essential for maintaining a psychosocially safe workplace. Assessing the availability of these problems, and the participation rates for and feedback from them, can help identify areas for enhancement.

Research from the *Journal of Occupational Health Psychology* indicates that organisations with comprehensive and well-implemented psychosocial safety policies report higher levels of employee satisfaction and lower rates of workplace stress and mental health issues (Dollard & Bakker, 2010).

Gathering Employee Feedback

Employee feedback is a vital component of any psychosocial safety assessment. It provides direct insights into employees' perceptions of their work environment, including their experiences with stress, support, and safety. Gathering feedback can be done through a variety of methods, including surveys, focus groups, and one-on-one interviews.

Effective Strategies for Gathering Feedback:

1. *Anonymous Surveys:* Conducting anonymous surveys allows employees to provide honest and candid feedback without fear of repercussions. Surveys should cover a range of topics, including job satisfaction, workplace stress, support from management, and perceptions of safety.

2. *Focus Groups:* Focus groups can provide deeper insights into specific issues identified in the surveys. These small, facilitated discussions allow employees to share their experiences and suggest improvements in a more interactive setting.

3. **One-on-One Interviews:** Individual interviews with employees can provide detailed and personal insights into their experiences and concerns. These interviews

should be conducted confidentially and with sensitivity to encourage open and honest communication.

4. *Suggestion Boxes:* Physical or digital suggestion boxes allow employees to anonymously submit ideas, concerns, or feedback at any time. This can be an effective way to gather ongoing input and address issues as they arise.

A study by the Chartered Institute of Personnel and Development (CIPD) found that organisations that actively seek and respond to employee feedback tend to have higher levels of employee engagement and satisfaction. The study also highlighted the importance of ensuring that feedback mechanisms are accessible, confidential, and followed by visible actions and improvements (CIPD, 2020).

Analysing Workplace Culture

Workplace culture plays a significant role in shaping the PSC. A positive and supportive culture can promote well-being, reduce stress, and enhance overall job satisfaction, while a toxic culture can have the opposite effect. Analysing workplace culture involves examining the underlying values, beliefs, and behaviours that characterise an organisation.

Key Aspects of Workplace Culture to Analyse:

1. *Leadership Style:* The behaviour and attitudes of leaders set the tone for the entire organisation. Analysing leadership styles can help identify whether leaders promote a supportive and inclusive environment or contribute to stress and conflict.

2. *Communication Patterns:* Effective communication is essential for a healthy workplace culture. This includes open and transparent communication between management and employees, as well as among peers. Assessing communication patterns can help identify areas for improvement.

3. *Employee Relationships:* Positive relationships among employees are a key component of a supportive work environment. Analysing the nature of these relationships, including levels of trust, collaboration, and support, can provide insights into the overall culture.

4. *Recognition and Rewards*: Recognising and rewarding employees for their contributions can enhance job satisfaction and motivation. Assessing the effectiveness and fairness of recognition and reward systems can assist to identify areas for enhancement.

5. *Inclusion, Equity and Diversity:* A culture that values inclusion, equity, and diversity is more likely to be supportive and respectful. Analysing the organisation's approach to diversity and inclusion can help identify strengths and areas for improvement.

A comprehensive analysis of workplace culture can be supported by tools such as the *Organisational Culture Assessment Instrument* (OCAI) developed by Kim Cameron and Robert Quinn.

Kim Cameron is a professor at the University of Michigan's Ross School of Business and is known for his pioneering work in the field of **Positive Organisational Scholarship**. His research focuses on leadership, organisational culture, and virtuous practices that enhance workplace performance and well-being.

Robert Quinn is a professor emeritus at the University of Michigan's Ross School of Business and a co-founder of the field of **Positive Organisational Scholarship**. He is recognised for his research on leadership, organisational change, and his development of the **Competing Values Framework** used for understanding organisational effectiveness.

Cameron and Quinn's tool helps organisations identify their current culture and desired future culture, providing a framework for making targeted improvements (Cameron & Quinn, 2011).

Implementing Changes Based on Findings

The findings from the psychosocial safety audit, policy evaluation, employee feedback, and culture analysis provide a comprehensive understanding of the current state of psychosocial safety in the workplace. Based on these findings, organisations can develop and implement targeted strategies to enhance psychosocial safety.

Key Steps for Implementing Changes:

1. *Develop an Action Plan:* Create a detailed action plan that outlines the specific steps needed to address the identified issues and enhance psychosocial safety. This plan should include clear objectives, timelines, and responsibilities.

2. *Engage Stakeholders:* Involve key stakeholders, including leadership, management, and employees, in the development and implementation of the action plan. Engaging stakeholders ensures buy-in and commitment to the changes.

3. *Provide Training and Resources:* Offer training and resources to support the implementation of new policies and practices. This might include mental health awareness training, stress management workshops, DFV support and resources for managers on bolstering employee well-being.

4. *Monitor and Evaluate Progress:* Regularly monitor and evaluate the progress of the implemented changes to ensure they are effective. Use feedback mechanisms, such as surveys and focus groups, to gather input from employees and make necessary adjustments.

5. *Celebrate Successes:* Recognise and celebrate the successes and improvements achieved through the implementation of the action plan. Celebrating successes reinforces positive changes and motivates continued efforts.

Case Studies

CASE STUDY 1: Identifying Burnout Risks in a Financial Services Firm

Company: A large financial services firm

Issue: Rising reports of employee burnout and high turnover among junior staff

Psychosocial Safety Audit Implementation: The firm conducted a comprehensive psychosocial safety audit to understand the root causes of burnout and turnover. The audit included anonymous employee surveys, focus groups, and one-on-one interviews with staff across all levels. The audit assessed work demands, work-life balance, management support, and the effectiveness of current mental health resources. The results revealed that excessive workloads, unrealistic deadlines, and poor communication from managers were the primary contributors to employee burnout.

Outcome: Based on the audit findings, the firm adjusted work expectations, set clearer performance goals, and introduced workload management policies to prevent excessive pressure. They also implemented leadership training focused on stress management and effective communication. Within six months, reports of burnout decreased by 20%, and employee turnover rates significantly improved. Employees reported feeling more supported by management, and the firm saw an improvement in overall job satisfaction and productivity.

CASE STUDY 2: Addressing Bullying and Toxic Culture in a Manufacturing Plant

Company: A mid-sized manufacturing plant

Issue: Widespread reports of workplace bullying and low employee morale

Psychosocial Safety Audit Implementation: The company conducted a psychosocial safety audit after receiving numerous complaints about workplace bullying and a toxic culture. The audit involved collecting data from anonymous employee surveys, reviewing exit interview feedback, and conducting safety assessments of communication channels. The audit also reviewed HR processes related to complaint handling, disciplinary actions, and the overall work environment. Results indicated a lack of trust in the company's reporting systems, frequent bullying incidents from line managers, and a culture that discouraged speaking up.

Outcome: The company immediately took action based on the audit findings. They established a confidential reporting system, implemented anti-bullying policies, and provided training for managers on fostering a respectful workplace. Six months after implementing changes, employee engagement surveys showed a 30% improvement in morale, and reported incidents of bullying dropped by 50%. The company's reputation as a supportive and safe workplace improved, resulting in higher retention rates and a positive shift in company culture.

CASE STUDY 3: Improving Mental Health and Reducing Presenteeism in a Tech Company

Company: A growing tech company

Issue: High levels of presenteeism and increased employee stress

Psychosocial Safety Audit Implementation: The company conducted a psychosocial safety audit to understand why employees were coming to work despite feeling unwell or disengaged, leading to presenteeism. The audit included reviewing current EAPs, mental health resources, and interviewing managers and employees to assess stress levels and work expectations. The findings showed that employees felt pressured to be constantly available and feared that taking time off for mental health would reflect poorly on their performance.

Outcome: As a result of the audit, the company introduced mental health awareness training, encouraged the use of EAP services, and promoted a flexible work policy allowing employees to take mental health days without fear of judgment. They also trained managers to recognise the signs of stress and burnout and to encourage open conversations about mental health. Within nine months, presenteeism dropped by 25%, and employee feedback highlighted a stronger sense of psychological safety. Employees felt more comfortable taking necessary time off, and overall productivity and morale improved as a result.

Key Takeaways

Assessing the psychosocial safety of your workplace is a critical step in creating a supportive and healthy work environment. By conducting a thorough psychosocial safety audit, evaluating existing policies and practices, gathering employee feedback, and analysing workplace culture, organisations can identify strengths and areas for improvement.

Implementing targeted changes based on these findings can significantly enhance psychosocial safety, leading to improved employee well-being, increased productivity and performance, and reduced turnover and absenteeism. Organisations that prioritise psychosocial safety and make continuous efforts to support their employees' mental health and well-being are more likely to succeed in creating a positive and resilient workplace.

References:

- Australian National Audit Office. (2020). Better practice guide: Public sector audit committees. Retrieved from https://www.anao.gov.au/work/better-practice-guide/public-sector-audit-committees

- Cameron, K. S., & Quinn, R. E. (2011). *Diagnosing and changing organisational culture: Based on the competing values framework*. John Wiley & Sons.

- Chartered Institute of Personnel and Development. (2020). Health and well-being at work survey. Retrieved from https://www.cipd.co.uk/knowledge/culture/well-being/health-well-being-work

Dollard, M. F., & Bakker, A. B. (2010). Psychosocial safety climate as a precursor to conducive work environments, psychological health problems, and employee engagement. *Journal of Occupational Health Psychology, 15*(3), 273-289.

CHAPTER 4

Recognising Psychosocial Hazards in the Workplace

In the modern workplace, psychosocial hazards pose a serious threat to employee well-being, productivity, and organisational success. Unlike physical hazards, which are often tangible and observable, psychosocial hazards are more insidious, arising from poor work design, organisation, and social interactions within the workplace. Recognising these hazards is essential for creating a psychosocially safe environment. This chapter will explore common psychosocial hazards, provide case studies, and outline early warning signs and red flags to help organisations take proactive measures in safeguarding their employees.

Common Psychosocial Hazards in the Workplace

Psychosocial hazards refer to elements of the work environment, the nature of the job, or interpersonal relationships that can lead to psychological or emotional harm. These hazards can vary depending on the industry and organisational culture, but there are several common categories of which all organisations should be aware:

1. *Job Insecurity:* Fear of losing one's job or not having stable employment is one of the most significant psychosocial hazards. Employees who feel that their jobs are at risk may experience chronic stress, anxiety, and reduced motivation, leading to decreased productivity and higher turnover rates. Research by Klandermans and Van Vuuren (1999) highlights the long-term effects

of job insecurity, which can result in both mental and physical health problems.

2. *High Job Demands and Low Control:* Workplaces that demand too much from employees without giving them adequate control over their tasks can cause severe psychological strain among employees. Karasek's Job Demands-Control model (Karasek, 1979) shows that jobs with high demands and low control increase the likelihood of stress, burnout, and mental health problems. Employees in these environments may feel overwhelmed, unable to meet expectations, and suffer from chronic exhaustion.

3. *Workplace Bullying and Harassment:* Interpersonal conflicts, bullying, harassment, and exclusion can create a toxic environment, impacting mental health and workplace morale. Research by Einarsen et al. (2003) highlights how prolonged exposure to bullying and harassment can lead to psychological distress, depression, and anxiety disorders. These behaviours can manifest in overt or covert forms, such as gossiping, exclusion from decision-making, or public humiliation.

4. *Poor Work-Life Balance:* In today's fast-paced world, employees often struggle to maintain a healthy work-life balance. Excessive working hours, pressure to be available outside regular working hours, and an inability to disconnect can result in burnout. The World Health Organization (WHO) (2019) recognises work-life imbalance as a significant contributor to mental health issues, emphasising that a lack of separation between work and personal life can lead to chronic stress.

5. *Lack of Social Support:* Workplaces where employees lack social support from colleagues or supervisors can be isolating and emotionally draining environments. The absence of meaningful relationships or guidance from leadership can exacerbate feelings of loneliness, anxiety, and job dissatisfaction (House, 1981). Organisations that fail to foster a culture of collaboration and support put their employees at risk of psychosocial harm.

Early Warning Signs and Red Flags

Recognising the early warning signs of psychosocial hazards is critical to prevent more serious issues from developing. These signs often manifest in subtle ways but can escalate if left unchecked. Here are some common red flags to watch for in the workplace:

1. *Increased Absenteeism:* A sudden rise in absenteeism may indicate that employees are struggling with stress, burnout, or other mental health challenges. Absenteeism is often a direct response to an overwhelming work environment or negative interpersonal dynamics.

2. *High Turnover Rates:* Frequent employee turnover is a clear indication that something is wrong within the organisation. Employees may be leaving due to job dissatisfaction, workplace bullying, or a toxic culture, all of which are psychosocial hazards.

3. *Decline in Productivity and Engagement:* A noticeable drop in productivity, creativity, or overall engagement can signal that employees are mentally or emotionally checked out. This can result from overwork, lack of control, or feeling undervalued in the workplace.

4. *Frequent Conflicts and Complaints:* An increase in inter-personal conflicts, complaints of harassment or bully-ing, or negative feedback during employee surveys can indicate the presence of psychosocial hazards. These is-sues often stem from a lack of communication, unclear expectations, or power imbalances.

5. *Emotional Distress and Fatigue:* Employees displaying signs of emotional distress, such as irritability, mood swings, or visible fatigue, may be struggling with psy-chosocial hazards. These symptoms are often indicators of burnout, anxiety, or depression caused by the work environment.

6. *Excessive Work Hours:* Employees consistently work-ing beyond their normal hours, or being available 24/7, may indicate a work-life imbalance or an unsustainable workload. Burnout and long-term health issues can arise if this issue is not addressed.

Proactive Measures and Leadership's Role

Recognising psychosocial hazards is just the first step. Leader-ship plays a pivotal role in addressing these hazards and cre-ating a workplace culture that prioritises mental health and well-being. This requires the development of comprehensive policies, the creation of a supportive environment, and the im-plementation of training programs to build awareness of these hazards among employees and managers.

For example, implementing regular employee surveys to moni-tor stress levels, providing mental health support services, and fostering open lines of communication can make a substantial difference in addressing these risks early. By proactively identifying and mitigating psychosocial hazards, organisations can enhance employee satisfaction, productivity, and overall workplace morale.

Real-World Examples

Addressing Work Pressure and Overtime

Company: Toyota

Issue: Overwork and extreme pressure leading to employee mental health crises

Psychosocial Hazard: Excessive work hours and overwhelming pressure to meet deadlines created a significant psychosocial hazard at Toyota, especially in the case of Akinori Yokoyama, a 30-year-old employee who tragically died by suicide after enduring excessive overtime. The culture at the time did not adequately recognise the strain being placed on workers, particularly younger employees and those working on tight production schedules.

Outcome: After this and other similar incidents came to light, Toyota acknowledged the issue and made efforts to reform its workplace culture. They began implementing stricter controls over working hours, increasing mental health awareness initiatives, and encouraging employees to take mandatory breaks. Recognising the psychosocial hazards related to excessive pressure, Toyota's new policies helped reduce the risk of burnout and fostered a healthier work-life balance.

Reference:

> BBC News. (2017). *Toyota suicide case highlights Japan's work culture crisis*. Retrieved from https://www.bbc.com

Identifying and Addressing Workplace Bullying

Company: Amazon

Issue: Allegations of bullying and toxic work culture leading to high turnover

Psychosocial Hazard: Amazon has faced numerous complaints about its high-pressure work environment, including accusations of workplace bullying and unrealistic performance expectations. Employees reported feeling micromanaged, bullied by supervisors, and pressured to work in emotionally and physically stressful conditions.

Outcome: Amazon responded to the growing criticisms by revisiting their workplace practices and pledging to address bullying concerns. In 2021, the company committed to a $300 million investment in safety and well-being initiatives to better support employee mental health and create safer, more supportive environments. This included reviewing feedback mechanisms, launching anti-bullying training, and expanding EAPs to help employees manage workplace stress and emotional health.

Reference:

- The Guardian. (2021). *Amazon pledges $300m on safety after accusations of workplace abuse*. Retrieved from https://www.theguardian.com

The Dangers of Isolation and Poor Mental Health Support

Company: Foxconn

Issue: Suicides and extreme isolation among workers

Psychosocial Hazard: Foxconn, one of the world's largest manufacturers, came under intense scrutiny in 2010 when a wave of employee suicides highlighted severe psychosocial hazards in their factories. Many employees worked long hours under harsh conditions, often isolated in dormitories far from their families. The company's lack of mental health support or avenues for employees to report distress created an environment where many felt trapped and hopeless.

Outcome: Following public outcry, Foxconn introduced significant changes, including raising wages, reducing work hours, and installing safety nets on buildings to prevent suicide attempts. They also started offering psychological support programs and establishing counselling services for their workforce. These efforts were part of a broader attempt to recognise and address the psychosocial hazards of isolation and overwhelming work pressure.

Reference:

- The New York Times. (2010). *After suicides, scrutiny of China's grim factories*. Retrieved from https://www.nytimes.com/2010/06/07/business/global/07suicide.html

Key Takeaways

Identifying and addressing stressors that can negatively impact employee mental health and well-being. Psychosocial hazards, such as excessive workloads, lack of support, and poor work environments, often go unnoticed but can lead to serious consequences for both employees and organisations. By actively recognising these hazards and implementing measures like open communication, mental health resources, and supportive leadership, workplaces can foster a safer, healthier environment that reduces stress and promotes productivity. This proactive approach not only improves employee morale but also mitigates long-term risks like absenteeism, high turnover, and reduced performance.

References and Resources:

- Clement, S., Schauman, O., Graham, T., Maggioni, F., Evans-Lacko, S., Bezborodovs, N., ... & Thornicroft, G. (2015). What is the impact of mental health-related stigma on help-seeking? A systematic review of quantitative and qualitative studies. *Psychological Medicine, 45*(1), 11-27.

- Einarsen, S., Hoel, H., Zapf, D., & Cooper, C. L. (2003). *Bullying and emotional abuse in the workplace: International perspectives in research and practice.* Taylor & Francis.

- House, J. S. (1981). *Work stress and social support.* Addison-Wesley Publishing.

- Klandermans, B., & Van Vuuren, T. (1999). Job insecurity: Review of the international literature on definitions, prevalence, and consequences. *European Journal of Work and Organisational Psychology, 8*(2), 145-160.

- Karasek, R. (1979). Job demands, job decision latitude, and mental strain: Implications for job redesign. *Administrative Science Quarterly, 24*(2), 285-308.

- World Health Organization (WHO). (2019). Mental health in the workplace. Retrieved from https://www.who.int/mental_health

Developing a Psychosocial Safety Plan

Creating a Psychosocial Safety Strategy

Developing a psychosocial safety strategy is a fundamental step toward ensuring employee well-being and fostering a supportive work environment. This strategy serves as a blueprint for implementing policies and practices that promote mental health, reduce stress, and prevent workplace harassment and bullying.

To create an effective psychosocial safety strategy, organisations should consider the following steps:

1. *Assess Current Conditions:* Begin by conducting a thorough assessment of the current psychosocial safety climate (PSC) in the workplace. This includes reviewing existing policies, gathering employee feedback, and identifying areas for improvement. Tools such as the Psychosocial Safety Climate Scale can help measure employees' perceptions regarding the organisational policies, practices, and procedures for protecting their psychological health (Dollard et al., 2010).

2. *Set Clear Goals and Objectives:* Establish specific, measurable, achievable, relevant, and time-bound (SMART) goals for the psychosocial safety strategy. These goals should align with the overall mission and values of the organisation and address identified areas for improvement. For example, a goal might be to reduce workplace stress levels by 20% within the next year.

3. *Involve Stakeholders:* Engage key stakeholders, including senior management, diversity, equity, and inclusion (DE&I) and human resources (HR) professionals, and employees, in the development of the strategy. Involving stakeholders ensures that the strategy is comprehensive, addresses the needs of all parties, and gains widespread support. Research by Nielsen and Randall (2012) emphasises the importance of participatory approaches in developing and implementing workplace interventions to ensure their success.

4. *Develop Policies and Procedures:* Create or update policies and procedures that support psychosocial safety. This includes anti-bullying and harassment policies, mental health support initiatives, and stress management programs. Policies should be clearly communicated to all employees and consistently enforced.

5. *Provide Training and Resources:* Offer training and resources to employees and managers to support the implementation of the psychosocial safety strategy. This might include workshops on stress management, Mental Health First Aid (MHFA), and resources for coping with workplace challenges.

6. *Implement Support Systems:* Establish support systems such as Employee Assistance Programs (EAPs), peer support networks, and mental health resources. These systems provide employees with access to confidential support and resources when they need them.

7. *Monitor and Evaluate:* Regularly monitor the implementation of the psychosocial safety strategy and evaluate its effectiveness. Use employee feedback, performance metrics, and other data to assess progress and make

- *Role Modelling:* Leaders should model the behaviours and attitudes they expect from their employees. This includes demonstrating respect, empathy, and support in their interactions with others.

- *Communication:* Open and transparent communication is essential for building trust and fostering a culture of psychosocial safety. Leaders should encourage dialogue, listen to employee concerns, and provide timely feedback and information.

- *Support and Resources:* Leaders must ensure that employees have access to the support and resources they need to maintain their psychological well-being. This includes providing access to mental health services, offering flexible work arrangements, and creating opportunities for professional development.

- *Continuous Improvement:* Psychosocial safety is an ongoing process that requires continuous evaluation and improvement. Leaders should regularly assess the effectiveness of their initiatives, seek feedback from employees, and make necessary adjustments to address emerging challenges and opportunities.

Why Psychosocial Safety Matters

Psychosocial safety benefits both employees and organisations. Studies indicate that workplaces with high psychosocial safety have lower absenteeism, improved productivity, and higher employee engagement (Safe Work Australia, 2018). Research by the **World Health Organization (WHO)** found that depression and anxiety cost the global economy an estimated $1 trillion annually due to lost productivity (WHO, 2019). Addressing these risks early fosters employee well-being, improves performance, and reduces turnover.

Legal Framework and Compliance

In Australia, psychosocial safety has been integrated into the regulatory framework, emphasising the importance of managing psychosocial hazards just as rigorously as physical ones. The **Model Work Health and Safety Regulations (2022)** include explicit requirements for employers to identify, manage, and mitigate risks related to stress, workload, bullying, and harassment (Safe Work Australia, 2022). This legislative focus reflects the growing recognition that psychological well-being is inseparable from occupational health and safety.

Real-World Implications

A proactive approach to psychosocial safety involves not only compliance but also fostering a culture where employees feel genuinely valued. For instance, research shows that workplaces that invest in psychological safety experience greater team innovation, enhanced collaboration, and better decision-making outcomes (Duhigg, 2016). Furthermore, organisations that integrate psychosocial safety into their core values are more likely to attract and retain top talent.

Real-World Examples

Examining real-world examples of organisations that have successfully implemented psychosocial safety initiatives can provide valuable insights and inspiration. Here are a few examples:

PART 3

Developing a Psychosocial Safety Plan

Developing a Psychosocial Safety Plan

Creating a Psychosocial Safety Strategy

Developing a psychosocial safety strategy is a fundamental step toward ensuring employee well-being and fostering a supportive work environment. This strategy serves as a blueprint for implementing policies and practices that promote mental health, reduce stress, and prevent workplace harassment and bullying.

To create an effective psychosocial safety strategy, organisations should consider the following steps:

1. *Assess Current Conditions:* Begin by conducting a thorough assessment of the current psychosocial safety climate (PSC) in the workplace. This includes reviewing existing policies, gathering employee feedback, and identifying areas for improvement. Tools such as the Psychosocial Safety Climate Scale can help measure employees' perceptions regarding the organisational policies, practices, and procedures for protecting their psychological health (Dollard et al., 2010).

2. *Set Clear Goals and Objectives:* Establish specific, measurable, achievable, relevant, and time-bound (SMART) goals for the psychosocial safety strategy. These goals should align with the overall mission and values of the organisation and address identified areas for improvement. For example, a goal might be to reduce workplace stress levels by 20% within the next year.

3. *Involve Stakeholders:* Engage key stakeholders, including senior management, diversity, equity, and inclusion (DE&I) and human resources (HR) professionals, and employees, in the development of the strategy. Involving stakeholders ensures that the strategy is comprehensive, addresses the needs of all parties, and gains widespread support. Research by Nielsen and Randall (2012) emphasises the importance of participatory approaches in developing and implementing workplace interventions to ensure their success.

4. *Develop Policies and Procedures:* Create or update policies and procedures that support psychosocial safety. This includes anti-bullying and harassment policies, mental health support initiatives, and stress management programs. Policies should be clearly communicated to all employees and consistently enforced.

5. *Provide Training and Resources:* Offer training and resources to employees and managers to support the implementation of the psychosocial safety strategy. This might include workshops on stress management, Mental Health First Aid (MHFA), and resources for coping with workplace challenges.

6. *Implement Support Systems:* Establish support systems such as Employee Assistance Programs (EAPs), peer support networks, and mental health resources. These systems provide employees with access to confidential support and resources when they need them.

7. *Monitor and Evaluate:* Regularly monitor the implementation of the psychosocial safety strategy and evaluate its effectiveness. Use employee feedback, performance metrics, and other data to assess progress and make

Developing a Psychosocial Safety Plan

Creating a Psychosocial Safety Strategy

Developing a psychosocial safety strategy is a fundamental step toward ensuring employee well-being and fostering a supportive work environment. This strategy serves as a blueprint for implementing policies and practices that promote mental health, reduce stress, and prevent workplace harassment and bullying.

To create an effective psychosocial safety strategy, organisations should consider the following steps:

1. *Assess Current Conditions:* Begin by conducting a thorough assessment of the current psychosocial safety climate (PSC) in the workplace. This includes reviewing existing policies, gathering employee feedback, and identifying areas for improvement. Tools such as the Psychosocial Safety Climate Scale can help measure employees' perceptions regarding the organisational policies, practices, and procedures for protecting their psychological health (Dollard et al., 2010).

2. *Set Clear Goals and Objectives:* Establish specific, measurable, achievable, relevant, and time-bound (SMART) goals for the psychosocial safety strategy. These goals should align with the overall mission and values of the organisation and address identified areas for improvement. For example, a goal might be to reduce workplace stress levels by 20% within the next year.

3. *Involve Stakeholders:* Engage key stakeholders, including senior management, diversity, equity, and inclusion (DE&I) and human resources (HR) professionals, and employees, in the development of the strategy. Involving stakeholders ensures that the strategy is comprehensive, addresses the needs of all parties, and gains widespread support. Research by Nielsen and Randall (2012) emphasises the importance of participatory approaches in developing and implementing workplace interventions to ensure their success.

4. *Develop Policies and Procedures:* Create or update policies and procedures that support psychosocial safety. This includes anti-bullying and harassment policies, mental health support initiatives, and stress management programs. Policies should be clearly communicated to all employees and consistently enforced.

5. *Provide Training and Resources:* Offer training and resources to employees and managers to support the implementation of the psychosocial safety strategy. This might include workshops on stress management, Mental Health First Aid (MHFA), and resources for coping with workplace challenges.

6. *Implement Support Systems:* Establish support systems such as Employee Assistance Programs (EAPs), peer support networks, and mental health resources. These systems provide employees with access to confidential support and resources when they need them.

7. *Monitor and Evaluate:* Regularly monitor the implementation of the psychosocial safety strategy and evaluate its effectiveness. Use employee feedback, performance metrics, and other data to assess progress and make

necessary adjustments. Continuous improvement is key to maintaining a safe and supportive work environment.

Setting Goals and Objectives

Setting clear and achievable goals is crucial for the success of any psychosocial safety plan. Goals provide direction, motivate employees, and help measure progress. When setting goals, organisations should consider the following:

1. *Align with Organisational Values:* Ensure that the goals of the psychosocial safety plan align with the organisation's values and mission. This alignment reinforces the importance of psychosocial safety and demonstrates the organisation's commitment to employee well-being.

2. *Make Goals Specific and Measurable:* Goals should be specific and measurable to provide a clear target and allow for accurate assessment of progress. For example, instead of setting a vague goal such as "Improve employee well-being", set a specific goal such as "Increase employee satisfaction scores by 15% within six months".

3. *Set Achievable and Realistic Goals:* Goals should be challenging yet achievable. Setting unrealistic goals can lead to frustration and disengagement, while achievable goals can motivate employees and build confidence.

4. *Ensure Relevance:* Goals should be relevant to the organisation's needs and priorities. For example, if workplace stress is a significant issue, a relevant goal might be to reduce reported stress levels by implementing stress management programs and providing resources for employees.

5. *Establish a Timeline:* Set a timeline for achieving each goal. A timeline provides a sense of urgency and helps keep the plan on track. For example, a goal might be to conduct a comprehensive psychosocial safety audit within the next three months.

Involving Stakeholders and Gaining Buy-In

Gaining buy-in from stakeholders is essential for the successful implementation of a psychosocial safety plan. Stakeholders include senior management, DE&I and HR professionals, employees, and external partners such as mental health experts or consultants. Here are some strategies for involving stakeholders:

1. *Engage Senior Management:* Senior management support is critical for the success of the psychosocial safety plan. Engage senior leaders early in the process, communicate the benefits of the plan, and seek their input and support. Research by Kelloway and Day (2005) highlights the positive impact of leadership commitment on the success of workplace health and safety initiatives.

2. *Create a Multidisciplinary Team:* Form a multidisciplinary team to develop and implement the psychosocial safety plan. This team should include representatives from HR, health and safety, employee representatives, and other relevant departments. A diverse team ensures that different perspectives and expertise are considered.

3. *Communicate the Benefits:* Clearly communicate the benefits of the psychosocial safety plan to all stakeholders. Highlight how the plan will improve employee well-being, enhance productivity, reduce turnover, and

create a positive work environment. Use data and evidence to support these claims.

4. *Seek Input and Feedback:* Involve stakeholders in the development of the plan by seeking their input and feedback. Conduct surveys, focus groups, and meetings to gather insights and suggestions. Involving stakeholders in the process increases their sense of ownership and commitment.

5. *Provide Training and Resources:* Offer training and resources to stakeholders to support their involvement in the psychosocial safety plan. This might include workshops on mental health awareness, stress management, and effective communication.

6. *Celebrate Successes:* Recognise and celebrate the successes and contributions of stakeholders in implementing the psychosocial safety plan. Celebrating successes reinforces positive behaviours and motivates continued efforts.

Aligning with Organisational Values and Mission

Aligning the psychosocial safety plan with the organisation's values and mission is essential for ensuring its success and sustainability. This alignment demonstrates the organisation's commitment to employee well-being and integrates psychosocial safety into the broader organisational culture. Here are some strategies for achieving alignment:

1. *Incorporate Psychosocial Safety into the Mission Statement:* Update the organisation's mission statement to reflect a commitment to psychosocial safety. This might

involve including language about promoting employee well-being, creating a supportive work environment, and prioritising mental health.

2. *Embed Psychosocial Safety in Organisational Values:* Ensure that psychosocial safety is a core organisational value. This involves integrating principles of respect, inclusion, and support into the organisation's values and communicating these values to all employees.

3. *Align Policies and Procedures:* Review and update organisational policies and procedures to ensure they align with the psychosocial safety plan. This might include updating HR policies, safety manuals, and employee handbooks to reflect the commitment to psychosocial safety.

4. *Promote a Culture of Safety:* Foster a culture of safety by encouraging open communication, mutual respect, and support among employees. This involves creating an environment where employees feel comfortable discussing mental health issues, seeking help, and supporting one another.

5. *Integrate Psychosocial Safety into Performance Metrics:* Include psychosocial safety metrics in performance evaluations and organisational assessments. This might involve measuring employee satisfaction, stress levels, and participation in mental health programs. Using these metrics to assess performance reinforces the importance of psychosocial safety.

6. *Provide Ongoing Training and Development:* Offer ongoing training and development programs to support the implementation of the psychosocial safety plan. This

might include workshops on stress management, mental health awareness, and effective communication.

Real-World Examples

Addressing Workplace Stress and Harassment

Company: France Telecom (now Orange S.A.)

Issue: High stress, bullying, and employee suicides

Psychosocial Hazard: Between 2008 and 2009, France Telecom faced a public crisis when more than 30 employees died by suicide, many of them leaving notes indicating that workplace stress and harassment were major contributing factors. The company was undergoing a significant restructuring process, which included forced mobility, job cuts, and an overall culture of fear and intimidation. Employees reported a toxic environment where they were micromanaged and pressured to relocate or change roles.

Outcome: Following an investigation, several top executives were found guilty of moral harassment, and France Telecom was fined for failing to prevent the psychosocial hazards. In response, the company made widespread changes to its HR policies, including the implementation of anti-harassment initiatives, a focus on employee well-being, and significant restructuring of their employee management approach. The company's approach became more focused on improving mental health resources, stress management, and fostering a healthier work culture.

Reference:

- The Guardian. (2019). *Ex-France Télécom bosses found guilty of moral harassment after wave of suicides.* Retrieved from https://www.theguardian.com

Reducing Stress and Improving Psychosocial Safety

Company: Barclays Bank

Issue: High levels of workplace stress and anxiety among employees

Psychosocial Hazard: Barclays Bank faced widespread complaints of stress and pressure among its workforce, particularly following the 2008 financial crisis. Employees at all levels reported struggling with unrealistic targets, heavy workloads, and a lack of support from managers. High expectations combined with an aggressive workplace culture led to increased absenteeism and a notable drop in employee morale.

Outcome: Barclays took action by conducting a comprehensive psychosocial safety audit and implementing a mental health and well-being strategy. The company introduced flexible work options, mental health support through EAPs, and training for managers on stress management and mental health awareness. The bank also encouraged an open-door policy, where employees could discuss workplace challenges in a confidential environment. These changes led to a significant improvement in employee well-being, a reduction in stress-related absences, and better overall performance.

Reference:

> Financial Times. (2019). *Barclays looks to reduce employee stress with mental health programs*. Retrieved from https://www.ft.com

Tackling Workplace Bullying and Emotional Exhaustion

Company: Walmart

Issue: Bullying and emotional exhaustion leading to high employee turnover

Psychosocial Hazard: Walmart experienced a surge in employee complaints related to workplace bullying, emotional exhaustion, and a lack of support for mental health. Many employees reported feeling overwhelmed by unrealistic productivity expectations, micromanagement, and bullying from supervisors. These conditions contributed to high turnover, increased absenteeism, and poor employee morale across various locations.

Outcome: Walmart launched a comprehensive initiative to address these psychosocial hazards by enhancing employee training on mental health and workplace bullying. They implemented stricter anti-bullying policies and introduced leadership programs to foster respectful and supportive management. Additionally, Walmart expanded its EAP services, offering more resources for employees dealing with stress, anxiety, and emotional exhaustion. Within a year, the company saw a decline in bullying complaints and a marked improvement in employee satisfaction and retention.

Reference:

- CNN Business. (2020). *Walmart tackles bullying and mental health with expanded Employee Assistance Programs*. Retrieved from https://www.cnn.com

Key Takeaways

Developing a psychosocial safety plan is a critical step in creating a supportive and healthy work environment. By following a structured approach that includes assessing current conditions, setting clear goals, involving stakeholders, and aligning with organisational values, organisations can develop a comprehensive and effective psychosocial safety strategy.

Research and evidence support the importance of psychosocial safety in the workplace. Studies have shown that organisations with strong PSCs report higher levels of employee well-being, increased productivity, and reduced turnover and absenteeism (Dollard & Bakker, 2010; Nielsen & Randall, 2012). Consider how implementing a psychosocial safety plan not only benefits employees but also contributes to the overall success and sustainability of the organisation.

References:

- Dollard, M. F., & Bakker, A. B. (2010). Psychosocial safety climate as a precursor to conducive work environments, psychological health problems, and employee engagement. *Journal of Occupational Health Psychology*, *15*(3), 273-289.

- Hall, G. B., Dollard, M. F., Tuckey, M. R., Winefield, A. H., & Thompson, B. M. (2010). Job demands, work-family conflict, and emotional exhaustion in police officers: A longitudinal test of competing theories. *Journal of Occupational and Organisational Psychology*, *83*(1), 237-250.

- Kelloway, E. K., & Day, A. L. (2005). Building healthy workplaces: Where we need to be. *Canadian Journal of Behavioural Science/Revue canadienne des sciences du comportement*, *37*(4), 309-312.

- Nielsen, K., & Randall, R. (2012). The importance of employee participation and perceptions of changes in procedures in a team working intervention. *Work & Stress*, *26*(2), 91-111.

CHAPTER 6

Policies and Procedures for Psychosocial Safety

Developing Comprehensive Policies

Well-defined, comprehensive policies that address various aspects of employee well-being are the cornerstones of a psychosocially safe workplace. These policies provide a structured approach to managing and mitigating psychosocial risks and promote a culture of safety and support within the organisation.

Different Types of Workplace Psychosocial Safety Policies

1. *Anti-Bullying and Harassment Policies:* Bullying and harassment are significant stressors in the workplace that can lead to serious mental health issues. Policies must clearly define what constitutes bullying and harassment, establish reporting mechanisms, and outline consequences for violators. According to a study by the Workplace Bullying Institute (WBI, 2017), 19% of U.S. workers experience bullying, highlighting the necessity for robust anti-bullying policies.

2. *Mental Health Support Policies:* These policies should encompass provisions for mental health days, access to mental health professionals, and accommodations for employees dealing with mental health issues. The World Health Organization (WHO) reports that depression and anxiety alone cost the global economy an estimated **$1 trillion per year** in lost productivity (WHO, 2017).

3. **Flexible Working Arrangements**: Policies that support flexible working hours, remote work, and job-sharing can significantly reduce stress and improve work-life balance. Research by the Chartered Institute of Personnel and Development (CIPD) in the UK shows that flexible working arrangements are associated with higher job satisfaction and reduced stress (CIPD, 2018).

4. *Inclusion and Diversity Policies:* Ensuring that the workplace is inclusive and diverse can help mitigate psychosocial risks associated with discrimination and bias. A McKinsey report found that companies in the top quartile for gender diversity are 21% more likely to outperform their peers on profitability (McKinsey & Company, 2018).

5. *Workload Management Policies:* Clear guidelines on workload management and expectations can help prevent burnout. These policies should include regular workload assessments, reasonable deadlines, and mechanisms for employees to report excessive workloads. A study by the American Psychological Association (APA) found that workload is a significant source of workplace stress, with 39% of employees reporting that workload is a major factor (APA, 2018).

6. *Domestic and Family Violence (DFV) Support Policies:* These policies should include provisions for paid leave for victims of DFV, access to counselling and support services, and the implementation of safety plans for affected employees. The Australian Human Rights Commission (AHRC) reports that domestic violence costs the Australian economy **$21.7 billion annually,** with workplaces bearing a significant portion of the financial impact due to absenteeism, reduced productivity, and staff turnover (AHRC, 2019).

Implementation Strategies

1. **Policy Communication and Training**: Once policies are developed, they must be effectively communicated to all employees. Training sessions, workshops, and regular reminders can help ensure that everyone understands the policies and how to apply them. The Occupational Safety and Health Administration (OSHA) emphasises the importance of training in creating a safe and healthy workplace (OSHA, 2015).

2. **Regular Review and Updates**: Policies should be regularly reviewed and updated to reflect changes in the organisation and the broader legal and social environment. This ensures that the policies remain relevant and effective. A report by the Society for Human Resource Management (SHRM) recommends annual policy reviews to ensure compliance and effectiveness (SHRM, 2020).

3. **Employee Involvement**: Involving employees in the development and review of policies can increase their effectiveness and acceptance. Employee feedback can provide valuable insights into potential issues and areas for improvement. A participatory approach is recommended by the National Institute for Occupational Safety and Health (NIOSH), which found that employee involvement in safety programs leads to better outcomes (NIOSH, 2019).

Implementing Support Systems

Support systems are essential for the practical application of psychosocial safety policies. They provide the necessary resources and assistance to employees, helping them navigate challenges and maintain their well-being.

Key Components of Support Systems

1. *Employee Assistance Programs (EAPs):* EAPs offer confidential counselling and support services for employees dealing with personal or work-related issues. These programs can address a range of issues, including mental health, substance abuse, and family problems. Research shows that EAPs can reduce absenteeism and improve productivity (Attridge, 2019).

2. *Peer Support Networks:* Establishing peer support networks can provide employees with a sense of community and belonging. These networks offer a platform for employees to share experiences, seek advice, and support each other. A study by the Australian Institute of Family Studies found that peer support programs can significantly improve mental health outcomes (AIFS, 2018).

3. *Mental Health Resources:* Providing access to mental health resources, such as self-help materials, online courses, and workshops, can empower employees to take charge of their mental health. The Mental Health Foundation reports that providing mental health resources can lead to increased employee engagement and reduced stigma (Mental Health Foundation, 2016).

4. *Crisis Intervention Services:* In cases of acute stress or trauma, immediate intervention is crucial. Crisis intervention services can provide timely support and prevent further escalation of issues. According to the International Critical Incident Stress Foundation (ICISF), early intervention can significantly reduce the long-term impact of traumatic events (ICISF, 2020).

Best Practices for Implementation

1. *Confidentiality and Accessibility:* Ensuring that support services are confidential and easily accessible is critical. Employees must feel safe and confident that their privacy will be respected. The Employee Assistance Professionals Association (EAPA) emphasises the importance of confidentiality in the success of EAPs (EAPA, 2018).

2. *Proactive Promotion:* Actively promoting support services through internal communications, posters, and regular reminders can increase awareness and utilisation. A study by Deloitte found that organisations with proactive mental health programs see a return on investment of $4 for every $1 spent (Deloitte, 2019).

3. *Integration with Health and Safety Programs:* Integrating psychosocial support services with existing health and safety programs can provide a holistic approach to employee well-being. The Centers for Disease Control and Prevention (CDC) recommend a coordinated approach to workplace health promotion (CDC, 2016).

4. *Ongoing Training for Support Providers:* Ensuring that those providing support, such as peer supporters, receive ongoing training can enhance the quality and effectiveness of support services. Training should cover current best practices, legal requirements, and emerging trends in psychosocial safety (American Counseling Association, 2020).

Ensuring Confidentiality and Trust

Confidentiality and trust are foundational elements of effective psychosocial safety policies and support systems. Without these, employees may be reluctant to seek help or report issues, undermining the effectiveness of the entire program.

Strategies for Ensuring Confidentiality

1. *Clear Confidentiality Policies:* Develop and communicate clear policies regarding confidentiality. These policies should outline what information will be kept confidential, how it will be protected, and under what circumstances, if any, it may be disclosed. In the USA, The *Health Insurance Portability and Accountability Act* (c) provides guidelines for maintaining the confidentiality of health information (HIPAA, 1996).

2. *Training for Managers and Support Providers:* Ensure that managers and those providing support services understand the importance of confidentiality and are trained in how to handle sensitive information. The APA provides guidelines for maintaining confidentiality in psychological services (APA, 2017). In Australia, the Australian Psychological Society (APS) provides guidelines for maintaining confidentiality in psychological services.

3. *Secure Communication Channels:* Use secure communication channels for sharing sensitive information. This might include encrypted emails, secure internal messaging systems, and confidential hotlines. The National Cyber Security Centre (NCSC) recommends best practices for securing communication channels (NCSC, 2020).

4. *Anonymous Reporting Mechanisms:* Provide mechanisms for employees to report issues anonymously if they choose. Anonymous reporting can encourage those who might fear retaliation or stigma to come for-

ward. A study by the Ethics Resource Centre found that anonymous reporting systems increase the likelihood of reporting misconduct (ERC, 2013).

Building Trust

1. *Transparency and Accountability:* Be transparent about how information will be used and ensure accountability in handling sensitive data. Regularly update employees on the measures taken to protect their privacy and the outcomes of reported issues. Transparency can build trust and confidence in the system.

2. *Consistent Enforcement:* Consistently enforce policies and procedures to demonstrate the organisation's commitment to psychosocial safety. Inconsistent enforcement can erode trust and undermine the effectiveness of the policies.

3. *Employee Involvement:* Involve employees in the development and review of policies and support systems. This inclusion can enhance their sense of ownership and trust in the system. The NIOSH emphasises the importance of employee involvement in workplace safety programs (NIOSH, 2019).

4. *Positive Reinforcement:* Recognise and reward behaviours that contribute to a positive psychosocial climate. This might include acknowledging employees who support their peers or managers who effectively implement psychosocial safety practices.

Real-World Examples

Pressure to Meet Unrealistic Targets Leading to Scandal

Company: Wells Fargo

Issue: Lack of psychosocial safety policies contributing to unethical behaviour and employee stress

Negative Impact: Wells Fargo faced a massive scandal in 2016 when it was revealed that employees had opened millions of unauthorised customer accounts to meet unrealistic sales targets set by management. The company fostered a high-pressure environment where employees were expected to meet impossible quotas, and there were few support systems in place to address the stress and anxiety this created. The lack of psychosocial safety policies, including mental health support and ethical safeguards, led employees to engage in unethical behaviours out of fear of losing their jobs.

Outcome: The fallout from this scandal was immense, resulting in **$3 billion** in fines and settlements, widespread layoffs, and significant damage to Wells Fargo's reputation. The bank's CEO resigned, and numerous top executives were forced out. The company was required to implement substantial changes, including stronger ethical oversight, reduced pressure on employees to meet targets, and new psychosocial safety measures. If Wells Fargo had recognised and addressed the psychosocial hazards created by unrealistic expectations, it could have prevented the unethical actions that followed and the resulting legal and financial consequences.

Reference:

- CNN Business. (2020). *Wells Fargo's $3 billion fake accounts settlement explained*. Retrieved from https://www.cnn.com

Ignoring Employee Concerns Leading to Emissions Scandal

Company: Volkswagen

Issue: Lack of transparency and psychosocial safety contributing to unethical decisions

Negative Impact: Volkswagen's 2015 emissions scandal, known as "Dieselgate", revealed the company's use of software to cheat emissions tests in its diesel vehicles. Employees were aware of the illegal practices but felt pressured to comply with unethical directives from upper management. The company's lack of clear whistleblower policies or psychosocial safety systems to support employees in reporting wrongdoing played a crucial role in allowing the scandal to unfold. Employees felt unable to speak out or question decisions, creating a culture of compliance without accountability.

Outcome: The scandal cost Volkswagen over **$30 billion** in fines, settlements, and vehicle recalls. The company's reputation was significantly damaged, and it faced lawsuits worldwide. In response, Volkswagen overhauled its corporate governance and introduced policies promoting transparency and ethical decision-making. The absence of a robust psychosocial safety net in the workplace allowed unethical behaviour to persist, leading to severe legal, financial, and reputational damage.

Reference:

- BBC News. (2015). *Volkswagen: The scandal explained*. Retrieved from https://www.bbc.com

Employee Stress and Absenteeism Due to Lack of Support

Company: Royal Mail

Issue: High absenteeism due to workplace stress and lack of mental health support

Negative Impact: The Royal Mail faced a period of high absenteeism and employee dissatisfaction in the mid-2000s, particularly related to workplace stress. With increasing pressure to meet delivery targets and frequent operational changes, employees reported feeling overwhelmed, unsupported, and under extreme pressure. There were no comprehensive psychosocial safety policies in place to help employees manage their stress, and the company lacked a formal structure to provide mental health resources or address burnout.

Outcome: Absenteeism rates soared, and productivity declined as employees struggled to cope with the mounting pressure. In response to rising concerns, the Royal Mail eventually implemented a series of well-being initiatives, including stress management programs and improved mental health resources for employees. The company also conducted regular health and safety audits to better understand the sources of workplace stress. Had these measures been introduced earlier, the company could have mitigated the loss in productivity and improved employee morale much sooner.

Reference:

❯ The Guardian. (2006). *Royal Mail faces surge in employee absenteeism*. Retrieved from https://www.theguardian.com

Key Takeaways

Developing comprehensive policies and support systems for psychosocial safety is crucial for creating a healthy and supportive work environment. By addressing key areas such as anti-bullying, mental health support, flexible working arrangements, and inclusion, organisations can mitigate psychosocial risks and promote employee well-being.

The implementation of these policies requires effective communication, regular reviews, employee involvement, and a strong emphasis on confidentiality and trust. Research and best practices from organisations such as the WHO, APA, and NIOSH provide valuable insights into the development and implementation of psychosocial safety policies.

Ultimately, a psychosocially safe workplace not only benefits employees but also enhances organisational performance, reduces turnover and absenteeism, and fosters a positive and inclusive work culture. By committing to the continuous improvement of psychosocial safety policies and support systems, organisations can create a work environment where employees feel valued, supported, and empowered.

References:

- American Psychological Association (APA). (2017). Ethical principles of psychologists and code of conduct. Retrieved from https://www.apa.org/ethics/code

- Attridge, M. (2019). Employee Assistance Programs: Evidence and current trends. *Journal of Workplace Behavioural Health, 34*(1), 1-28.

- Centers for Disease Control and Prevention (CDC). (2016). Workplace health promotion. Retrieved from https://www.cdc.gov/workplacehealthpromotion/index.html

- Chartered Institute of Personnel and Development (CIPD). (2018). Flexible working practices. Retrieved from https://www.cipd.org/en/

- Deloitte. (2019). Mental health and employers: The case for investment. Retrieved from https://www.deloitte.com/au/en.html

- Employee Assistance Professionals Association (EAPA). (2018). Standards and guidelines for Employee Assistance Programs. Retrieved from https://eapassn.org/

- Ethics Resource Center. (2013). National business ethics survey. Retrieved from https://www.ethics.org/

- International Critical Incident Stress Foundation (ICISF). (2020). Critical incident stress management. Retrieved from https://icisf.org/

- McKinsey & Company. (2018). Delivering through diversity. Retrieved from https://www.mckinsey.com/

- Mental Health Foundation. (2016). Added value: Mental health as a workplace asset. Retrieved from https://www.mentalhealth.org.uk/

- National Institute for Occupational Safety and Health (NIOSH). (2019). Total worker health. Retrieved from https://www.cdc.gov/niosh/twh/default.html https://www.cdc.gov/niosh/twh/default.html

- National Cyber Security Centre. (2020). Securing your communications. Retrieved from https://www.ncsc.gov.uk/

- Occupational Safety and Health Administration (OSHA). (2015). Safety and health programs. Retrieved from https://www.osha.gov/

- Society for Human Resource Management (SHRM). (2020). Employee handbook creation and review. Retrieved from https://www.shrm.org/

- World Health Organization (WHO). (2017). Depression and other common mental disorders: Global health estimates. Retrieved from https://www.who.int

PART 4

Recognising Coercive Behaviours and the impact on the Workplace

CHAPTER 7

Coercive Behaviours in the Workplace and Their Impact

Coercive behaviours in the workplace are manipulative tactics used by individuals to control, dominate, or exploit others. Regardless of whether these behaviours are subtle or overt, they all have detrimental effects on both individuals and organisations. Understanding these behaviours is crucial for fostering a healthy, safe, and productive work environment. Below is a more in-depth examination of various coercive behaviours commonly found in the workplace.

Blackmail

Blackmail involves threatening to reveal damaging information about someone unless they comply with certain demands. In the workplace, blackmail can be used to coerce an employee into unethical behaviour, silence them about misconduct, or force them to comply with the blackmailer's demands. Blackmail is a serious form of manipulation that can have devastating consequences for the victim, including damage to their reputation, career, and mental health. It also creates a culture of fear and mistrust in the workplace, where employees are afraid to speak up or challenge unethical behaviour. Organisations that allow blackmail to occur risk facing legal consequences, losing valuable talent, and damaging their reputation.

Bullying

Bullying is repeated, aggressive behaviour intended to hurt, intimidate, or dominate another person. In the workplace, bullying can take many forms, including verbal abuse, physical threats, sabotage, or exclusion. Bullying often involves an imbalance of power, where the bully holds a position of authority or influence over the victim. This behaviour creates a hostile work environment, leading to increased stress, anxiety, and depression for the victim. It also undermines team morale, collaboration, and productivity, as employees become focused on self-preservation rather than working together. Organisations that tolerate bullying risk facing legal consequences, losing valuable talent, and damaging their reputation. losing valuable talent and damaging their reputation.

Covert Control

Covert control involves subtle, indirect attempts to control or manipulate others. This might include passive-aggressive behaviour, withholding information, or using guilt to influence decisions. In the workplace, covert control can be difficult to detect because it is often disguised as concern, helpfulness, or adherence to rules and procedures. However, the underlying intent is to maintain control over others without appearing overtly controlling. This behaviour can create a tense and distrustful work environment, where employees feel manipulated and uncertain about their standing. Covert control can also result in conflicts, as the manipulator's true intentions become apparent over time, causing resentment and frustration among team members.

Crazy Making

Crazy making is a form of psychological manipulation designed to make the victim question their reality or sanity. This behaviour involves a mix of contradictory messages, shifting expectations, and gaslighting, where the manipulator denies events or twists facts to confuse the victim. In the workplace, crazy making can occur when a manager or colleague gives conflicting instructions, changes deadlines without notice, or denies making certain requests, leaving the employee feeling frustrated, anxious, and unsure of themselves. The purpose of crazy making is to destabilise the victim's confidence, making them more dependent on the manipulator for direction and approval. Over time, this behaviour can erode the victim's self-esteem and mental health, leading to a sense of helplessness and resignation.

Discrimination

Discrimination in the workplace is a pervasive form of coercive behaviour, where individuals or groups are unfairly treated based on characteristics such as race, gender, age, disability, or sexual orientation. This behaviour not only undermines the dignity of the targeted individuals but also serves as a tool for exerting control and power within the organisation. Discriminatory practices can manifest in various forms, including biased hiring processes, unequal pay, limited opportunities for advancement, and exclusion from important meetings or projects. The psychological impact of discrimination is profound, leading to decreased job satisfaction, lower self-esteem, and increased stress, which can result in higher turnover rates and reduced organisational productivity.

Exclusion

Exclusion involves deliberately keeping someone out of groups, conversations, or decisions. This can be as overt as not inviting someone to meetings or social events, or as subtle as ignoring their input, withholding important information, or giving them the silent treatment. In the workplace, exclusion is often used as a form of punishment or control, making the victim feel marginalised and powerless. This behaviour can lead to feelings of loneliness, anxiety, and depression, and it can have a significant impact on the victim's job performance and job satisfaction. Exclusion also undermines team cohesion and collaboration, as it creates divisions and fosters a culture of exclusion and mistrust.

Over time, exclusion can result in high turnover, decreased job satisfaction, and a toxic work environment.

Flying Monkeys

Flying monkeys are individuals who act on behalf of a manipulator, often unwittingly, to carry out the manipulator's agenda. In the workplace, flying monkeys might include colleagues who support or enforce the toxic behaviour of a manipulative leader without fully understanding the harm to which they are contributing. These individuals may spread rumours, enforce unfair policies, or sabotage others on the manipulator's behalf, all while believing they are acting in the organisation's best interest. Flying monkeys are dangerous because they amplify the manipulator's power and influence, making it more difficult for victims to challenge or escape the toxic behaviour. The long-term impact of flying monkeys includes increased conflict, division, and dysfunction within the organisation.

Gaslighting

Gaslighting is a form of psychological manipulation that causes someone to doubt their perception, memory, or reality. In the workplace, this might involve a manager or colleague denying events, twisting facts, or blaming the victim for misunderstandings, making the employee feel confused, anxious, and unsure of themselves. Gaslighting is often used to gain control over someone by undermining their confidence and making them reliant on the manipulator for guidance and validation. This behaviour can have a devastating impact on the victim's mental health, leading to anxiety, depression, and a loss of self-esteem. It also creates a toxic work environment where trust is eroded, and employees are afraid to speak up or challenge the status quo.

Ghosting

Ghosting, traditionally associated with personal relationships, is increasingly recognised as a coercive behaviour in the workplace. When leaders or colleagues intentionally ignore, exclude, or cease communication with an individual, it can be a form of psychological manipulation designed to undermine confidence, exert control, or marginalise the target. This behaviour can lead to severe emotional distress, eroding trust and creating a hostile work environment. The silence associated with ghosting can leave the victim in a state of uncertainty and anxiety, questioning their value and role within the organisation. It can also disrupt team dynamics and productivity, as the affected employee becomes disengaged and demoralised.

Grooming

While the term grooming is commonly used in the context of exploitation of minors by adults and in domestic and family violence (DFV) relationships, it can also apply to some workplace dynamics. It involves building a relationship of trust and dependence with someone, often to exploit or manipulate them later. In the workplace, grooming might involve a manager or colleague giving special attention to an employee, offering them opportunities, or mentoring them, with the intention of gaining their loyalty or compliance. Once the target is emotionally invested or reliant on the relationship, the manipulator may begin to exploit the employee by asking for favours, bending rules, or encouraging unethical behaviour. Grooming is particularly insidious because it often starts with positive, supportive behaviours, making it difficult for the victim to recognise the manipulation until it is too late. The long-term impact of grooming can include damaged relationships, ethical breaches, and a toxic work environment.

Guilt Tripping

Guilt tripping is a subtle yet powerful coercive tactic where an individual manipulates others by making them feel responsible for problems or failures. In the workplace, this often manifests when managers or colleagues imply that employees' lack of dedication or effort is harming the team or the organisation (Ryan & Deci, 2017). This creates a culture of fear and obligation, pressuring employees to overextend themselves to avoid guilt or potential repercussions. Over time, guilt tripping leads to burnout, decreased job satisfaction, and increased absenteeism, as employees struggle to maintain a healthy work-life balance while being manipulated into overcommitting (Greenberg, 2019).

Harassment

Harassment involves unwanted and unwelcome behaviour that is intimidating, hostile, or offensive. Harassment can take many forms, including verbal, physical, and sexual, and is often targeted at someone's gender, race, or other personal characteristics. In the workplace, harassment creates a toxic environment where employees feel unsafe, disrespected, and unsupported. This behaviour can lead to increased stress, anxiety, and depression for the victim, as well as decreased job satisfaction and productivity. Organisations that fail to address harassment may risk legal consequences, losing valuable talent, and damaging their reputation. It is essential for organisations to have clear policies and procedures in place to prevent and address harassment.

Humiliation

Humiliation involves deliberately belittling or demeaning someone in front of others. In the workplace, this could include public reprimands, mocking, or spreading rumours about an employee. Humiliation is often used as a tool to assert dominance and control over others, making the victim feel powerless and inferior. This behaviour can have a profound impact on the victim's self-esteem, mental health, and job performance. It also creates a hostile work environment where employees are afraid to express themselves or take risks for fear of being humiliated. Organisations that tolerate humiliation risk losing valuable talent, facing legal consequences, and damaging their reputation.

Inclusion

Inclusion, while typically a positive concept, can be weaponised as a coercive behaviour in the workplace when it is used selectively or manipulatively. In such cases, inclusion is offered as a conditional privilege rather than a fundamental right, creating an environment where employees feel pressured to conform or align with certain behaviours, attitudes, or group dynamics to be "included". This form of coercion can lead to feelings of exclusion, isolation, and psychological distress among those who are not favoured or who resist conforming. Ultimately, this damages team cohesion and undermines trust within the organisation. The misuse of inclusion in this manner can be subtle yet profoundly harmful, as it exploits the basic human need for belonging to manipulate and control workplace dynamics.

Intimidation

Intimidation involves the use of threats, aggression, or fear to control others. In the workplace, intimidation can take many forms, ranging from overt actions such as yelling, making threats of termination, or public humiliation, to more subtle behaviours like giving someone the silent treatment, staring them down, or spreading rumours. Intimidation is often used by individuals in positions of power to maintain control over their subordinates or to coerce them into compliance. This tactic creates a culture of fear, where employees are too scared to speak up, challenge ideas, or report unethical behaviour. The long-term impact of such a culture can be devastating, leading to decreased employee morale, increased turnover, and a toxic work environment that stifles innovation and productivity.

Invalidation

Invalidation involves dismissing or undermining someone's thoughts, feelings, or experiences. In the workplace, this might manifest as a manager or colleague consistently downplaying an employee's contributions or concerns, making them feel unimportant or insignificant. Invalidation can take many forms, including dismissive comments, sarcastic remarks, or ignoring someone's input altogether. This behaviour can have a significant impact on the victim's self-esteem and job satisfaction, as it makes them feel devalued and unappreciated. Invalidation also stifles creativity and innovation, as employees are less likely to share their ideas or take risks when they feel their contributions are not valued.

Isolation

Isolation involves excluding someone from communication, decision-making, or social activities. This can be done overtly, such as not inviting someone to meetings or social events, or covertly, such as ignoring their input or withholding important information. In the workplace, isolation can be used as a form of punishment or control, making the victim feel marginalised and powerless. This behaviour can foster feelings of loneliness, anxiety, and depression, and it can have a significant impact on the victim's job performance and job satisfaction. Isolation also undermines team cohesion and collaboration, as it creates divisions and fosters a culture of exclusion and mistrust.

Justification

Justification involves rationalising or excusing harmful behaviour. In the workplace, this might manifest as a leader explaining away abusive or unethical actions as necessary for high performance or the greater good. For example, a manager might justify micromanagement by claiming it ensures quality, or they might excuse aggressive behaviour as a form of "tough love" to push employees to excel. Justification is a dangerous behaviour because it normalises harmful actions and creates a culture where such behaviour is accepted or even encouraged. Over time, this can lead to a toxic work environment where employees feel powerless to challenge the status quo and where abusive behaviour becomes entrenched in the organisational culture.

Learned Helplessness

Learned helplessness occurs when someone becomes conditioned to believe they are powerless to change their situation, even when opportunities for change exist. This often happens after repeated failures, constant criticism, or exposure to a controlling environment where the individual feels they have no control or influence. In the workplace, learned helplessness can result from a toxic culture where employees feel disempowered, unsupported, and unable to effect change. Over time, this can lead to a lack of motivation, decreased job satisfaction, and increased absenteeism. Organisations that perpetuate learned helplessness risk creating a stagnant work environment where employees are disengaged, innovation is stifled, and turnover is high.

Love Bombing

Love bombing is a form of manipulation that involves overwhelming someone with excessive attention, flattery, and affection to gain control over them. This tactic is often used in personal relationships, but it can also manifest in professional settings. In the workplace, a manager or colleague might use love bombing to create a false sense of security and loyalty. For example, a boss might excessively praise an employee, offer them special opportunities, or show extraordinary kindness, all with the intention of making the employee feel indebted or beholden to them. Once the target is emotionally invested or reliant on the relationship, the manipulator may withdraw the positive reinforcement, leaving the employee confused and desperate to regain favour. The ultimate goal is to create dependency, where the employee feels they must comply with the manipulator's demands to maintain the relationship or their status within the organisation.

Micromanagement

Micromanagement, while often intended to maintain control and ensure high standards, can quickly turn into a coercive behaviour when it becomes excessive. Research shows that micromanagement leads to significant stress and dissatisfaction among employees, stripping them of their autonomy and diminishing their job satisfaction (White, 2010). This lack of trust stifles creativity and innovation, as employees may feel their contributions are undervalued or constantly scrutinised (Williams, 2022). The constant pressure to meet unrealistic expectations, combined with the inability to make decisions independently, often results in burnout, reduced productivity, and increased turnover rates (Chambers, 2019).

No Disconnection from Work After Hours

The expectation that employees remain connected to work outside of regular hours is another form of coercive behaviour that blurs the boundaries between personal and professional life. Studies show that this constant connectivity leads to significant stress and disrupts employees' ability to recharge and maintain a healthy work-life balance (Derks & Bakker, 2014). The impact is severe, with research indicating that this constant connectivity contributes to burnout, reduced productivity, and long-term health issues (Sonnentag et al., 2017). Organisations committed to psychosocial safety must address this issue to prevent the erosion of employee well-being and morale.

Overt Control

Overt control involves direct and obvious attempts to control or dominate others. This might include micromanagement, strict rules, or dictating how tasks should be done without input from the employee. Overt control is often justified as necessary for maintaining order, ensuring quality, or achieving goals, but it can lead to resentment and disengagement among employees. In the workplace, overt control stifles creativity, innovation, and collaboration, as employees are afraid to take initiative or offer new ideas. It can also create a high-pressure environment where employees feel constantly scrutinised and unable to perform at their best. Over time, overt control can manifest as a high turnover rate, decreased job satisfaction, and a toxic work environment.

Sabotage

Sabotage in the workplace is a particularly insidious form of coercive behaviour, where individuals deliberately undermine the efforts of others to gain a competitive edge or cause harm. This behaviour can manifest in various ways, such as withholding critical information, spreading false rumours, or intentionally causing errors in someone else's work (Kramer & Harris, 2020). The impact of sabotage is profound, leading to a toxic work environment characterised by distrust, fear, and hostility. Research indicates that sabotage erodes team cohesion, lowers morale, and severely impacts organisational effectiveness (Pfeffer & Cialdini, 2021), as employees become more focused on self-preservation than on collaboration and innovation.

Scapegoating

Scapegoating involves unfairly blaming one person for the problems or failures of the group. In the workplace, a scapegoated employee may be held responsible for mistakes or issues that are not their fault, often to deflect blame from higher-ups or to protect the group's image. Scapegoating can be a form of bullying, where the targeted individual is consistently singled out for criticism, ostracised, or punished. This behaviour can cause severe psychological distress for the victim, including anxiety, depression, and a sense of isolation. Additionally, scapegoating undermines team cohesion, as it creates a culture of fear where employees are afraid to make mistakes or speak up for fear of being blamed. Organisations that allow scapegoating to persist risk losing valuable talent, damaging their reputation, and creating a toxic work environment.

Stonewalling

Stonewalling is a toxic behaviour in the workplace characterised by one party refusing to communicate, engage, or acknowledge the concerns of others. This behaviour can manifest as non-responsiveness, ignoring requests, or deliberately withholding critical information needed to move a project or conversation forward. Stonewalling creates a hostile environment where collaboration and productivity are hindered, leaving employees frustrated and demoralised. It can damage team dynamics and significantly undermine trust within the organisation. Research shows that stonewalling is often a form of emotional manipulation used to assert control or avoid accountability (Gottman, 1999). When this behaviour becomes normalised in the workplace, it can lead to long-term issues such as increased employee turnover, reduced morale, and overall decreased productivity (Einarsen, Hoel, Zapf, & Cooper, 2011).

Triangulation

Triangulation occurs when one person manipulates communication between two others to control or influence them. In the workplace, this might involve a manager pitting employees against each other by selectively sharing information or creating competition for resources, opportunities, or praise. The manipulator may also use one employee as a messenger to avoid direct communication with others, thereby maintaining control over the flow of information and keeping the employees off balance. Triangulation creates a divisive atmosphere where trust is eroded, collaboration is stifled, and employees are more focused on protecting themselves than on working together. This behaviour can also lead to long-term conflicts and resentment among team members, further damaging the organisational culture.

Weaponised Incompetence

Weaponised incompetence occurs when an individual intentionally pretends to be less capable or knowledgeable than they actually are, in order to avoid responsibility or shift work onto others. This tactic often leads to an uneven distribution of work, causing frustration and added stress for colleagues who must compensate for the individual's deliberate inefficiency. Common examples of weaponised incompetence include feigning ignorance, making repeated avoidable mistakes, or consistently asking for excessive help with straightforward tasks. Over time, this behaviour not only undermines productivity but also breeds resentment, erodes team cohesion, and fosters a toxic work environment.

Impacts of Coercive Behaviours in the Workplace

The coercive behaviours described above can have a profound and far-reaching impact on the workplace environment. These behaviours create a culture of fear, mistrust, and dysfunction that undermines morale, productivity, and overall organisational health. Employees who are subjected to such behaviours often experience increased stress, anxiety, and depression, leading to decreased job satisfaction and higher turnover rates. The presence of coercive behaviours also damages team cohesion and collaboration, as employees are pitted against each other or isolated from support networks.

Organisations that allow these behaviours to persist may face significant legal and financial risks, including lawsuits, reputational damage, and loss of key talent. Moreover, the long-term effects of a toxic workplace culture can lead to decreased innovation, stagnation, and an inability to attract and retain top talent.

Addressing and eliminating coercive behaviours is not only essential for fostering a psychosocially safe and productive work environment, but also for mitigating the serious financial and legal risks that can arise if these behaviours are left unchecked. In the following sections, we will explore the wide-ranging impacts of unchecked coercive behaviours, including reduced staff retention, increased absenteeism and presenteeism, poor employee morale, decreased collaboration, and the overall undermining of psychosocial safety. These factors not only harm employees but also significantly hinder an organisation's long-term success and stability.

Financial and Legal Risks

The financial repercussions of coercive behaviours in the workplace can be extensive. One of the primary ways in which these behaviours affect an organisation's bottom line is through increased turnover. Employees who experience coercive behaviours are more likely to leave the organisation, either by resigning or by being driven out. The cost of turnover is high, as it includes expenses related to recruiting, hiring, and training new employees, as well as the loss of institutional knowledge and expertise. According to the Society for Human Resource Management (SHRM), the cost of replacing an employee can range from six to nine months of the employee's salary, depending on their role within the organisation.

Coercive behaviours also contribute to decreased productivity, which can have a direct impact on revenue. When employees are subjected to coercive behaviours, their ability to focus and perform effectively is compromised. They may spend more time worrying about their safety and well-being than on their work tasks, leading to a decline in overall output. This reduction in productivity can result in missed deadlines, lower quality of work, and a decline in customer satisfaction—all of which can negatively affect an organisation's profitability.

Moreover, coercive behaviours heighten legal and reputational risks. Organisations that fail to address or prevent these behaviours may find themselves facing workers compensation costs, lawsuits, fines, and settlements related to workplace harassment, discrimination, or wrongful termination. The financial impact of legal actions can be substantial, not only in terms of direct costs but also in terms of damage to the organisation's reputation. A tarnished reputation can mean lost business opportunities, decreased customer trust, and difficulty attracting top talent.

Reduced Staff Retention

Staff retention is a critical concern for any organisation, and coercive behaviours can severely undermine efforts to retain employees. When employees experience coercive behaviours, they are likely to feel unsupported, unsafe, and undervalued, leading them to seek employment elsewhere. High turnover rates can create a vicious cycle, as the departure of experienced employees places additional stress on those who remain, potentially leading to further resignations.

Coercive behaviours also contribute to a toxic work environment, which can drive employees away. A toxic culture characterised by these coercive behaviours erodes trust and loyalty, making it difficult for employees to feel a sense of belonging or commitment to the organisation. Employees who do not feel psychologically safe are unlikely to stay with an organisation, as they prioritise their mental and emotional well-being over job stability.

In addition to losing valuable employees, organisations that fail to address coercive behaviours may struggle to attract new talent. Prospective employees are increasingly looking for workplaces that prioritise psychological safety and employee well-being. If an organisation develops a reputation for tolerating or perpetuating coercive behaviours, it may find it difficult to attract the skilled and motivated individuals needed to drive the organisation forward.

Absenteeism and Presenteeism Issues

Coercive behaviours in the workplace contribute to both absenteeism and presenteeism, each of which can have significant negative effects on organisational performance.

Absenteeism occurs when employees frequently miss work due to stress, anxiety, or illness related to the toxic work environment. Employees subjected to coercive behaviours may take time off to recover from the emotional and psychological toll, to avoid the abusive environment, or to seek medical or therapeutic help. High levels of absenteeism disrupt workflow, increase the burden on other employees, and reduce overall productivity. Additionally, chronic absenteeism can lead to increased costs related to temporary staffing, overtime pay, and decreased efficiency.

Presenteeism, on the other hand, occurs when employees come to work despite being unwell, distracted, or disengaged due to the effects of coercive behaviours. While these employees may be physically present, their ability to perform their duties effectively is compromised. Presenteeism can result in reduced productivity, mistakes, and accidents, as well as long-term health issues for the affected employees. The cost of presenteeism is often difficult to quantify, but it can have a substantial impact on an organisation's overall performance and profitability.

Both absenteeism and presenteeism are indicators of an unhealthy work environment where employees do not feel safe or supported. Addressing coercive behaviours is essential for reducing these issues and ensuring that employees are both physically and mentally present at work, contributing to the organisation's success.

Poor Employee Morale

Employee morale is a crucial determinant of workplace productivity, engagement, and overall organisational health. Coercive behaviours have a deeply corrosive effect on morale, leading to widespread dissatisfaction, disengagement, and disillusionment among employees.

When employees are subjected to coercive behaviours, they often feel powerless, unsupported, and demoralised. This can lead to a decline in motivation, as employees no longer see the value in putting forth their best efforts if they are being manipulated, intimidated, or harassed. Low morale can manifest in a variety of ways, including decreased productivity, increased absenteeism, and a lack of enthusiasm for work tasks.

In addition to affecting individual employees, low morale can spread throughout the organisation, creating a pervasive sense of negativity and hopelessness. Teams may become fractured, with employees distrustful of one another and reluctant to collaborate. The overall atmosphere of the workplace may become toxic, leading to further declines in morale and productivity.

High morale, on the other hand, is associated with increased job satisfaction, higher levels of engagement, and a more positive work environment. To foster high morale, organisations must address and eliminate coercive behaviours, ensuring that employees feel valued, respected, and supported in their roles.

Less Collaboration

Effective collaboration is essential for innovation, problem-solving, and achieving organisational goals. However, coercive behaviours can severely undermine collaboration by creating an environment of fear, mistrust, and competition rather than cooperation.

Coercive behaviours such as triangulation, exclusion, and scapegoating can pit employees against one another, leading to conflicts and divisions within teams. When employees are focused on protecting themselves from manipulation or harassment, they are less likely to collaborate openly and honestly with their colleagues. This lack of collaboration can result in missed opportunities, inefficiencies, and a decline in the overall quality of work.

Furthermore, when employees do not feel psychologically safe, they are less likely to share ideas, offer feedback, or take risks. Innovation and creativity are stifled in an environment where employees fear retribution or criticism for their contributions. To foster a culture of collaboration, organisations must prioritise the elimination of coercive behaviours and create a safe space for open communication, idea-sharing, and teamwork.

Undermined Psychosocial Safety

Psychosocial safety refers to the extent to which employees feel safe from psychological harm in the workplace. This includes protection from bullying, harassment, discrimination, and other forms of coercive behaviour. Psychosocial safety is a key component of a healthy work environment, as it enables employees to perform at their best without fear of harm or retribution.

Coercive behaviours directly undermine psychosocial safety by creating an environment of fear, anxiety, and insecurity. When employees do not feel safe, they are more likely to experience stress, burnout, and other mental health issues. This not only affects their individual well-being but also negatively impacts the organisation as a whole.

A lack of psychosocial safety can lead to a range of negative outcomes, including decreased productivity, higher turnover rates, and increased absenteeism. Employees who do not feel safe are less likely to be engaged, motivated, or committed to their work. This can result in a decline in the overall performance of the organisation, as well as increased costs related to turnover, absenteeism, and health care.

To create a psychologically safe work environment, organisations must take proactive steps to identify and eliminate coercive behaviours. This includes implementing clear policies and procedures for addressing misconduct, providing training on respectful communication and conflict resolution, and fostering a culture of openness, support, and accountability.

Case Studies

Case Study 1: Addressing Micromanagement and Building Trust

Company: A global IT services company

Issue: Micromanagement causing low employee morale and high turnover

Coercive Behaviour: A senior manager in the company was engaging in micromanagement, constantly overseeing and controlling the team's tasks down to the smallest detail. This led to frustration, low morale, and a 25% turnover rate within the team over a year.

Solution: The human resources (HR) department conducted an anonymous employee feedback survey and identified the manager's behaviour as the root cause of the issue. To address the problem, they provided the manager with leadership coaching focused on trust-building, delegation, and communication. The company also introduced a transparent performance management system where employees set their own goals and tracked their progress, reducing the need for constant oversight.

Outcome: Within six months, employee turnover in the team dropped by 15%, and engagement surveys indicated a marked improvement in job satisfaction. The manager was able to develop better trust with their team, empowering employees to take ownership of their work. As a result, team productivity increased, and the overall work environment became more collaborative and positive.

Case Study 2: Eliminating Gaslighting to
Improve Team Dynamics

Company: A large healthcare provider

Issue: Gaslighting by a senior team member eroding trust and causing conflict

Coercive Behaviour: A senior team member was engaging in gaslighting, manipulating situations to make colleagues doubt their judgment and create confusion. This led to a toxic work environment where team members began to mistrust one another and question their own capabilities, resulting in decreased collaboration and rising tension.

Solution: The company introduced mandatory training on identifying and addressing workplace bullying and gaslighting. HR intervened directly, conducting one-on-one sessions with the affected team and implementing conflict resolution practices. The senior team member was given a clear warning and required to participate in a mediation process to address their behaviour. Leadership emphasised a zero-tolerance policy for bullying and manipulative behaviour.

Outcome: After addressing the issue head-on, the company saw a significant improvement in team dynamics. Trust was gradually rebuilt, and employees reported feeling more confident in their roles. Collaboration within the team improved, and productivity levels returned to normal. The employee responsible for gaslighting either changed their behaviour or faced eventual termination, ensuring the organisation upheld a culture of respect and accountability.

Case Study 3: Confronting Sabotage and
Fostering Accountability

Company: A regional marketing agency

Issue: Sabotage leading to project delays and team conflicts

Coercive Behaviour: An employee in a competitive position within the marketing team was intentionally withholding critical information and making strategic errors to sabotage the progress of colleagues, hoping to improve their own standing. This led to repeated project delays, frustration among team members, and strained relationships.

Solution: The company identified the issue through a performance review process and multiple complaints from the employee's colleagues. They implemented clear accountability measures, such as transparent project management software that tracked individual contributions and progress. Additionally, the employee was required to undergo performance improvement training focused on teamwork, accountability, and ethical behaviour.

Outcome: The sabotage stopped as the individual's actions were made visible and the company implemented stronger oversight on project workflows. Over time, the team's performance improved as trust was restored. The employee involved either adapted to the new system of accountability or was let go, ensuring that the team's collaborative environment and productivity were no longer compromised by coercive behaviour. The company also strengthened its overall culture of accountability to prevent future incidents.

Key Takeaways

Coercive behaviours in the workplace have far-reaching negative impacts on both employees and organisations. From financial losses and high turnover rates to decreased morale and weakened collaboration, the effects of these behaviours are profound and damaging. Additionally, coercive behaviours undermine psychosocial safety, leading to increased stress, anxiety, and other mental health issues among employees.

To create a healthy, productive, and innovative workplace, organisations must prioritise the elimination of coercive behaviours. This requires a commitment to fostering a culture of respect, accountability, and support, where employees feel safe, valued, and empowered to perform at their best. By addressing these issues, organisations can not only improve the well-being of their employees but also enhance their overall performance and success.

References:

- Chambers, H. (2019). The impact of micromanagement on workplace productivity. *Journal of Organisational Behavior*, *40*(4), 511-528.

- Cherry, K. (2023). What causes learned helplessness. Retrieved from https://www.verywellmind.com/what-is-learned-helplessness-2795326

- Derks, D., & Bakker, A. B. (2014). Smartphone use, work-home interference, and burnout: A diary study on the role of recovery. *Applied Psychology*, *63*(3), 411-440.

- Einarsen, S., Hoel, H., Zapf, D., & Cooper, C. L. (2003). *Bullying and emotional abuse in the workplace: International perspectives in research and practice.* CRC Press.

Ferris, D. L., Brown, D. J., Berry, J. W., & Lian, H. (2008). The development and validation of the workplace ostracism scale. *Journal of Applied Psychology, 93*(6), 1348-1366.

Gottman, J. (1999). *The seven principles for making marriage work*. Three Rivers Press.

Greenberg, J. (2019). The psychological costs of guilt tripping in the workplace. *Journal of Applied Psychology, 104*(3), 328-342.

Jones, K. P., Peddie, C. I., Gilrane, V. L., King, E. B., & Gray, A. L. (2016). Not so subtle: A meta-analytic investigation of the correlates of subtle and overt discrimination. *Journal of Management, 42*(6), 1588-1613.

Kramer, M., & Harris, S. (2020). The dark side of competition: Understanding sabotage in the workplace. *Organisational Dynamics, 49*(2), 100748.

MacIntosh, J. A. (2006). Workplace bullying influences women's engagement in the workplace. *Advances in Nursing Science*, 29(3), E51-E61. https://doi.org/10.1097/00012272-200607000-00009

Morrison, E. W., & Milliken, F. J. (2000). Organisational silence: A barrier to change and development in a pluralistic world. *Academy of Management Review, 25*(4), 706-725.

Pfeffer, J., & Cialdini, R. B. (2021). Toxic work environments: The consequences of sabotage and mistrust. *Leadership Quarterly, 32*(1), 101476.

Ryan, R. M., & Deci, E. L. (2017). *Self-determination theory: Basic psychological needs in motivation, development, and wellness*. Guilford Press.

⊙ Sonnentag, S., Binnewies, C., & Mojza, E. J. (2017). Recovery, work engagement, and proactive behaviour: A new look at the interface between nonwork and work. *Journal of Applied Psychology, 92*(3), 617-628.

⊙ Spector, P. E., & Fox, S. (2005). *Counterproductive work behaviour: Investigations of actors and targets.* American Psychological Association.

⊙ StopBullying.gov. (2023). What is bullying? Retrieved from https://www.stopbullying.gov/what-is-bullying

⊙ Triana, M. d. C., Jayasinghe, M., & Pieper, J. R. (2015). Perceived workplace racial discrimination and its correlates: A meta-analysis. *Journal of Organisational Behaviour, 36*(4), 491-513.

⊙ U.S. Equal Employment Opportunity Commission. (2024). Harassment. Retrieved from https://www.eeoc.gov/harassment

⊙ White, R. (2010). Micromanagement: The consequences of over-control in the workplace. *Management Review, 25*(3), 89-102.

⊙ Williams, P. (2022). Leadership and Innovation: The role of trust and autonomy. *Business Leadership Quarterly, 58*(2), 145-162.

CHAPTER 8

Dealing with Coercive Behaviours

Coercive behaviours, such as bullying, harassment, and manipulation, are detrimental to workplace environments, impacting employee morale, productivity, and overall organisational health. These behaviours can create a toxic atmosphere, leading to higher turnover rates, decreased job satisfaction, and increased absenteeism. Addressing and preventing coercive behaviours requires a comprehensive approach that includes strong leadership, clear policies, consistent and continuing training, and a supportive environment for employees. This chapter explores the critical elements of dealing with coercive behaviours in the workplace, emphasising the importance of leadership buy-in, the development of robust policies, the role of Employee Assistance Programs (EAPs), and the need for ongoing training.

Leadership Buy-In: The Foundation of Change

Leadership buy-in is crucial for successfully addressing coercive behaviours. Without the commitment of leaders, efforts to create a respectful and safe workplace are likely to fall short. Leaders set the tone for organisational culture and are responsible for modelling the behaviours they want to see in their employees. According to the Australian Human Rights Commission (AHRC, 2020), effective leadership is essential in preventing and managing workplace bullying and harassment.

Leaders must demonstrate a clear commitment to eradicating coercive behaviours by:

- Undergoing training to recognise and address these behaviours.

- Establishing open communication channels that allow employees to report concerns without fear of retribution.

- Participating in the development and implementation of policies that clearly define and prohibit coercive behaviours.

- Holding themselves and others accountable for maintaining a respectful workplace.

Leadership commitment also involves promoting a culture of respect and inclusivity, where all employees feel valued and supported. This can be achieved by regularly engaging with employees, seeking feedback on workplace culture, and taking swift action when coercive behaviours are reported.

Developing Comprehensive Policies

Clear and comprehensive policies are the backbone of any effort to address coercive behaviours. These policies should provide a clear definition of what constitutes coercive behaviour, outline the procedures for reporting such behaviour, and specify the consequences for those who engage in it. According to Safe Work Australia (2019), effective policies are critical for managing psychosocial risks in the workplace, including bullying, harassment, and other forms of coercion.

Key components of effective policies include:

- *Definitions and Examples:* Clearly define coercive behaviours, including those listed in Chapter 8. Provide examples to help employees understand what these behaviours look like in practice.

- *Reporting Procedures:* Outline the steps employees should take to report coercive behaviours, ensuring that the process is accessible, confidential, and protects employees from retaliation.

- *Investigation Process:* Describe how reports of coercive behaviour will be investigated, including timelines, the role of HR, and the involvement of external investigators if necessary.

- *Consequences and Disciplinary Actions:* Specify the consequences for engaging in coercive behaviours, ranging from warnings to termination, depending on the severity of the behaviour.

- *Support for Victims:* Detail the resources available to employees who have experienced coercive behaviours, including access to EAPs, counselling, and other support services.

Policies should be regularly reviewed and updated to reflect changes in workplace dynamics, legal requirements, and best practices. Involving employees in the policy development process can also enhance buy-in and ensure that the policies are relevant and effective.

Procedures and Toolkits for Addressing Coercive Behaviours

In addition to clear policies, organisations need robust procedures and practical toolkits to effectively respond to reports of coercive behaviours. These resources help ensure that incidents are handled promptly, fairly, and consistently. The Fair Work Ombudsman (2021) emphasises the importance of having well-defined procedures to build trust in the system and encourage employees to come forward with their concerns.

Effective procedures and toolkits should include:

- *Investigation Guidelines:* Provide a step-by-step guide for investigating reports of coercive behaviours, including how to interview the complainant, the accused, and any witnesses.

- *Documentation Templates:* Include templates for documenting incidents, investigation findings, and any actions taken. Proper documentation is crucial for maintaining transparency and accountability.

- *Support Resources:* Offer resources for managers and HR professionals on how to support employees during and after the investigation process. This may include information on EAPs, referral to external counselling services, or guidance on how to facilitate a return to work after a traumatic incident.

- *Communication Tools:* Develop communication strategies for informing the wider workforce about the outcome of investigations, while maintaining confidentiality. Transparency in how incidents are handled can help to build trust and reinforce the organisation's commitment to a safe workplace.

The Role of Employee Assistance Programs (EAPs)

Employee Assistance Programs (EAPs) are a vital resource for employees affected by coercive behaviours. EAPs provide confidential counselling and support services, helping employees navigate the emotional and psychological impact of such behaviours. According to a study by the Employee Assistance Professional Association of Australia (2020), organisations with robust EAPs see improvements in employee well-being, reduced absenteeism, and increased productivity.

EAPs can assist employees by:

- *Offering Confidential Support:* Employees can access counselling services to discuss their experiences and receive guidance on how to cope with the impact of coercive behaviours.

- *Providing Resources for Managers:* EAPs often offer training and resources for managers on how to handle reports of coercive behaviours and support affected employees.

- *Facilitating Mediation:* In some cases, EAPs can provide mediation services to help resolve conflicts between employees before they escalate into more serious issues.

Promoting the uptake of EAP services is crucial to ensuring that employees feel supported. Organisations should regularly remind employees of the availability of EAPs, provide information on how to access these services, and ensure that the services are accessible to all employees, including those in remote or dispersed locations.

Barriers to Employees Uptaking EAPs

EAPs are designed to offer employees support with personal and work-related issues, providing services such as counselling, financial advice, and legal assistance. Despite the benefits EAPs offer, many employees choose not to engage with these programs.

Several factors contribute to this reluctance, each rooted in the broader workplace culture and perceptions surrounding EAPs:

Stigma and Perceived Weakness: One of the primary reasons employees avoid using EAPs is the stigma associated with seeking help. Employees may fear that utilising these services will be perceived as a sign of weakness or an inability to manage their responsibilities. This concern is particularly acute in high-pressure environments where there is an unspoken expectation to maintain a facade of resilience. Research by Clement et al. (2015) indicates that the stigma surrounding mental health services is a significant barrier to seeking help, which can extend to EAP utilisation.

Confidentiality Concerns: Confidentiality is another major concern that prevents employees from accessing EAPs. Employees may fear that their use of the program will be reported to management, potentially affecting their job security or career progression. Even when EAPs are explicitly described as confidential, a lack of trust in the organisation's commitment to privacy can deter employees from using these services. A study by Attridge (2019) highlights that concerns about confidentiality are one of the most commonly cited reasons for low EAP engagement.

Lack of Awareness and Accessibility: Another issue is the lack of awareness or understanding of what EAPs offer. Some employees may not be fully informed about the scope of services available to them or how to access these services. In addition, if EAPs are not well-promoted within the organisation or if employees find it difficult to navigate the process of getting help, they are less likely to engage. The SHRM Foundation (2019) emphasises the importance of effective communication and easy access to EAP services to improve engagement rates.

Perceived Irrelevance: Some employees may view EAPs as irrelevant to their specific needs, believing that the program is not equipped to address the particular issues they are facing. This perception can arise if EAP services are not tailored to the unique challenges of the workforce or if employees have had previous experiences where EAPs did not meet their expectations. A report by the Employee Assistance Professionals Association (EAPA) (2020) suggests that organisations should regularly assess and update their EAP offerings to ensure they remain relevant and effective for the workforce.

Addressing Barriers to Uptaking EPAs

Addressing these barriers requires a multifaceted approach that includes reducing stigma, ensuring confidentiality, raising awareness, and tailoring EAP services to meet the specific needs of the workforce. By understanding and mitigating the factors that prevent employees from engaging with EAPs, organisations can foster a more supportive environment where employees feel safe seeking the help they need.

Training: Building Awareness and Skills

Training is a key component of any strategy to address coercive behaviours in the workplace. Comprehensive training programs help employees recognise coercive behaviours, understand their impact, and learn how to respond effectively. According to the Workplace Bullying Institute (WBI, 2021), organisations that invest in regular, targeted training see a reduction in the incidence of workplace bullying and other coercive behaviours.

Effective training programs should:

- *Be Mandatory for All Employees:* Everyone in the organisation, from entry-level employees to senior executives, should participate in training on coercive behaviours.

This ensures that all employees are aware of the organisation's policies and know how to respond to incidents.

- ◉ **Be Part of the Onboarding Process:** It is important employees know the culture of the organisation and the expectations of their behaviour. The onboarding process should reflect this, as well as how employees can expect to be treated and the processes in place if these expectations are not met.

- ◉ *Include Practical Scenarios:* Use role-playing exercises and case studies to help employees practise recognising and responding to coercive behaviours in a safe environment.

- ◉ **Be Ongoing:** Training should not be a one-time event. Regular refresher courses help reinforce learning and ensure that employees stay informed about new developments in workplace safety.

- ◉ *Tailored for Different Roles:* While all employees should receive basic training, additional sessions should be tailored for leaders and HR, DE&I professionals, and stakeholders who may need to handle reports of coercive behaviours and conduct investigations.

Creating a Culture of Engagement and Safety

Creating a culture where coercive behaviours are not tolerated requires the active engagement of all employees. Engaged employees are more likely to report incidents and participate in initiatives to create a safer workplace. According to Gallup (2021), organisations with high levels of employee engagement experience fewer incidents of workplace bullying and harassment.

To foster a culture of engagement and safety:

- ⊙ *Encourage Open Communication:* Create multiple channels for employees to voice their concerns, whether through anonymous reporting systems, regular check-ins with managers, or dedicated employee feedback sessions.

- ⊙ *Involve Employees in Policy Development:* Engage employees in the development and review of policies and procedures to increase buy-in and ensure that the policies reflect the real needs and concerns of the workforce.

- ⊙ *Recognise and Reward Positive Behaviours:* Acknowledge and reward employees who contribute to a positive workplace culture. This can include recognising those who report coercive behaviours, those who support colleagues through difficult times, and those who actively promote respect and inclusivity.

The Importance of a Top-Down Approach

Addressing coercive behaviours in the workplace requires a holistic, top-down approach. Leadership commitment, clear policies, effective procedures, comprehensive training, and active employee engagement must all be aligned to create a cohesive strategy. The International Labour Organization (ILO, 2020) highlights that a coordinated approach to managing workplace behaviours is essential for creating safe and respectful environments.

A top-down approach involves:

- ⊙ *Leadership Accountability:* Leaders must be held accountable for maintaining a safe workplace and addressing coercive behaviours promptly and effectively.

- *Policy Integration:* Ensure that policies on coercive behaviours are integrated into the organisation's broader HR strategy, aligning with other policies on workplace safety, diversity, and inclusion.

- *Continuous Improvement:* Regularly assess the effectiveness of the organisation's approach to coercive behaviours and make adjustments as needed. This may involve conducting employee surveys, reviewing incident reports, and benchmarking against best practices.

Dealing with coercive behaviours in the workplace is a complex and ongoing challenge. However, by taking a comprehensive, top-down approach, organisations can create a safe and supportive environment where such behaviours are not tolerated. Leadership buy-in, clear policies, effective procedures, ongoing training, and the promotion of EAP services are all critical components of this strategy. By committing to these efforts, organisations can protect their employees, enhance their workplace culture, and ultimately improve their overall performance.

Case Studies

Case Study 1: Improving Employee Well-Being through Increased EAP Utilisation

Company: A mid-sized manufacturing company

Issue: High levels of absenteeism and burnout among employees

EAP Implementation: The company noticed a spike in absenteeism, particularly related to stress and mental health issues. Despite having an EAP in place, utilisation was low due to a lack of awareness and perceived stigma. To address this, the HR department launched an internal campaign promoting EAP services, including anonymous counselling, mental health support, and stress management resources. They held workshops to destigmatise seeking help and encouraged managers to regularly remind their teams about the available services.

Outcome: Within six months, EAP usage increased by 40%. Absenteeism rates dropped significantly as more employees sought help for stress-related issues early on, preventing burnout. Employee satisfaction surveys showed improved morale, and the company reported a noticeable boost in productivity as employees began to feel more supported in managing their work-life balance.

Case Study 2: Using EAPs to Address Domestic and Family Violence (DFV)

Company: A large retail chain

Issue: Employees impacted by DFV

EAP Implementation: The organisation recognised that many employees were facing personal challenges related to DFV but were reluctant to seek help. In response, the company enhanced its EAP by adding specialised support for DFV victims, including trauma counselling, legal advice, and assistance with safety planning. They also trained managers to recognise signs of DFV and proactively offer EAP resources to affected employees confidentially.

Outcome: The targeted support led to a significant increase in EAP engagement among employees dealing with DFV. Feedback from those who accessed the program indicated that the counselling and legal assistance provided a lifeline during difficult times. The company saw improved retention among employees who might otherwise have been forced to leave due to personal struggles, and workplace safety improved as the organisation actively supported its staff through confidential resources.

Case Study 3: Reducing Presenteeism through EAP Mental Health Programs

Company: A global financial services firm

Issue: High levels of presenteeism among employees due to stress and anxiety

EAP Implementation: The firm noticed that many employees were showing up to work but were disengaged, likely due to chronic stress and anxiety related to workload and performance pressure. To combat this, the company bolstered its EAP offerings by including targeted mental health programs, stress management workshops, and mindfulness training. They encouraged employees to use the EAP not only for crisis situations but also for preventive mental health support. Leaders were trained to promote EAP usage as a positive step toward well-being, rather than a sign of weakness.

Outcome: The EAP mental health programs led to a 25% reduction in presenteeism over a year. Employees who participated in the programs reported lower stress levels, higher job satisfaction, and better focus at work. The firm saw improvements in both individual and team performance, demonstrating that proactive mental health support could help address presenteeism while improving overall productivity.

Key Takeaways

There critical need to identify and address coercive behaviours in the workplace to protect employee well-being and maintain a healthy organizational culture. Coercive behaviours—such as manipulation, bullying, gaslighting, and intimidation—undermine trust, collaboration, and morale, leading to increased stress, anxiety, and even mental health issues among employees. Organisations must establish clear policies and provide training to help leaders and staff recognise and respond to these toxic behaviours. By creating a culture of accountability and support, businesses can foster a safer, more inclusive environment where coercive tactics are not tolerated, ensuring the psychosocial safety of all employees.

References and Resources:

- Attridge, M. (2019). Employee Assistance Programs: Evidence and current practices. *Workplace Health & Safety, 67*(5), 203-212.

- Australian Human Rights Commission (AHRC). (2020). Good practice, good business: Preventing discrimination and harassment. Retrieved from https://www.humanrights.gov.au/our-work/employers/good-practice-good-business-preventing-discrimination-and-harassment

- Clement, S., Schauman, O., Graham, T., Maggioni, F., Evans-Lacko, S., Bezborodovs, N., ... & Thornicroft, G. (2015). What is the impact of mental health-related stigma on help-seeking? A systematic review of quantitative and qualitative studies. *Psychological Medicine, 45*(1), 11-27.

- Employee Assistance Professionals Association (EAPA). (2020). Employee Assistance Programs: Enhancing the employee experience. Retrieved from www.eapassn.org

- Employee Assistance Professional Association of Australia. (2020). The benefits of Employee Assistance Programs. Retrieved from https://www.eapaa.org.au/

● Fair Work Ombudsman. (2021). Bullying in the workplace. Retrieved from https://www.fairwork.gov.au/employee-entitlements/bullying-in-the-workplace

● Gallup. (2021). The relationship between engagement at work and organisational outcomes. Retrieved from https://www.gallup.com/workplace/321247/engagement-work-organisational-outcomes.aspx

● International Labour Organization (ILO). (2020). Ending violence and harassment in the world of work. Retrieved from https://www.ilo.org/global/topics/violence-harassment/lang--en/index.htm

● Safe Work Australia. (2019). Guide for preventing and responding to workplace bullying. Retrieved from https://www.safeworkaustralia.gov.au/doc/guide-preventing-and-responding-workplace-bullying

● SHRM Foundation. (2019). Creating a workplace culture that values mental health. Retrieved from www.shrm.org/foundation

● Workplace Bullying Institute (WBI). (2021). Workplace bullying training. Retrieved from https://www.workplacebullying.org/solutions/training/

CHAPTER 9

From Bystanders to Upstanders

Workplace toxicity, including behaviours like bullying, exclusion, discrimination, and harassment, can significantly damage employee well-being, organisational culture, and overall productivity. When left unaddressed, such behaviours lead to low morale, high turnover, and poor performance. While leadership and HR departments play pivotal roles in cultivating a safe work environment, empowering employees to shift from passive bystanders to proactive upstanders is crucial in disrupting toxic dynamics and fostering a respectful, inclusive, and psychosocially safe workplace.

This chapter will explore why upstanders are essential in the workplace, provide strategies for training employees to effectively intervene, and highlight real-world examples of how organisations have benefited from upstander programs. Additionally, we will address the specific challenges of handling toxic behaviours, particularly when managers or those in leadership positions are the perpetrators, plus how to deal with discriminatory actions such as sexism, racism, and harassment.

The Importance of Upstanders in the Workplace

Upstander intervention is a vital tool for preventing the escalation of toxic behaviours and fostering an inclusive and supportive workplace. Encouraging employees to become upstanders serves multiple functions:

1. **Preventing Escalation via Early Intervention:** Toxic behaviours often start small but can escalate quickly if left unchecked. Whether it's overt bullying, exclusion, or

covert manipulation, these actions can erode the psychological safety of employees, leading to increased turnover and absenteeism. Research indicates that early intervention by upstanders can prevent toxic behaviours from escalating and becoming ingrained in the workplace culture (Lutgen-Sandvik, 2006).

2. **Promotes a Psychosocially Safe Culture:** Psychosocial safety refers to a workplace environment where employees feel secure, respected, and able to voice concerns without fear of retaliation. Upstanders contribute to this culture by demonstrating that toxic behaviours will not be tolerated and that employees will support one another in maintaining a respectful environment. When upstanders act, it encourages others to follow suit, creating a ripple effect of positive behaviour.

3. **Demonstrates Accountability and Ethical Leadership:** Upstanders model accountability by holding their peers, and sometimes managers, to higher standards of behaviour. By stepping in to correct harmful actions, they help maintain ethical standards and foster a culture where everyone feels responsible for contributing to a respectful and productive workplace. This proactive approach also aligns with organisational values and reinforces the importance of psychosocial safety as a shared responsibility.

4. **Challenges Power Imbalances:** In cases where toxic behaviour stems from someone in a position of authority, such as a manager, upstander intervention is especially critical. Employees often feel powerless when the perpetrator is their superior but providing them with the tools and confidence to address inappropriate behaviour—even from leaders—can help correct power imbalances.

Organisations need to ensure that upstanders are supported through clear reporting mechanisms and anti-retaliation policies, especially when a manager is involved.

How to Train Employees to Become Upstanders

Training employees to become upstanders requires a multi-faceted approach that includes education, practice, leadership modelling, and clear policies. Below are strategies organisations can adopt to create a culture of upstanding behaviour:

1. Training on Recognising Toxic Behaviours

Before employees can become upstanders, they need to know how to identify toxic behaviours. Toxicity in the workplace takes many forms, from overt actions such as verbal abuse and harassment to more covert behaviours like gossiping, exclusion, and gaslighting. Training should cover:

- **Overt bullying**: Behaviours that are openly aggressive, including shouting, public humiliation, or verbal threats.

- **Covert bullying**: Subtle, often hidden behaviours, such as sabotaging a colleague's work, exclusion from important meetings, or spreading malicious rumours.

- **Discriminatory behaviour**: Harassment based on gender, race, sexual orientation, or any other characteristic that marginaliss individuals.

- **Upward bullying**: When employees undermine or resist managers, creating a hostile work environment for their superiors.

Employees must understand how these behaviours harm not only the individuals directly involved but also the organisation's culture and success.

2. Role-Playing and Scenario-Based Training

Role-playing exercises are one of the most effective ways to teach employees how to intervene in real-life situations. By practicing upstander interventions in a controlled environment, employees gain confidence in their ability to confront toxic behaviour. Scenarios might include:

- **Intervening in gossip**: Teaching employees how to redirect conversations away from harmful gossip.

- **Addressing discriminatory remarks**: Helping employees learn how to confront sexist or racist comments respectfully but firmly.

- **Supporting colleagues who are excluded**: Training on how to involve colleagues who are systematically excluded from projects or discussions.

These practical exercises equip employees with the skills they need to act in the moment, reinforcing that small actions—such as stepping in to stop gossip—can have a significant impact on workplace dynamics.

3. Providing Clear Reporting Channels and Support Systems

Employees need to feel confident that they will be supported if they choose to intervene or report toxic behaviour. Organisations should provide:

- **Anonymous reporting options**: Allowing employees to report inappropriate behaviour without fear of retaliation.

- **Transparent procedures**: Ensuring that all reports are taken seriously and acted upon promptly.

- **Anti-retaliation policies**: Clearly stating that employees who report toxic behaviours or intervene as upstanders will be protected from negative consequences.

When employees know that their concerns will be addressed without repercussion, they are more likely to step in and act.

4. Leadership Buy-In and Modelling Upstanding Behaviour

Leaders play a critical role in creating a culture of upstanding behaviour. When leaders visibly intervene against toxic behaviours or praise employees for their courage in doing so, they set a standard for the entire organisation. Leadership buy-in also reinforces that upstander behaviour aligns with company values and expectations.

Organisations should ensure that leaders are trained to recognise and address toxic behaviours within their teams and are held accountable for their role in maintaining a healthy work environment.

Addressing Toxic Managers and Discriminatory Behaviours

One of the greatest difficulties employees face is when the perpetrator of toxic behaviour is their manager or someone in a position of authority. Employees may hesitate to speak up due to fear of retaliation or career consequences, but this is where upstander intervention becomes even more critical. To address these challenges:

- **Provide anonymous reporting options**: To address issues where the manager is involved without fear of retaliation.

- **HR transparency**: Ensure that HR departments handle complaints involving leadership with transparency and impartiality.

- **Encourage upward communication**: Equip employees with the tools to communicate concerns constructively to their superiors, including training on managing up.

- **Establish open-door policies**: Employees should feel comfortable reporting issues directly to senior leadership if their immediate manager is involved in toxic behaviour.

Similarly, addressing discriminatory behaviour, such as sexism, racism, or harassment, is critical in creating a safe workplace. Upstanders must be prepared to step in when they witness discriminatory comments or actions, especially when the behaviour is targeted at marginalised groups.

Addressing Gossip and Exclusionary Behaviours

Gossip and exclusion are common yet harmful behaviours that can create a toxic work environment. Employees often engage in gossip without realising the damage it causes, but upstanders can help shift the narrative and create a more respectful workplace.

Upstanders can:

- **Call out gossip**: Calmly redirect conversations when gossip occurs, such as, "I don't think it's fair to talk about [Name] behind their back. Let's focus on the task at hand."

- **Ignore gossip**: Refusing to participate in gossip and walking away from harmful conversations sends a strong message that such behaviour is unacceptable.

- ⊘ **Report gossip**: If gossip crosses the line into bullying or exclusion, upstanders can report it to HR or management to prevent further harm.

Addressing gossip and exclusionary behaviours contributes to a more inclusive and psychologically safe environment for all employees.

Overcoming Barriers to Upstander Intervention

Despite the benefits of upstander behaviour, many employees hesitate to act due to fear of retaliation, uncertainty about the proper course of action, or discomfort with confrontation. Organisations must address these barriers to foster a culture of upstanding behaviour by:

1. *Building Confidence through Training:* Role-playing exercises and scenario-based training help employees practice interventions, giving them the confidence to act when needed.

2. *Reinforcing Anti-Retaliation Policies:* Employees need assurance that they will not face negative consequences for reporting or intervening in toxic behaviour, particularly when addressing managerial misconduct.

3. *Encouraging Small Actions:* Even minor interventions, such as redirecting a conversation away from gossip, can have a significant impact. Training should emphasise that every action counts, regardless of scale.

4. *Recognising and Rewarding Upstanding Behaviour:* Publicly acknowledging employees who act as upstanders reinforces the importance of intervention and encourages others to follow suit.

Real-World Examples

1. University of California, Berkeley

The University of California, Berkeley, faced criticism after mishandling several high-profile sexual harassment cases. In response, the university launched an upstander training program that educated students and staff on how to intervene when they witnessed harassment or inappropriate behaviour. This program improved reporting of incidents and increased trust between the university administration and the student body.

Outcome: After implementing upstander training, UC Berkeley saw an increase in reported incidents of harassment and bullying. Students and staff felt more empowered to speak out, and trust in the administration improved.

Reference:

- The Guardian (2016). *Sexual harassment cases raise questions about University of California's response.* Retrieved from https://www.theguardian.com.

2. Uber Technologies, Inc.

Uber experienced a public relations crisis in 2017 after reports surfaced about rampant sexism and harassment in the workplace. The company responded by introducing mandatory upstander training that encouraged employees to intervene when they witnessed inappropriate behaviour, including discrimination and bullying. This initiative was part of a broader effort to overhaul Uber's toxic work culture.

Outcome: Following the implementation of upstander training, Uber began to repair its workplace culture. Employees reported feeling more empowered to speak up, and the company saw a marked improvement in employee engagement and satisfaction.

Reference:

- New York Times (2017). *Inside Uber's aggressive, unrestrained workplace culture.* Retrieved from https://www.nytimes.com

3. NHS England: Combatting Workplace Bullying

The NHS launched the "Civility Saves Lives" campaign to address widespread bullying and harassment within the healthcare sector. This initiative included upstander training, teaching employees to recognise and address bullying, even when it came from senior medical staff. By emphasising civility and intervention, the NHS was able to significantly reduce incidents of workplace bullying.

Outcome: NHS England saw a reduction in reported bullying incidents and improvements in staff morale and well-being. The campaign fostered a more respectful and inclusive environment where employees felt empowered to address toxic behaviour without fear of retaliation, even in hierarchical situations. The training also improved collaboration and trust within teams, contributing to better patient care.

Reference:

- The Guardian (2019). *NHS launches new campaign to tackle workplace bullying.* Retrieved from https://www.theguardian.com

Key Takeaways

Empowering employees to shift from being passive bystanders to proactive upstanders is essential for building a respectful, inclusive, and psychosocially safe workplace. Upstanders play a crucial role in disrupting toxic behaviours, whether they stem from peers or managers, and help foster a culture of account-ability and trust. With clear policies, leadership support, and effective training, employees gain the tools and confidence needed to intervene safely and effectively.

Organisations that invest in upstander programs not only create safer work environments but also enjoy higher employee engagement, reduced turnover, and improved productivity. As demonstrated by the case studies from education, healthcare, and corporate sectors, upstander interventions can have transformative effects on workplace culture, promoting well-being and resilience.

Creating a culture of upstanding behaviour is a shared responsibility, requiring ongoing commitment from employees, managers, and leaders alike. When individuals take ownership of maintaining a respectful and inclusive workplace, organisations thrive both ethically and financially, ensuring long-term success.

References:

- Accenture (2019). *Diversity and Inclusion Report: Bystander Training and Workplace Culture.*

- Edmondson, A. C. (1999). Psychological safety and learning behavior in work teams. *Administrative Science Quarterly, 44*(2), 350-383.

- Lutgen-Sandvik, P. (2006). Take this job and…: Quitting and other forms of resistance to workplace bullying. *Communication Monographs, 73*(4), 406-433.

- The Guardian (2016). *Sexual harassment cases raise questions about University of California's response.* Retrieved from https://www.theguardian.com

- The Guardian (2019). *NHS launches new campaign to tackle workplace bullying.* Retrieved from https://www.theguardian.com

- New York Times (2017). *Inside Uber's aggressive, unrestrained workplace culture.* Retrieved from https://www.nytimes.com

PART 5

Navigating Trauma in Leaders and Employees

CHAPTER 10

Leaders with Unresolved Trauma

Unresolved trauma in leaders can profoundly influence their leadership styles, the cultures they cultivate, and the well-being of their teams. While the effects of trauma can vary widely, the presence of unresolved emotional wounds often manifests in maladaptive behaviours that ripple throughout the organisation. This chapter explores the complex relationship between unresolved trauma in leaders, the cultures they create, and the impact on their teams. It will also provide insight into how organisations can support leaders in addressing their trauma to foster healthier work environments.

Understanding Unresolved Trauma in Leaders

Trauma, particularly when unresolved, can shape a person's worldview, behaviours, and interactions with others. Leaders, by virtue of their positions, have a significant influence on the culture and dynamics within their organisations. When leaders carry unresolved trauma, it can manifest in various ways, including hyper-vigilance, emotional reactivity, control issues, or difficulty trusting others.

Research shows that trauma can have long-lasting effects on the brain, particularly in areas responsible for emotional regulation, decision-making, and interpersonal relationships. Leaders who have experienced trauma might struggle with these aspects, leading to inconsistent leadership behaviours, poor decision-making, or an inability to connect with or understand the needs of their team members. This, in turn, can create a work environment characterised by fear, instability, or lack of trust.

The Impact of Unresolved Trauma on Leadership Styles

Leaders with unresolved trauma may unconsciously adopt leadership styles that mirror their internal struggles. For example, a leader with a history of trauma might exhibit authoritarian tendencies, using control as a way to manage their own anxieties. This can create a rigid, top-down leadership style that stifles creativity and open communication within the team. Employees in such environments may feel micromanaged, undervalued, or fearful of making mistakes, leading to decreased morale and productivity.

Alternatively, some leaders with unresolved trauma may become overly accommodating or avoidant, fearing confrontation or rejection. This can lead to a lack of clear direction, inconsistent decision-making, or an inability to address conflicts effectively. Teams under such leadership might experience confusion, a lack of accountability, or a culture where issues are swept under the rug rather than addressed openly and constructively.

A leadership style influenced by unresolved trauma often results in a work environment that reflects the leader's internal chaos. This can create a culture where employees feel unsafe, unsure of expectations, and disconnected from their leader and their peers.

The Cultures Created by Traumatised Leaders

The culture of an organisation is often a direct reflection of its leadership. Leaders with unresolved trauma may inadvertently create toxic work cultures that mirror their unresolved emotional wounds. Such cultures are often characterised by high levels of stress, poor communication, and a lack of psychological safety.

In toxic work cultures, employees may feel that they are constantly walking on eggshells, unsure of how their leader will react in any given situation. This can create a culture of fear, where employees are afraid to speak up, share ideas, or report issues. Over time, this can result in high turnover, decreased employee engagement, and a decline in overall organisational performance.

Moreover, leaders with unresolved trauma may struggle to build trusting relationships with their team members. This lack of trust can permeate the organisation, leading to a culture where employees are hesitant to collaborate, share information, or support one another. The absence of trust and psychological safety can also hinder innovation, as employees may be reluctant to take risks or think outside the box.

The Effects on Team Members

The impact of a leader's unresolved trauma extends beyond the organisational culture—it also affects individual team members. Employees working under a traumatised leader may experience increased levels of stress, anxiety, and job dissatisfaction. This is particularly true in environments where the leader's unresolved trauma manifests in volatile or unpredictable behaviour.

Research has shown that employees in toxic work environments are more likely to experience burnout, a state of chronic stress that can lead to physical and mental health issues. Burnout not only affects an employee's well-being but also their productivity, creativity, and overall job performance. In extreme cases, prolonged exposure to a toxic work environment can even cause long-term psychological trauma for the employees themselves.

Furthermore, team members may struggle to connect with a leader who is emotionally distant or inconsistent. This can produce feelings of isolation, frustration, and a lack of support. When employees do not feel supported or valued by their leader, it can erode their commitment to the organisation and reduce their motivation to perform at their best.

Addressing Unresolved Trauma in Leadership

Recognising the impact of unresolved trauma in leaders is the first step toward creating healthier work environments. Organisations have a responsibility to support their leaders in addressing their trauma, not only for the well-being of the leader but for the overall health of the organisation.

One effective approach is to provide leaders with access to mental health resources, such as counselling or therapy, that can help them process and heal from their trauma. This can be done through EAPs, offering mental health days, or providing financial support for mental health services. Leaders who take the time to work through their trauma can develop greater self-awareness, emotional regulation, and resilience, which in turn can enhance their leadership abilities.

In addition to providing mental health resources, organisations should consider implementing leadership development programs that include training on emotional intelligence (EI), conflict resolution, and trauma-informed leadership. These programs can equip leaders with the skills they need to manage their emotions, build trust with their team, and foster a psychologically safe work environment.

Creating a Trauma-Informed Work Environment

To support leaders and employees alike, organisations can benefit from adopting a trauma-informed approach to their workplace culture. A trauma-informed work environment recognises the prevalence and impact of trauma and integrates this understanding into policies, practices, and interactions.

This approach involves creating a culture of safety, trustworthiness, and empowerment, where all employees feel valued and supported. It also includes providing training for all staff on how to recognise signs of trauma and respond appropriately, promoting a culture of empathy and understanding.

By fostering a trauma-informed work environment, organisations can not only support their leaders in healing from unresolved trauma but also prevent the creation of toxic work cultures that harm employees. This approach can lead to a more resilient, engaged, and high-performing workforce.

Unresolved trauma in leaders can have far-reaching effects on their leadership style, the culture of their organisation, and the well-being of their team members. Recognising and addressing this trauma is crucial for creating a healthy work environment where all employees can thrive. By providing leaders with the necessary resources and support, organisations can help them heal from their trauma and develop into more effective, empathetic, and resilient leaders. In turn, this can foster a workplace culture characterised by trust, safety, and collaboration, leading to better outcomes for the organisation as a whole.

Case Studies

Case Study 1: Financial Services Firm - Leader with Unresolved Trauma Creating a Culture of Fear

Scenario:

John, the CEO of a large financial services firm, experienced significant trauma in his personal life, including the loss of a family member and an abusive upbringing. However, he never sought support to address these issues, and as a result, brought this unresolved trauma into his leadership style. John was known for his unpredictable behaviour, often reacting harshly to mistakes and publicly berating employees. His leadership approach created a culture of fear and intimidation, where employees were afraid to speak up or report problems.

Impact on the Workplace:

This toxic leadership led to high levels of employee turnover, as staff members felt undervalued and emotionally drained. The fear of making mistakes stifled innovation and creativity within the company, and the work environment became hostile. Productivity declined as employees disengaged, and the firm began to lose top talent to competitors. The company's reputation as an employer also suffered, making it harder to attract skilled professionals. Had the organisation recognised John's unresolved trauma and provided leadership coaching and support, it could have mitigated these negative outcomes and fostered a more positive work environment.

Case Study 2: Retail Chain - Manager's Unresolved Trauma Causing Micromanagement and Burnout

Scenario:

Sarah, a regional manager for a national retail chain, grew up in a household where she had to constantly prove her worth to an emotionally distant parent. She carried this trauma into her professional life, where she overcompensated by exerting excessive control over her team. Sarah's need for control manifested in extreme micromanagement, where she closely monitored every detail of her subordinates' work, leaving them little autonomy or trust. This behaviour stemmed from her unresolved trauma, as she felt the need to assert control to feel secure.

Impact on the Workplace:

Sarah's micromanagement led to burnout and frustration among her team. Employees became disengaged, feeling that their skills and contributions were undervalued. The constant pressure from Sarah resulted in increased absenteeism, as employees took more time off to cope with the stress of their work environment. Over time, the region Sarah managed saw a decline in sales and customer satisfaction as store managers struggled to maintain morale. If Sarah had received trauma-informed leadership training and psychological support, she could have learned healthier ways to manage her team, avoiding the financial and operational costs associated with her behaviour.

Case Study 3: Tech Company – CTO's Unresolved Trauma Leading to Poor Conflict Resolution

Scenario:

Alex, the Chief Technology Officer (CTO) of a fast-growing tech startup, experienced significant trauma during a previous job, where he was unfairly blamed for the failure of a major project. This unresolved trauma made Alex highly defensive and unable to handle criticism, even when it was constructive. His leadership style was marked by a reluctance to engage in open conversations about challenges and issues, often deflecting blame onto others and avoiding difficult conversations. This avoidance led to escalating conflicts between departments, as Alex failed to address the root causes of interpersonal tensions.

Impact on the Workplace:

The unresolved conflicts and lack of effective communication among teams began to negatively affect project timelines and deliverables. Employees, frustrated by the lack of leadership and Alex's defensiveness, started to lose trust in the company's ability to resolve internal issues. Tensions grew, leading to a toxic atmosphere where employees were unwilling to collaborate or raise concerns. This directly impacted productivity and led to missed opportunities, as key projects were delayed due to unresolved internal conflicts. If Alex had received trauma-informed leadership coaching, the company could have avoided these costly disruptions and maintained a more cohesive, collaborative workplace.

Key Takeaways

As is evident from the above case studies, unresolved trauma in leaders results in significant negative impacts on the workplace, including increased employee turnover, decreased productivity, and a toxic work culture. These examples highlight the importance of trauma-informed leadership training and providing mental health support for leaders, ensuring that their unresolved issues do not adversely affect the entire organisation.

References:

- Bloom, S. L. (2013). Creating sanctuary: Toward the evolution of sane societies. Routledge.

- Dutton, J. E., & Heaphy, E. D. (2003). The power of high-quality connections. *Positive Organisational Scholarship,* 263-278.

- Goleman, D. (2006). *Emotional intelligence: Why it can matter more than IQ.* Bantam.

- Herman, J. L. (1997). *Trauma and recovery: The aftermath of violence—from domestic abuse to political terror.* Basic Books.

⏩ Kahn, W. A. (1990). Psychological conditions of personal engagement and disengagement at work. *Academy of Management Journal, 33*(4), 692-724.

⏩ Litz, B. T., & Roemer, L. (2007). Post-traumatic stress disorder: An overview. In *The Oxford handbook of clinical psychology* (pp. 316-340). Oxford University Press.

⏩ Maslach, C., & Leiter, M. P. (2016). *The truth about burnout: How organisations cause personal stress and what to do about it.* Jossey-Bass.

⏩ van der Kolk, B. A. (2014). *The body keeps the score: Brain, mind, and body in the healing of trauma.* Penguin Books.

CHAPTER 11

Leading Employees with Unresolved Trauma

Trauma, whether it stems from personal experiences or work-related incidents, has a significant impact on individuals and their interactions within a team or organisation. For leaders, managing employees with unresolved trauma presents unique challenges that can affect team dynamics, productivity, and overall organisational culture. While trauma-informed practices have gained attention in recent years, many leaders are still navigating the complexities of leading individuals with trauma histories without a full understanding of the implications.

This chapter will explore the challenges leaders face when managing employees and teams with unresolved trauma, how trauma affects behaviour and team performance, and the strategies leaders can adopt to create a supportive, productive environment while addressing these challenges effectively.

Understanding Unresolved Trauma and Its Impact

Unresolved trauma refers to past emotional, psychological, or physical wounds that continue to affect an individual's behaviour, emotions, and interactions. Trauma can stem from various sources, such as childhood abuse, domestic violence, loss, or workplace harassment. When these traumatic experiences remain unresolved, they can manifest in the workplace in a variety of ways, such as anxiety, hypervigilance, mood swings, and difficulties in interpersonal communication.

According to the Substance Abuse and Mental Health Services Administration (SAMHSA), unresolved trauma can result in negative coping mechanisms like avoidance, aggression, or emotional withdrawal (SAMHSA, 2014). This is particularly challenging for leaders who must balance productivity and team cohesion while considering the well-being of their employees.

Leadership Challenges with Employees' Unresolved Trauma

1. Emotional and Behavioural Volatility

One of the most immediate challenges leaders face when managing individuals with unresolved trauma is emotional and behavioural volatility. Employees with trauma histories may be prone to heightened emotional reactions, such as anger, frustration, or intense sadness, in response to stress or perceived threats. This volatility can disrupt team dynamics and lead to interpersonal conflict, affecting overall productivity.

Leaders are often unprepared to handle these reactions, which may be unpredictable or out of proportion to the situation. Without adequate training, leaders might misinterpret these behaviours as poor performance, lack of commitment, or even insubordination, rather than understanding them as trauma responses.

2. Distrust of Authority and Leadership

Individuals with unresolved trauma, especially those who have experienced trauma involving authority figures, may exhibit a deep-seated distrust of leadership. This can manifest in resistance to direction, refusal to engage in collaborative efforts, or a reluctance to open up about concerns. In such cases, leaders may find it difficult to establish rapport, provide constructive feedback, or effectively manage performance issues.

This lack of trust can undermine team cohesion and cause friction between the leader and the employee. It can also create an environment where the employee feels isolated, further compounding the effects of trauma.

3. Impacts on Team Dynamics and Collaboration

Unresolved trauma can also impact the broader team dynamic, as employees with trauma may struggle to engage in open communication or collaborative efforts. For example, someone with a history of trauma may avoid group interactions, feel easily overwhelmed by conflict, or have difficulty setting boundaries with colleagues.

This lack of engagement can hinder collaboration, lead to misunderstandings, or cause resentment among team members who do not understand the employee's trauma-related challenges. Moreover, unresolved trauma can create an atmosphere of tension within the team, where others may feel they are walking on eggshells to avoid triggering emotional outbursts.

4. Difficulty with Feedback and Performance Management

Providing feedback and managing performance are essential aspects of leadership, but they can become complex when working with individuals who have unresolved trauma. Trauma can affect an employee's ability to receive feedback constructively; they may perceive criticism as a personal attack or experience heightened anxiety when discussing performance issues.

Leaders must navigate the delicate balance between maintaining productivity and addressing trauma-related sensitivities. Standard performance management approaches may not work effectively, and leaders may struggle to find ways to provide feedback that does not exacerbate the employee's trauma-related challenges.

5. Increased Absenteeism and Presenteeism

Trauma can also lead to increased absenteeism or presentee-ism, where employees are physically present but mentally dis-engaged. This can occur as a result of burnout, anxiety, or de-pression linked to their unresolved trauma. Employees may call in sick more frequently, take extended breaks, or exhibit a lack of focus during work hours.

Leaders must balance the need for productivity with an under-standing of the underlying reasons for these behaviours. With-out proper intervention, absenteeism and presenteeism can become chronic issues that affect team performance and organ-isational outcomes.

The Importance of Trauma-Informed Leadership

To address these challenges, it is crucial for leaders to adopt a trauma-informed approach to leadership. Trauma-informed leadership recognises the presence of trauma and its effects on behaviour, relationships, and work performance. It involves cre-ating an environment of safety, trust, and support, where em-ployees feel empowered to perform at their best while navigat-ing their personal challenges.

1. Creating a Safe and Supportive Environment

A trauma-informed leader prioritises creating a psychological-ly safe workplace where employees feel valued, respected, and supported. According to Brown and Shanafelt (2017), psycholog-ical safety is critical for fostering open communication and trust within teams. Leaders must establish clear boundaries, provide regular check-ins, and ensure that employees have access to mental health resources such as EAPs counselling services.

2. Building Trust and Transparency

Building trust with employees is fundamental in trauma-informed leadership. Leaders should strive to be transparent in their decision-making, consistent in their actions, and approachable in their communication. Trust is built over time through empathy, active listening, and a genuine interest in the well-being of employees. For employees with unresolved trauma, knowing they can rely on their leader for support and understanding can be transformative.

3. Flexibility in Performance Management

Traditional performance management approaches may not be suitable for employees with trauma. Leaders should adopt flexible strategies that take the employee's emotional and mental state into account. For example, providing feedback in private, offering specific guidance for improvement, and using a strengths-based approach can help employees manage their work more effectively without feeling overwhelmed or criticised.

4. Training and Education for Leaders

Trauma-informed leadership requires continuous learning and training. Leaders should seek out training on trauma, mental health, and psychological safety to better understand how to manage employees with unresolved trauma. Many organisations offer workshops, courses, or certifications on trauma-informed practices, and engaging in this education can empower leaders to navigate complex emotional dynamics within their teams.

5. Collaborating with Mental Health Professionals

In cases where an employee's trauma significantly impacts their work performance, leaders should collaborate with mental health professionals or human resources (HR) specialists. Engaging EAPs or other workplace wellness initiatives can provide employees with access to counselling, therapy, or coaching, helping them manage their trauma while maintaining productivity.

Case Studies

Case Study 1: Trauma-Informed Leadership in Action

Consider a case study where a manager in a mid-sized tech company was struggling to manage an employee, Sarah, who had been a high performer but was exhibiting erratic behaviour, frequently calling in sick, and becoming withdrawn from her team. Sarah's work quality had declined, and the manager was unsure how to address the situation without alienating her.

After engaging in a conversation with Sarah, the manager learned that she had been dealing with unresolved trauma from a recent personal loss. The manager, who had attended trauma-informed leadership training, responded with empathy and provided Sarah with access to the company's EAP for counselling support. Additionally, the manager restructured Sarah's workload temporarily, allowing her to manage stress more effectively while receiving the support she needed.

Over time, Sarah began to re-engage with her work, and her performance improved. By adopting a trauma-informed approach, the manager was able to retain a valuable employee and create an environment where Sarah felt safe and supported.

Key Takeaways

Leading employees with unresolved trauma requires a deep sense of empathy, flexibility, and a willingness to adapt leadership practices. While the challenges can be significant, adopting a trauma-informed approach can foster a healthier, more productive work environment. By creating spaces of safety, trust, and support, leaders can help employees navigate their trauma while maintaining their performance and engagement.

Trauma-informed leadership is not just about addressing individual trauma; it's about building a resilient and compassionate organisational culture where all employees feel valued and empowered to thrive.

References and Resources:

- Brown, B. & Shanafelt, T. (2017). *Cultivating a culture of well-being in the workplace.* Harvard Business Review.

- Brown, B. (2018). *Dare to lead: Brave work. Tough conversations. Whole hearts.* Random House.

- Substance Abuse and Mental Health Services Administration (SAMHSA). (2014). *Trauma-informed care in behavioural health services.* Retrieved from https://store.samhsa.gov/product/TIP-57-Trauma-Informed-Care-in-Behavioural-Health-Services

CHAPTER 12

Trauma-Informed Communication

Trauma-informed communication is a critical component of creating a psychosocially safe workplace. It involves recognising the prevalence of trauma, understanding its impact on individuals, and adapting communication strategies to foster a safe and supportive environment. By adopting trauma-informed communication practices, leaders and employees can build trust, reduce the risk of re-traumatisation, and promote a culture of empathy and understanding. This chapter delves into the principles of trauma-informed communication, practical strategies for implementation, and the benefits of this approach in the workplace.

Understanding Trauma and Its Impact on Communication

Trauma is an emotional response to a distressing or disturbing event that overwhelms an individual's ability to cope. It can stem from various sources, including abuse, violence, accidents, being bullied or humiliated—especially as a child by a teacher or parent, or natural disasters. The effects of trauma can be long-lasting, affecting a person's emotional regulation, cognitive functioning, and interpersonal relationships. In the workplace, trauma can manifest in various ways, such as heightened anxiety, difficulty concentrating, or challenges in trusting others.

Communication is a fundamental aspect of workplace interactions, but for individuals with a history of trauma, certain communication styles or behaviours can trigger negative emotional responses. For example, aggressive or authoritative tones, sudden changes in plans, or ambiguous instructions can evoke feelings of fear, confusion, or helplessness. Trauma-informed communication seeks to minimise these triggers by adopting a compassionate, clear, and consistent approach that prioritises the psychological safety of all individuals.

Principles of Trauma-Informed Communication

The Substance Abuse and Mental Health Services Administration (SAMHSA) outlines six key principles of trauma-informed care, which can be directly applied to communication in the workplace:

1. *Safety:* Creating an environment where individuals feel physically and psychologically safe is paramount. This involves being mindful of both verbal and non-verbal cues and ensuring that communication does not inadvertently cause distress.

2. *Trustworthiness and Transparency:* Building trust. This can be achieved through clear, consistent, and honest communication. Being transparent about decisions, processes, and expectations helps individuals feel secure and reduces anxiety.

3. *Peer Support:* Encouraging peer support and collaboration fosters a sense of community and shared understanding. Open communication channels between colleagues can provide emotional support and reduce feelings of isolation.

4. *Collaboration and Mutuality:* Emphasising collaboration and shared decision-making. Recognising that everyone has a role in the communication process and

valuing each person's input helps create a more inclusive and respectful environment.

5. *Empowerment, Voice, and Choice:* Empowering individuals by giving them a voice and a choice in communication. This can help mitigate the effects of trauma and involves actively listening, validating their experiences, and respecting their autonomy.

6. *Cultural, Historical, and Gender Issues:* Recognising the importance of cultural sensitivity and acknowledging the diverse backgrounds and experiences of individuals. This includes being aware of how historical and social contexts may influence communication preferences and needs.

Strategies for Trauma-Informed Communication in the Workplace

Implementing trauma-informed communication in the workplace requires a commitment to ongoing learning and adaptation. The following strategies can help leaders and employees adopt trauma-informed practices:

1. Active Listening:

What it is: Active listening involves fully concentrating, understanding, and responding to what the speaker is saying without judgement or interruption. It is a foundational element of trauma-informed communication.

How to implement: Practice reflective listening by summarising what the speaker has said to ensure understanding. Use non-verbal cues, such as nodding or maintaining eye contact, to show engagement. Avoid interrupting or rushing the conversation and provide space for the speaker to express themselves fully.

2. Clear and Consistent Communication:

What it is: Trauma-informed communication requires clarity and consistency to avoid misunderstandings and reduce anxiety.

How to implement: Use simple, straightforward language that is free of jargon or ambiguity. Provide clear instructions and set expectations from the outset. If changes occur, communicate them promptly and explain the reasons behind them. Ensure that all relevant information is shared with the necessary individuals to prevent feelings of exclusion or uncertainty.

3. Creating a Safe Environment:

What it is: A safe environment is one where individuals feel comfortable expressing themselves without fear of judgement, criticism, or repercussions.

How to implement: Foster a culture of respect and inclusivity by promoting open dialogue and encouraging diverse perspectives. Set boundaries for communication that prevent aggressive or harmful behaviours, such as bullying or harassment. Offer private spaces for sensitive conversations and respect confidentiality.

4. Being Mindful of Non-Verbal Communication:

What it is: Non-verbal communication, including body language, facial expressions, and tone of voice, can significantly impact how a message is received.

How to implement: Be aware of your non-verbal cues and ensure they align with your verbal message. For example, maintaining an open posture, using a calm tone of voice, and making appropriate eye contact can convey empathy and attentiveness. Avoid crossing your arms, rolling your eyes, or using a harsh tone, as these can be perceived as dismissive or confrontational. Leaning back, looking away or slouching may be perceived as disinterest.

5. Providing Choices and Encouraging Autonomy:

What it is: Empowering individuals by offering choices and respecting their autonomy helps to build trust and reduce feelings of helplessness.

How to implement: Whenever possible, provide options for how and when communication takes place. For example, ask if the individual prefers to communicate via email, in person, or over the phone. Encourage them to share their thoughts and opinions and involve them in decision-making processes that affect them. Respect their right to decline participation in certain conversations if they feel uncomfortable.

6. Responding to Emotional Distress with Compassion:

What it is: Trauma-informed communication requires a compassionate response to emotional distress, recognising that such reactions may be linked to past trauma.

How to implement: If someone becomes visibly upset or anxious during a conversation, acknowledge their feelings and offer support. Avoid dismissing or minimising their emotions. Instead, ask how you can help and provide reassurance. If necessary, suggest taking a break or rescheduling the conversation to give them time to process their emotions.

The Benefits of Trauma-Informed Communication

Adopting trauma-informed communication practices offers numerous benefits for both individuals and organisations. These include:

1. Increased Psychological Safety:

When individuals feel that their emotional and psychological well-being is respected, they are more likely to engage openly in communication and contribute to the workplace. This sense of safety can lead to higher levels of employee satisfaction and retention.

2. Improved Trust and Collaboration:

Trauma-informed communication fosters trust between leaders, employees, and colleagues. When trust is established, collaboration becomes more effective, and teams can work together more cohesively toward common goals.

3. Reduced Risk of Re-Traumatisation:

By being mindful of the potential impact of trauma on communication, organisations can reduce the risk of re-traumatising employees, which can lead to improved mental health outcomes and a more supportive work environment.

4. Enhanced Organisational Culture:

A trauma-informed approach to communication can transform the overall culture of an organisation, making it more inclusive, empathetic, and responsive to the needs of all employees. This can result in a more positive workplace atmosphere and stronger organisational performance.

Implementing Trauma-Informed Communication Training

To fully integrate trauma-informed communication into the workplace, organisations should consider providing training for all employees, particularly leaders and managers. This training should cover the following areas:

1. Understanding Trauma:

Educate employees about the nature of trauma, its effects on individuals, and how it can influence communication. This foundational knowledge is essential for recognising the need for trauma-informed approaches.

2. Practical Communication Skills:

Provide hands-on training in active listening, clear communication, non-verbal communication, and responding to emotional distress. Role-playing exercises can be particularly effective in helping employees practice these skills in a safe environment.

3. Cultural Competency:

Ensure that the training addresses the importance of cultural sensitivity in communication, recognising that individuals from different backgrounds may have unique communication needs and preferences.

4. Ongoing Support and Development:

Offer continuous learning opportunities, such as workshops, webinars, or discussion groups, to help employees refine their trauma-informed communication skills over time. Encourage leaders to model these practices and provide feedback and support to their teams.

Real-World Examples

Government Department Implementing
Trauma-Informed Communication

Sector: Government (US Veterans Affairs Department)

Issue: High levels of PTSD and mental health challenges among veterans

Trauma-Informed Communication Implementation: The US Department of Veterans Affairs (VA) serves veterans, many of whom experience post-traumatic stress disorder (PTSD) and other mental health issues related to their military service. Historically, veterans found interactions with VA staff stressful due to a lack of understanding and empathy regarding trauma. In response, the VA implemented a trauma-informed communication training program for all employees, focusing on active listening, avoiding re-traumatisation, and creating safe spaces for veterans to share their experiences.

Outcome: After adopting trauma-informed communication practices, the VA saw improved trust between veterans and staff. Veterans reported feeling more supported and understood, leading to increased participation in mental health services. Employee satisfaction also improved as staff felt better equipped to handle sensitive interactions. A report on the program showed that adopting trauma-informed communication helped reduce veterans' anxiety when accessing services, improved mental health outcomes, and led to better overall care experiences.

Reference:

> U.S. Department of Veterans Affairs. (2020). VA adopts trauma-informed care for veterans with PTSD. Retrieved from https://www.va.gov

Healthcare Industry Using Trauma-Informed Communication

Sector: Healthcare (Kaiser Permanente)

Issue: Improving patient care for trauma survivors in medical settings

Trauma-Informed Communication Implementation: Kaiser Permanente, one of the largest healthcare providers in the US, recognised that many patients, especially survivors of abuse or violence, often avoided or delayed medical care due to fears of re-traumatisation during clinical visits. To address this, the organisation implemented a trauma-informed communication strategy across its hospitals and clinics. This included training healthcare professionals on how to ask questions without causing distress, listening actively, and offering patients more control during their medical care to foster a sense of safety and respect.

Outcome: After implementing trauma-informed communication practices, Kaiser Permanente reported increased patient satisfaction, particularly among trauma survivors. Patients felt more empowered and comfortable during medical procedures, which led to more frequent use of preventive healthcare services. Clinicians also noted that trauma-informed communication improved patient trust and rapport, leading to better patient outcomes and stronger adherence to treatment plans.

Reference:

> Kaiser Permanente. (2018). Trauma-informed care for survivors of violence: Implementing best practices across healthcare systems. Retrieved from https://www.kaiserpermanente.org

Hospitality Industry Implementing Trauma-Informed Communication for Guest Relations

Sector: Hospitality (Marriott International)

Issue: Improving guest relations by addressing trauma and stress-related concerns

Trauma-Informed Communication Implementation: Marriott International, a global leader in the hospitality industry, noticed that some guests exhibited heightened anxiety or discomfort due to personal trauma or stressful travel experiences. In response, the company implemented trauma-informed communication training for staff members at key customer touchpoints, including front desk employees, concierges, and event planners. The training emphasised empathy, patience, and respectful communication, with staff learning how to de-escalate potentially stressful situations and avoid triggering trauma responses.

Outcome: Marriott saw a significant improvement in guest satisfaction, particularly among those who had previously reported anxiety or negative experiences during their stay. Frontline employees were better equipped to manage difficult guest interactions, and the hotel's reputation for providing compassionate service improved. The implementation of trauma-informed communication also reduced the frequency of guest complaints related to service quality and created a more inclusive and welcoming environment for all guests.

Reference:

- Marriott International. (2019). Enhancing guest experiences through trauma-informed service and communication practices. Retrieved from https://www.marriott.com

Key Takeaways

Trauma-informed communication is not just a set of techniques; it is a mindset that prioritises empathy, respect, and understanding in all interactions. By adopting trauma-informed communication practices, organisations can create a more inclusive and supportive work environment that promotes psychological safety, trust, and collaboration. This approach benefits not only individuals who have experienced trauma but also the organisation as a whole, leading to a healthier and more productive workplace.

References:

⊙ Bloom, S. L. (2013). Creating sanctuary: Toward the evolution of sane societies. Routledge.

⊙ Goleman, D. (2006). *Emotional intelligence: Why it can matter more than IQ.* Bantam.

⊙ Herman, J. L. (1997). *Trauma and Recovery: The aftermath of violence—From domestic abuse to political terror.* Basic Books.

⊙ Litz, B. T., & Roemer, L. (2007). Post-traumatic stress disorder: An overview. In *The Oxford handbook of clinical psychology* (pp. 316-340). Oxford University Press.

⊙ Maslach, C., & Leiter, M. P. (2016). *The truth about burnout: How organisations cause personal stress and what to do about it.* Jossey-Bass.

⊙ Substance Abuse and Mental Health Services Administration (SAMHSA). (2014). *SAMHSA's concept of trauma and guidance for a trauma-informed approach.* https://store.samhsa.gov/sites/default/files/d7/priv/sma14-4884.pdf

⊙ van der Kolk, B. A. (2014). *The body keeps the score: Brain, mind, and body in the healing of trauma.* Penguin Books.

CHAPTER 13

Bullying Caused by Unresolved Trauma in the Workplace

Unresolved trauma can manifest in various detrimental ways within a workplace, one of the most harmful being bullying. Employees with unresolved trauma may inadvertently or deliberately become bullies as a result of their psychological wounds, using controlling or aggressive behaviours as coping mechanisms. These individuals may lack the emotional regulation needed to navigate stress, anger, or perceived threats, and consequently, their unresolved trauma may drive them to lash out at colleagues, subordinates, or even superiors.

How Trauma Can Lead to Bullying

Trauma can deeply affect an individual's ability to interact with others in a healthy and constructive way. Those who have experienced trauma, particularly if it involved power imbalances—such as in cases of abuse, neglect, or violence—may develop maladaptive behaviours to regain a sense of control. According to Herman (1992), trauma survivors often struggle with feelings of powerlessness and vulnerability, which can cause them to act out in ways that re-establish dominance over others, often in harmful or aggressive ways.

For example, an employee who has unresolved trauma stemming from past abuse may become hypervigilant to perceived slights or threats, even when none exist. This heightened sensitivity may cause them to react disproportionately to minor conflicts, using bullying as a form of self-protection. By belittling or intimidating others, these individuals feel as though they are regaining control over their environment.

1. Trauma-Induced Hypervigilance and Control

One of the hallmarks of unresolved trauma is hypervigilance— an exaggerated state of awareness where individuals are constantly on guard, anticipating danger or conflict. In the workplace, this can cause traumatised employees to perceive neutral situations as threatening. This overreaction can lead them to adopt bullying tactics as a way to assert control and pre-empt perceived threats.

For instance, a manager with unresolved trauma might micromanage their team, impose unrealistic demands, or berate subordinates for minor mistakes. Their behaviour is not necessarily rooted in a desire to harm but rather in a deeply ingrained need to control their surroundings to avoid further emotional injury. This form of bullying can create a toxic work environment, where employees feel belittled, disempowered, and unable to perform to their potential.

2. Emotional Dysregulation and Aggression

Trauma often impacts emotional regulation, making it difficult for individuals to manage their feelings in a healthy way. When faced with stress, conflict, or feelings of inadequacy, those with unresolved trauma may react with anger, hostility, or aggression. This emotional volatility can lead to bullying behaviour, where individuals lash out at colleagues as a means of externalising their inner turmoil.

In some cases, individuals may not even be consciously aware that they are engaging in bullying. Their emotional responses may feel automatic or justified in the moment, but the long-term effects on the workplace can be devastating. Bullying disrupts team cohesion, undermines morale, and leads to increased absenteeism and turnover.

3. Projection of Trauma onto Others

Traumatised individuals may also project their unresolved feelings onto others, perceiving their own insecurities or fears in the behaviour of colleagues. This can result in scapegoating or singling out specific individuals as targets for bullying. The bully may exaggerate perceived flaws in others or hold them to impossible standards, projecting their own trauma-induced need for perfection or control onto their colleagues.

For example, an employee who was subjected to harsh criticism as a child may unconsciously replicate this dynamic in the workplace, bullying coworkers as a way to avoid feeling inferior themselves. By putting others down, they temporarily alleviate their own sense of inadequacy or shame, albeit in a destructive and harmful manner.

Impact of Trauma-Induced Bullying

The presence of trauma-induced bullying can severely disrupt workplace dynamics. The impact on both the individuals involved and the organisation as a whole is substantial, leading to decreased productivity, higher turnover, and long-lasting damage to the work culture.

1. Psychological Harm to Targets

Bullying has well-documented negative effects on the mental health of its victims, leading to anxiety, depression, stress, and burnout. When the bullying stems from someone's unresolved trauma, the effects on the target can be even more complex. In these cases, the bully's erratic behaviour may be difficult to predict, leaving the target feeling constantly on edge, unable to determine how to avoid triggering negative responses.

According to Einarsen, Hoel, Zapf, and Cooper (2011), bullying can cause long-term psychological harm to employees, diminishing their self-esteem, work satisfaction, and overall well-being. In extreme cases, bullying can lead to PTSD in the victim, compounding the cycle of trauma in the workplace.

2. Disruption to Team Dynamics

Trauma-induced bullying not only affects the direct target but also has broader consequences for the team. Bullying can create an environment of fear and mistrust, where employees are hesitant to collaborate or share ideas out of fear of retaliation. In this toxic environment, team cohesion breaks down, and communication suffers.

Additionally, when unresolved trauma is the root cause of bullying, it can make it harder for team members to address the problem. Colleagues may feel empathy for the bully's trauma but be unsure how to hold them accountable for their harmful behaviour. This confusion can generate further tension and inaction, allowing the bullying to persist unchecked.

3. Organisational Costs

The costs of bullying, particularly when rooted in unresolved trauma, extend far beyond the individual and team levels. Organisations dealing with trauma-induced bullying may face increased absenteeism, presenteeism, and turnover. Employees who are bullied or who witness bullying are more likely to disengage from their work, contributing to lower productivity and reduced overall performance.

Furthermore, organisations with bullying problems face reputational risks. High employee turnover and poor workplace culture can harm the company's ability to attract and retain top talent. In more severe cases, unresolved workplace bullying can prompt legal issues, as employees may seek recourse through employment law channels.

Addressing Trauma-Induced Bullying

Effectively addressing bullying caused by unresolved trauma requires a multifaceted approach that considers both the individual experiencing trauma and the organisational culture that enables or tolerates bullying.

1. Trauma-Informed Leadership

Trauma-informed leadership is crucial for recognising and addressing the root causes of bullying. Leaders should receive training on how trauma affects behaviour and learn to recognise signs of trauma in their teams. By understanding the connection between unresolved trauma and bullying, leaders can take proactive steps to intervene and provide support.

Leaders should also create a culture where open communication is encouraged, and employees feel safe discussing issues related to mental health or trauma. Providing access to EAPs and mental health resources can help employees work through their trauma without resorting to bullying behaviour.

2. Establish Clear Anti-Bullying Policies

Organisations must establish and enforce clear anti-bullying policies that apply to all employees, regardless of their personal histories. While it's important to acknowledge and support employees with trauma, this should not excuse or allow harmful behaviour. Anti-bullying policies should be clear, accessible, and consistently applied, ensuring that all employees understand what constitutes bullying and how it will be addressed.

3. Provide Mental Health Support

Organisations should prioritise mental health support for both those affected by bullying and those with unresolved trauma. Providing access to mental health professionals through EAPs, offering trauma-informed training programs, and creating a culture that encourages seeking help can prevent trauma from manifesting as bullying.

Real-World Examples

Managing Unresolved Trauma in Law Enforcement

Sector: Government (Law Enforcement - NSW Police Force, Australia)

Issue: High levels of unresolved trauma leading to PTSD and absenteeism among officers

Managing Unresolved Trauma: The New South Wales Police Force (NSWPF) recognised that police officers frequently experience traumatic events, leading to unresolved trauma that manifests in PTSD, anxiety, and depression. The force struggled with high rates of absenteeism and officers taking early retirement due to mental health issues. To address this, NSWPF introduced a comprehensive mental health and wellness program, which included trauma counselling, peer support groups, and early intervention strategies. Officers were encouraged to seek help early, with dedicated resources provided through EAPs and confidential mental health services.

Outcome: The NSWPF saw a significant reduction in absenteeism and psychological injury claims following the introduction of the trauma support program. Officers who participated in trauma-informed counselling reported better mental health outcomes, and retention rates improved. The program has since been expanded to provide ongoing support and resilience training, helping officers manage the emotional toll of their work and preventing the escalation of unresolved trauma.

Reference:

- ❯ NSW Police Force. (2018). Employee Mental Health and Wellness Program. Retrieved from https://www.police.nsw.gov.au

Managing Trauma in Healthcare Workers

Sector: Healthcare (Johns Hopkins Hospital, USA)

Issue: Burnout and unresolved trauma among healthcare workers during and after the COVID-19 pandemic

Managing Unresolved Trauma: During the COVID-19 pandemic, healthcare workers at Johns Hopkins Hospital experienced immense stress and trauma, leading to severe burnout, anxiety, and PTSD. Many staff members were overwhelmed by the high number of critically ill patients, the loss of colleagues, and the long hours spent in high-risk environments. The hospital launched a comprehensive mental health initiative specifically aimed at addressing unresolved trauma in its workforce. This initiative included on-site mental health counsellors, peer support groups, access to trauma-informed therapy, and mindfulness training. Leadership also implemented "resilience rounds" where staff could debrief and share experiences in a safe space.

Outcome: The trauma support program significantly improved the mental well-being of healthcare workers. Staff reported feeling more supported and engaged in their work, leading to reduced turnover and absenteeism rates. The proactive management of unresolved trauma among healthcare professionals helped maintain team cohesion and morale, particularly during

the most intense periods of the pandemic. This initiative became a model for other hospitals managing employee trauma
in high-stress situations.

Reference:

- Johns Hopkins Medicine. (2021). Addressing COVID-19
  trauma in healthcare workers: A comprehensive approach.
  Retrieved from https://www.hopkinsmedicine.org

Managing Trauma and Stress in Hospitality Workers

Sector: Hospitality (Hilton Hotels)

Issue: Unresolved trauma and stress among hospitality workers
due to customer-facing roles

Managing Unresolved Trauma: Hilton Hotels identified unresolved trauma and chronic stress as key issues affecting frontline hospitality workers, particularly those dealing with difficult
guests, high workloads, and workplace harassment. Many employees reported feeling emotionally drained and experiencing
burnout, leading to high turnover and absenteeism. To address
these issues, Hilton launched a trauma-informed care and
well-being program for its staff. The program included confidential access to mental health services, trauma training for managers, and peer support networks. Employees were encouraged to
participate in mindfulness and stress management workshops
to help them cope with the emotional challenges of their roles.

Outcome: The initiative led to a marked improvement in employee retention and a reduction in stress-related absenteeism.
Employees reported feeling more empowered to manage the
emotional demands of their work and appreciated the availability of mental health resources. Hilton also saw an improvement
in guest satisfaction, as staff who had previously struggled with

burnout were better equipped to handle customer interactions. The success of this program led Hilton to expand its mental health support services across more of its locations worldwide.

Reference:

- Hilton Hotels. (2020). Employee well-being and trauma support initiatives in hospitality. Retrieved from https://www.hilton.com

Key Takeaways

Unresolved trauma can have serious repercussions in the workplace, especially when it manifests as bullying behaviour. Leaders need to be equipped with the tools to recognise the signs of trauma-induced bullying and create a supportive environment that promotes healing and collaboration. By fostering a trauma-informed workplace, organisations can prevent bullying, support employees through their trauma, and cultivate a healthier, more productive work environment.

References and Resources:

- Einarsen, S., Hoel, H., Zapf, D., & Cooper, C. L. (2011). *Bullying and harassment in the workplace: Developments in theory, research, and practice*. CRC Press.

- Herman, J. L. (1992). *Trauma and recovery: The aftermath of violence—from domestic abuse to political terror*. Basic Books.

- Substance Abuse and Mental Health Services Administration (SAMHSA). (2014). Trauma-informed care in behavioural health services. Retrieved from https://store.samhsa.gov/product/TIP-57-Trauma-Informed-Care-in-Behavioural-Health-Services

PART 6

Aspects of Leadership and Employee Training

CHAPTER 14

Training Leaders and Managers

Training leaders and managers is a critical component of fostering a psychosocially safe workplace. Effective leadership training equips managers with the skills necessary to support their teams, identify and mitigate psychosocial risks, and promote a culture of safety and respect.

Aspects of Leadership Training

1. *Role Modelling:* Leaders and managers serve as role models in the workplace. Their behaviour sets the tone for organisational culture. According to a study by the Chartered Institute of Personnel and Development (CIPD), 80% of employees believe that their direct manager's behaviour significantly impacts their job satisfaction and performance (CIPD, 2020).

2. *Conflict Resolution:* Effective leaders are skilled in conflict resolution, which is essential for maintaining a psychosocially safe environment. Training programs that focus on mediation and conflict management can reduce workplace tensions and foster a more collaborative atmosphere. The American Management Association (AMA) highlights that conflict management training can lead to a 58% improvement in team dynamics (AMA, 2017).

3. *Mental Health Awareness:* Leaders must be knowledgeable about mental health issues and how to support employees who may be struggling. Training in Mental Health First Aid (MHFA) and awareness can help managers identify early signs of mental health problems

and provide appropriate support. The MHFA program in Australia has shown that its participants are more likely to recognise and respond to mental health issues effectively (MHFA Australia, 2018).

4. *Compliance and Legal Awareness:* Leaders need to understand legal and ethical considerations related to workplace safety, including anti-bullying laws, discrimination policies, and occupational health and safety (OHS) regulations. This knowledge ensures that they can enforce policies effectively and maintain a safe work environment. In the US, the Occupational Safety and Health Administration (OSHA) emphasises the importance of legal compliance in maintaining workplace safety (OSHA, 2016).

Components of Leadership Training Programs

1. *Emotional Intelligence:* Training programs should include modules on emotional intelligence (EI), which is crucial for effective leadership. EI helps leaders manage their own emotions and understand and influence the emotions of others. Research by Daniel Goleman suggests that EI is a key factor in leadership success, with emotionally intelligent leaders achieving higher team performance and job satisfaction (Goleman, 1998).

2. *Communication Skills:* Effective communication is essential for leaders to convey policies, provide feedback, and resolve conflicts. Training should cover active listening, non-verbal communication, and effective feedback techniques. The Harvard Business Review reports that leaders who communicate effectively can improve team performance by up to 25% (HBR, 2019).

3. *Stress Management:* Leaders must manage their own stress and help their teams cope with workplace pressures. Training in stress management techniques, such as mindfulness and resilience-building, can enhance leaders' ability to maintain a supportive work environment. The American Psychological Association (APA) highlights the benefits of stress management training in reducing burnout and improving job satisfaction (APA, 2018).

4. *Equity, Inclusivity and Diversity:* Leaders should be trained to foster an inclusive and diverse workplace. This training should address unconscious bias, cultural competency, and strategies for promoting equity, diversity, and inclusion. A report by McKinsey & Company found that inclusive workplaces are 35% more likely to outperform their peers (McKinsey, 2015).

The Role of Leadership in Psychosocial Safety

Leadership plays a pivotal role in creating and sustaining a psychosocially safe workplace. Leaders influence organisational culture, employee engagement, and overall workplace well-being.

Creating a Supportive Leadership Culture

1. *Leading by Example:* Leaders must demonstrate the behaviours they expect from their employees. This includes showing respect, empathy, and commitment to psychosocial safety. According to a study by the Centre for Creative Leadership, leaders who model positive behaviours can significantly influence their teams' attitudes and behaviours (CCL, 2017).

2. *Building Trust:* Trust is the foundation of a psychosocially safe workplace. Leaders can build trust by being

transparent, consistent, and fair in their actions. Research by the Edelman Trust Barometer indicates that trust in leadership is strongly correlated with employee engagement and performance (Edelman, 2019).

3. *Encouraging Open Communication:* Leaders should create an environment where employees feel safe to voice their concerns and share their ideas. Open communication channels can help identify and address psychosocial risks early. A study by Gallup found that employees who feel heard by their leaders are 4.6 times more likely to feel empowered to perform their best work (Gallup, 2018).

4. *Providing Support and Resources:* Leaders must ensure that employees have access to the necessary resources and support systems, such as mental health services, EAPs, and flexible working arrangements. The availability of these resources can significantly impact employees' well-being and productivity.

Leadership Training Programs

1. *Executive Coaching:* Executive coaching can help leaders develop the skills needed to support a psychosocially safe workplace. Coaches work with leaders on a one-on-one basis to address specific challenges and enhance their leadership capabilities. The International Coach Federation (ICF) reports that executive coaching can lead to a 70% improvement in work performance (ICF, 2016).

2. *Workshops and Seminars:* Regular workshops and seminars on topics related to psychosocial safety can keep leaders informed about the latest trends, research, and best practices. These sessions can also provide a plat-

form for leaders to share experiences and learn from each other.

3. *Online Training Modules:* Online training modules offer flexibility and accessibility for leaders to learn at their own pace. These modules can cover a wide range of topics, including mental health awareness, conflict resolution, and inclusive leadership. A study by the eLearning Industry found that online training can increase knowledge retention by 25-60% compared to traditional classroom training (eLearning Industry, 2019).

4. *Peer Support Groups:* Peer support groups for leaders can provide a space for sharing experiences, discussing challenges, and offering mutual support. These groups can enhance leaders' resilience and ability to manage psychosocial risks effectively.

Measuring the Impact of Leadership Training

1. *Employee Feedback:* Regular surveys and feedback mechanisms can help measure the impact of leadership training on employee well-being and organisational culture. The Society for Human Resource Management (SHRM) recommends using employee feedback to assess the effectiveness of training programs and identify areas for improvement (SHRM, 2020).

2. *Performance Metrics:* Tracking key performance metrics, such as employee engagement, productivity, and turnover rates, can provide insights into the effectiveness of leadership training. A study by the Human Capital Institute (HCI) found that organisations with strong leadership development programs experience 29% higher employee engagement (HCI, 2017).

3. ***Behavioural Observations:*** Observing leaders' behaviours and interactions with their teams can help assess the impact of training. Behavioural assessments and 360-degree feedback can provide valuable information about how leaders are applying their training in practice.

4. ***Organisational Outcomes:*** Analysing organisational outcomes, such as financial performance, customer satisfaction, and innovation, can help measure the broader impact of leadership training. Research by the Conference Board found that organisations with effective leadership development programs outperform their peers in key business metrics (Conference Board, 2018).

Key Strategies for Building a Supportive Leadership Team

Creating a supportive leadership team involves selecting and developing leaders who are committed to psychosocial safety and employee well-being. The following strategies can assist in building a supporting leadership team:

1. ***Selecting the Right Leaders:*** Recruitment and selection processes should prioritise candidates who demonstrate strong interpersonal skills, EI, and a commitment to psychosocial safety. Behavioural interviews and psychometric assessments can help identify these qualities.

2. ***Ongoing Development:*** Providing ongoing development opportunities for leaders can help them continuously improve their skills and stay updated on best practices. This can include advanced leadership training, mentoring programs, and participation in professional networks.

3. *Recognising and Rewarding Supportive Leaders: Recognising* and rewarding leaders who actively promote psychosocial safety can reinforce positive behaviours and encourage others to follow suit. Recognition programs can include awards, public acknowledgment, and career advancement opportunities.

4. *Fostering Collaboration and Teamwork:* Encouraging collaboration and teamwork among leaders can help create a unified approach to psychosocial safety. Regular leadership meetings, team-building activities, and cross-functional projects can strengthen relationships and promote a cohesive leadership team.

Real-World Examples

Poor Leadership in Managing Hospital Workforce and Patient Care

Sector: Government (Healthcare - NHS, UK)

Issue: Untrained leadership failing to manage workforce stress and patient care quality

Negative Impact: The UK's National Health Service (NHS) experienced a crisis in 2013 when a public inquiry revealed that poor leadership contributed to catastrophic failures in patient care at Stafford Hospital. Senior leaders and managers lacked the training and skills necessary to recognise and address the staff's high levels of stress, burnout, and low morale. The hospital's leadership failed to manage resources effectively, and employees were not provided adequate support to handle the increasing pressure. This led to significant lapses in patient safety, resulting in avoidable deaths and neglect.

Outcome: The report highlighted the lack of leadership training in areas such as EI, crisis management, and employee support. The scandal led to widespread public outrage, legal investigations, and significant reputational damage to the NHS. The findings from the Stafford Hospital inquiry prompted reforms across the NHS, including a greater emphasis on leadership training, patient safety protocols, and better workforce management. However, the damage to public trust and the emotional toll on both patients and healthcare workers took years to recover.

Reference:

- The Guardian. (2013). *NHS Mid Staffordshire scandal: Public inquiry report.* Retrieved from https://www.theguardian.com

Poor Leadership and Communication Leading to the 737 MAX Crisis

Sector: Aviation (Boeing)

Issue: Ill-equipped leadership and poor crisis management

Negative Impact: Boeing faced one of the largest crises in aviation history after two fatal crashes involving the 737 MAX aircraft in 2018 and 2019. An internal investigation revealed that the company's leadership, including top executives, had failed to act on safety concerns raised by employees. Leaders were untrained in proper crisis communication and prioritising safety over profits, which resulted in critical software issues being ignored. Boeing's leadership also failed to foster a culture where employees felt empowered to voice safety concerns, further exacerbating the problem.

Outcome: The fallout from the 737 MAX crisis was immense. Boeing faced billions of dollars in losses, grounded fleets worldwide, and a significant loss of public trust. The company's CEO was ousted, and Boeing implemented sweeping changes to its leadership structure, including a stronger focus on safety and more transparent communication. Leadership training programs were also introduced to better equip managers in handling crises and prioritising employee and passenger safety.

Reference:

⊙ The New York Times. (2020). *Boeing's 737 Max crisis: What's happened and what's next?* Retrieved from https://www.nytimes.com

Poor Crisis Leadership During the Deepwater Horizon Spill

Sector: Energy Industry (BP)

Issue: Ill-equipped leadership exacerbating a crisis

Negative Impact: In 2010, BP faced one of the largest environmental disasters in history when the Deepwater Horizon oil rig exploded, causing a massive oil spill in the Gulf of Mexico. One of the primary criticisms of BP's handling of the disaster was the poor leadership displayed by then-CEO Tony Hayward and other senior executives. BP's leadership was ill-equipped to handle the crisis, failing in key areas such as crisis communication, coordination with regulatory authorities, and employee engagement. Hayward's public comments, such as "I'd like my life back", were seen as insensitive and further damaged the company's reputation.

The leadership team was criticised for downplaying the severity of the disaster, which not only delayed effective responses but also increased the environmental, legal, and financial costs. Internally, BP's leadership was also found to have failed in creating a culture that prioritised safety. Before the spill, employees had raised concerns about safety practices on the oil rig, but these warnings were not acted upon by management, demonstrating a lack of accountability and oversight.

Outcome: The Deepwater Horizon disaster resulted in 11 worker fatalities, severe environmental damage, and a financial cost of over **$65 billion** in fines, settlements, and clean-up expenses. BP's share price plummeted, and the company's brand suffered significant long-term damage. CEO Tony Hayward resigned in the aftermath of the crisis. BP was forced to implement wide-ranging safety reforms, strengthen its leadership accountability, and enhance crisis management training. The disaster highlighted the critical need for skilled leadership in crisis situations and the importance of fostering a culture of safety and transparency.

References:

- BBC News. (2010). *BP oil spill: The Deepwater Horizon disaster*. Retrieved from https://www.bbc.com

- The New York Times. (2018). *BP pays $65 billion in penalties and clean-up for Deepwater Horizon spill*. Retrieved from https://www.nytimes.com

Key Takeaways

Training and education are essential components of creating and sustaining a psychosocially safe workplace. By investing in leadership training, organisations can equip their leaders with the skills and knowledge necessary to support their teams, manage psychosocial risks, and promote a culture of safety and respect.

Effective leadership training programs should focus on key areas such as EI, communication skills, stress management, and inclusivity. Measuring the impact of these programs through employee feedback, performance metrics, and organisational outcomes can help ensure their effectiveness and identify areas for improvement.

Building a supportive leadership team involves selecting the right leaders, providing ongoing development opportunities, recognising and rewarding supportive behaviours, and fostering collaboration and teamwork. By creating a strong and committed leadership team, organisations can drive positive change and create a work environment where employees feel valued, supported, and empowered.

Investing in training and education for leaders is not just a one-time effort but an ongoing commitment to continuous improvement and adaptation. As workplace dynamics and psychosocial risks evolve, so too must the strategies and practices that support psychosocial safety. By staying proactive and responsive, organisations can ensure that they remain at the forefront of creating safe, healthy, and productive work environments.

References:

- American Management Association. (2017). Conflict management: The key to effective leadership. Retrieved from https://www.amanet.org/

- American Psychological Association (APA). (2018). Stress in America: Generation Z. Retrieved from https://www.apa.org/news/press/releases/stress/2018/stress-gen-z.pdf

- Center for Creative Leadership. (2017). Leading through change. Retrieved from https://www.ccl.org/

⏩ Chartered Institute of Personnel and Development (CIPD). (2020). The importance of leadership in employee engagement. Retrieved from https://www.cipd.org/en/

⏩ Conference Board. (2018). The business case for leadership development. Retrieved from https://conference-board.org/

⏩ Deloitte. (2019). The ROI of leadership development. Retrieved from https://www.deloitte.com/au/en.html

⏩ eLearning Industry. (2019). Benefits of online training. Retrieved from https://elearningindustry.com/

⏩ Edelman Trust Barometer. (2019). Trust at work. Retrieved from https://www.edelman.com/trust/2019-trust-barometer

⏩ Gallup. (2018). The importance of employee voice. Retrieved from https://www.gallup.com/home.aspx

⏩ Goleman, D. (1998). *Emotional intelligence: Why it can matter more than IQ*. Bantam Books.

⏩ Harvard Business Review. (2019). The impact of effective communication. Retrieved from https://hbr.org/

⏩ Human Capital Institute (HCI). (2017). The impact of leadership development on employee engagement. Retrieved from https://www.hci.org/

⏩ International Coach Federation (ICF). (2016). The benefits of executive coaching. Retrieved fromhttps://coachfederation.org/ https://coachfederation.org/

⏩ McKinsey & Company. (2015). Diversity matters. Retrieved from https://www.mckinsey.com

Mental Health First Aid Australia (MHFA). (2018). Mental health first aid program. Retrieved from https://mhfa.com.au/

Occupational Safety and Health Administration (OSHA). (2016). Leadership in safety and health. Retrieved from https://www.osha.gov/

Society for Human Resource Management (SHRM). (2020). Employee feedback mechanisms. Retrieved from https://www.shrm.org/

CHAPTER 15

Employee Training and Awareness

Educating Employees on Psychosocial Safety

Creating a psychosocially safe workplace begins with educating employees about the importance of psychosocial safety and how they can contribute to a positive work environment. This education involves raising awareness about psychosocial risks, promoting mental health literacy, and equipping employees with the tools to support their own well-being and that of their colleagues.

Importance of Employee Education

1. *Awareness of Psychosocial Risks:* Employees need to understand the various psychosocial risks that can affect their mental health and well-being. These risks include workplace bullying, harassment, excessive workload, lack of support, and poor work-life balance. According to the World Health Organization (WHO), awareness of psychosocial risks is crucial for preventing work-related stress and promoting a healthy work environment (WHO, 2020).

2. *Promoting Mental Health Literacy:* Mental health literacy involves recognising, understanding, and responding to mental health issues. Educating employees about mental health can reduce stigma and encourage individuals to seek help when needed. A study by Jorm et al. (2019)

found that mental health literacy programs significantly improve knowledge and attitudes toward mental health, leading to better outcomes for employees.

3. ***Building Resilience:*** Resilience is the ability to adapt to and recover from stress and adversity. Training programs that focus on resilience-building can help employees develop coping strategies and maintain their well-being in the face of challenges. Research by the APA shows that resilience training can boost employees' ability to manage stress and improve overall job satisfaction (APA, 2018).

4. ***Encouraging Peer Support:*** Peer support is a critical component of a psychosocially safe workplace. Educating employees on how to support their colleagues and create a supportive network can foster a sense of community and enhance collective well-being. The Centers for Disease Control and Prevention (CDC) highlight the importance of peer support programs in promoting mental health and reducing isolation (CDC, 2019).

Components of Employee Training Programs

1. ***Workshops and Seminars:*** Interactive workshops and seminars on psychosocial safety can engage employees and provide them with practical knowledge and skills. These sessions can cover topics such as stress management, conflict resolution, and mental health awareness. A study by the Harvard Business Review found that interactive training programs are more effective in changing behaviours and improving workplace culture (HBR, 2019).

2. *Online Training Modules:* Online training modules offer flexibility and accessibility for employees to learn at their own pace. These modules can include videos, quizzes, and interactive content to enhance engagement and retention. According to a report by the eLearning Industry, online training can increase knowledge retention by up to 60% compared to traditional classroom training (eLearning Industry, 2019).

3. *Regular Training Updates:* Psychosocial safety training should not be a one-time event. Regular updates and refresher courses can help reinforce key concepts and keep employees informed about new developments and best practices. The Society for Human Resource Management (SHRM) recommends annual training updates to maintain employee awareness and engagement (SHRM, 2020).

4. *Tailored Training Programs:* Training programs should be tailored to the specific needs and context of the organisation. This can involve customising content to address particular psychosocial risks, organisational culture, and employee demographics. The customisation of training programs can enhance relevance and effectiveness, as highlighted by a study from the Journal of Occupational Health Psychology (JOHP, 2018).

Creating Safe Spaces for Open Communication

Open communication is essential for identifying and addressing psychosocial risks in the workplace. Creating safe spaces where employees feel comfortable sharing their concerns and experiences can lead to early intervention and support.

Importance of Open Communication

1. *Early Identification of Issues:* Open communication allows for the early identification of psychosocial risks and mental health issues. Employees are more likely to speak up about their concerns if they feel safe and supported. The National Institute for Occupational Safety and Health (NIOSH) emphasises that early intervention can prevent minor issues from escalating into major problems (NIOSH, 2019).

2. *Reducing Stigma:* Creating a culture of open communication can reduce the stigma associated with mental health and psychosocial risks. When employees see that their concerns are taken seriously and addressed, they are more likely to seek help and support. The Mental Health Foundation reports that open communication can significantly reduce mental health stigma in the workplace (Mental Health Foundation, 2020).

3. *Building Trust:* Trust is a fundamental element of a psychosocially safe workplace. Open communication fosters trust between employees and management, as it demonstrates that the organisation values and respects employee well-being. A study by the Edelman Trust Barometer found that trust in the workplace is strongly linked to employee engagement and productivity (Edelman, 2019).

4. *Enhancing Collaboration:* Open communication encourages collaboration and teamwork. When employees feel safe to share their ideas and concerns, it can lead to more innovative solutions and a more cohesive work environment. Research by the Institute for Corporate Productivity (i4cp) shows that high-performance

organisations prioritise open communication and collaboration (i4cp, 2018).

Strategies for Creating Safe Spaces

1. *Regular Check-Ins and Feedback:* Implementing regular check-ins and feedback sessions can provide employees with opportunities to voice their concerns and receive support. These sessions can be formal, such as performance reviews, or informal, such as weekly team meetings. A study by Gallup found that regular feedback significantly improves employee engagement and performance (Gallup, 2018).

2. *Anonymous Reporting Mechanisms:* Anonymous reporting mechanisms, such as suggestion boxes or online platforms, can encourage employees to report psychosocial risks and concerns without fear of retaliation. The Occupational Safety and Health Administration (OSHA) recommends implementing anonymous reporting systems to enhance workplace safety (OSHA, 2016).

3. *Open-Door Policies:* Encouraging an open-door policy where employees feel comfortable approaching management with their concerns can promote open communication. This policy should be supported by a culture of respect and non-judgment. The Chartered Institute of Personnel and Development (CIPD) highlights the benefits of open-door policies in fostering a supportive work environment (CIPD, 2020).

4. *Employee Resource Groups:* Employee resource groups (ERGs) can provide safe spaces for employees to discuss specific issues related to psychosocial safety, such as mental health, diversity, and inclusion. ERGs can offer

peer support, advocacy, and resources to help employees navigate challenges. Research by the Diversity Council Australia (DCA) shows that ERGs contribute to a more inclusive and supportive workplace culture (DCA, 2019).

Ongoing Training and Development Programs

Ongoing training and development programs are essential for maintaining a psychosocially safe workplace. These programs ensure that employees remain informed and engaged with psychosocial safety practices.

Importance of Ongoing Training

1. *Continuous Improvement:* Ongoing training allows for continuous improvement and adaptation of psychosocial safety practices. As workplace dynamics and psychosocial risks evolve, so too must the strategies to address them. The International Labour Organization (ILO) emphasises the need for continuous learning and development in promoting OHS (ILO, 2019).

2. *Reinforcement of Key Concepts:* Regular training reinforces key concepts and practices related to psychosocial safety. This reinforcement helps ensure that employees retain important information and apply it in their daily work. A study by the Journal of Occupational Health Psychology found that regular training updates lead to better knowledge retention and application (JOHP, 2018).

3. *Engagement and Motivation:* Ongoing training keeps employees engaged and motivated to contribute to a psychosocially safe workplace. Training programs that are interactive, relevant, and engaging can enhance

employee motivation and commitment. The AMA reports that ongoing training is a key factor in employee engagement and retention (AMA, 2017).

4. *Adapting to New Challenges:* Ongoing training programs allow organisations to address new challenges and emerging risks. For example, the COVID-19 pandemic introduced new psychosocial risks related to remote work, isolation, and health concerns. Ongoing training can equip employees with the knowledge and skills to navigate these challenges effectively.

Components of Ongoing Training Programs

1. *Onboarding and Refresher Courses:* Onboarding and regular refresher courses can help employees stay updated on the latest psychosocial safety practices and research. These courses can be delivered through workshops, webinars, or online modules. The eLearning Industry recommends offering refresher courses at least annually to maintain knowledge and engagement (eLearning Industry, 2019).

2. *Advanced Training Modules:* Advanced training modules can provide in-depth knowledge and skills on specific aspects of psychosocial safety, such as conflict resolution, MHFA, and resilience-building. These modules can be tailored to different roles and levels within the organisation. The Harvard Business Review highlights the benefits of advanced training in enhancing employee expertise and performance (HBR, 2019).

3. *Peer Learning and Mentorship:* Peer learning and mentorship programs can facilitate knowledge sharing and support among employees. These programs can

include peer coaching, mentoring relationships, and knowledge-sharing sessions. The Center for Creative Leadership (CCL) reports that peer learning and mentorship programs can significantly enhance employee development and organisational culture (CCL, 2017).

4. **Certification Programs:** Offering certification programs in psychosocial safety can provide employees with formal recognition of their knowledge and skills. Certification can enhance employee credibility and motivation. The OSHA recommends certification programs as a way to validate and enhance workplace safety training (OSHA, 2016).

Real-World Examples

Lack of Employee Training on Psychosocial Safety Leading to High Turnover and Injuries

Sector: Logistics and E-commerce (Amazon Warehouses)

Issue: Lack of employee training on psychosocial safety contributing to stress, burnout, and workplace injuries

Negative Impact: Amazon's warehouse operations are known for high productivity demands, with employees working long shifts under strict time constraints. However, the company faced widespread criticism for failing to provide adequate psychosocial safety training to its warehouse staff. Workers were not trained on how to manage workplace stress, mental health challenges, or how to seek help when feeling overwhelmed. Additionally, supervisors lacked training in identifying psychosocial hazards, leading to an unaddressed culture of stress and burnout.

Outcome: This lack of psychosocial safety training led to high employee turnover, with many workers leaving due to stress-related health problems and burnout. Amazon experienced a spike in absenteeism, presenteeism, and workplace injuries, as employees were pushed to meet unrealistic targets without the necessary support or resources. The negative media coverage, employee protests, and worker walkouts caused reputational damage, and the company faced pressure from regulatory bodies to improve working conditions. Financially, the high turnover and the cost of hiring and training new employees strained operations, ultimately impacting productivity and profitability.

Reference:

- BBC. (2020). Amazon workers protest over conditions at New York warehouse. Retrieved from https://www.bbc.com

Lack of Psychosocial Safety Training Leading to a Toxic Work Culture

Sector: Automotive (Tesla)

Issue: Lack of employee training on psychosocial safety, resulting in high stress and a toxic work environment.

Negative Impact: Tesla's aggressive production targets and fast-paced work environment led to numerous reports of employee burnout, high stress levels, and a toxic workplace culture. Employees at all levels, from factory workers to office staff, faced immense pressure to meet deadlines, with little to no training on how to manage psychosocial hazards such as stress, conflict, or workplace bullying. There was also a lack of training on how to foster open communication and a safe environment where employees could raise concerns about mental health without fear of retaliation.

Outcome: The absence of psychosocial safety training contributed to a toxic culture where employees were afraid to speak up about stress or bullying, which led to disengagement and increased employee turnover. Tesla faced negative media attention, public scrutiny, and legal challenges due to employee complaints about working conditions. The company's failure to address psychosocial hazards also led to diminished productivity, lower employee morale, and a tarnished reputation as an employer. Had Tesla implemented proper training programs on psychosocial safety, it could have mitigated these costly outcomes.

Reference:

- CNBC. (2019). *Tesla workers cite high stress, long hours, and a culture of fear in lawsuits*. Retrieved from https://www.cnbc.com

Lack of Psychosocial Safety Training Leading to Increased Psychological Injury Claims

Sector: Government (Victoria Police, Australia)

Issue: Lack of training in psychosocial safety contributing to rising mental health issues and stress-related claims

Negative Impact: The high-stress nature of policing exposes officers to significant psychosocial hazards, including trauma, stress, and mental health challenges. However, for many years, Victoria Police did not provide sufficient psychosocial safety training to its officers or leadership. Without proper training in recognising and managing psychosocial hazards, officers faced significant challenges in coping with trauma and stress. Additionally, leaders were not trained in how to support employees facing mental health issues or how to create a work environment that prioritised psychosocial safety.

Outcome: The lack of training contributed to a rise in psychological injury claims, absenteeism, and long-term sick leave among officers. Many employees experienced burnout and PTSD, which were left untreated due to the lack of proper support systems. The financial cost to the organisation was significant, with millions spent on psychological injury claims and overtime payments to cover for absent officers. The situation also negatively impacted officer morale, with many leaving the force due to stress and lack of support. Eventually, Victoria Police had to implement new training programs and mental health initiatives, but the damage to employee well-being and organisational performance was already significant.

Reference:

- The Age. (2019). *Victoria Police faces rising mental health claims and burnout issues*. Retrieved from https://www.theage.com.au

Key Takeaways

Employee training and awareness are foundational elements of a psychosocially safe workplace. Educating employees about psychosocial risks, mental health, and resilience can empower them to contribute to a positive and supportive work environment. Creating safe spaces for open communication and providing ongoing training and development opportunities are essential for maintaining and enhancing psychosocial safety. By investing in employee training and awareness, organisations can foster a culture of well-being, trust, and collaboration, ultimately leading to improved employee satisfaction, performance, and organisational success.

References:

- American Management Association. (2017). Employee engagement and retention. Retrieved from https://www.amanet.org/

- American Psychological Association (APA). (2018). Building your resilience. Retrieved from https://www.apa.org/helpcenter/road-resilience

- Centers for Disease Control and Prevention (CDC). (2019). Peer support programs. Retrieved from https://www.cdc.gov/

- Chartered Institute of Personnel and Development (CIPD). (2020). The importance of leadership in employee engagement. Retrieved from https://www.cipd.org/en/

- Diversity Council Australia. (2019). The impact of employee resource groups. Retrieved from https://www.dca.org.au/

- eLearning Industry. (2019). Benefits of online training. Retrieved from https://elearningindustry.com/

- Edelman Trust Barometer. (2019). Trust at work. Retrieved from https://www.edelman.com/trust/trust-barometer

- Gallup. (2018). The importance of employee voice. Retrieved from https://www.gallup.com/home.aspx

- Harvard Business Review. (2019). The impact of effective communication. Retrieved from https://hbr.org/

⊙ Institute for Corporate Productivity. (2018). High-performance organisations. Retrieved from https://www.i4cp.com/

⊙ International Labour Organization (ILO). (2019). Continuous learning and development. Retrieved from https://www.ilo.org/

⊙ Journal of Occupational Health Psychology. (2018). The impact of training updates. Retrieved from https://www.apa.org/pubs/journals/ocp/

⊙ Mental Health Foundation. (2020). Reducing mental health stigma. Retrieved from https://www.mental-health.org.uk/

⊙ National Institute for Occupational Safety and Health (NIOSH). (2019). Psychosocial risk factors. Retrieved from https://www.cdc.gov/niosh/

⊙ Occupational Safety and Health Administration (OSHA). (2016). Leadership in safety and health. Retrieved from https://www.osha.gov/

⊙ Society for Human Resource Management (SHRM). (2020). Employee feedback mechanisms. Retrieved from https://www.shrm.org/

⊙ World Health Organization (WHO). (2020). Psychosocial risks and work-related stress. Retrieved from https://www.who.int/occupational_health/topics/stressatwp/en/

PART 7

Implementing and Sustaining Psychosocial Safety

CHAPTER 16

Integrating Psychosocial Safety into Daily Operations

Creating a workplace that prioritises psychosocial safety requires more than just policies and training sessions; it demands the integration of psychosocial safety into daily operations. This means embedding psychosocial safety principles into every aspect of the workplace, from management practices to employee interactions.

Embedding Psychosocial Safety in Work Practices

1. *Work Design and Job Control:* Research indicates that job control—giving employees the autonomy to make decisions about their work—significantly impacts mental health and job satisfaction. A study by Karasek and Theorell (1990) found that high job demands paired with low job control are linked to higher stress levels and poor health outcomes. To mitigate this, organisations should design jobs that offer employees a degree of control over their tasks and schedules.

2. *Supportive Management Practices:* The role of management in fostering a psychosocially safe environment cannot be overstated. According to a report by the Chartered Institute of Personnel and Development (CIPD, 2020), supportive management practices, such as regular check-ins, constructive feedback, and recognition of employee achievements, are crucial for employee

well-being. Managers should be trained to recognise signs of distress and to provide appropriate support.

3. *Inclusive Policies:* Inclusive workplace policies that respect diversity and promote equity are fundamental to psychosocial safety. The World Economic Forum (WEF, 2021) emphasises that diversity and inclusion (D&I) initiatives not only improve organisational culture but also enhance business performance. By fostering an inclusive environment, organisations can reduce discrimination and bullying, leading to a safer and more supportive workplace.

Encouraging Collaboration and Teamwork

1. *Team-Building Activities:* Regular team-building activities can strengthen relationships and build trust among employees. A meta-analysis by Klein et al. (2009) found that team-building interventions improve team outcomes, including communication, cohesion, and performance. These activities should be designed to be inclusive and engaging for all team members.

2. *Collaborative Workspaces:* Physical and virtual collaborative workspaces can facilitate communication and teamwork. Open-plan offices, for instance, can promote interaction, though they must be designed to balance collaboration with the need for privacy and focused work. A study by Bernstein and Turban (2018) highlights the importance of carefully considering the layout and design of workspaces to support both individual and collaborative work.

3. *Shared Goals and Objectives:* Setting shared goals and objectives can unite employees and foster a sense of col-

lective purpose. The Goal-Setting Theory by Locke and Latham (2002) suggests that specific, challenging goals enhance performance and motivation. Teams should be encouraged to set and work toward common goals that align with the organisation's mission and values.

Monitoring and Evaluating Progress

Effective implementation of psychosocial safety requires ongoing monitoring and evaluation to ensure that initiatives are effective and to identify areas for improvement. This involves collecting data, analysing outcomes, and making necessary adjustments.

Continuous Improvement and Adaptation

1. *Regular Assessments:* Conducting regular assessments of psychosocial safety initiatives can help track progress and identify areas for improvement. Tools such as surveys, focus groups, and interviews can provide valuable insights into employee experiences and perceptions. The Health and Safety Executive (HSE, 2017) recommends using validated assessment tools to measure psychosocial risk factors and outcomes.

2. *Data-Driven Decision-Making:* Utilising data to drive decision-making ensures that initiatives are evidence-based and tailored to the organisation's specific needs. A report by McKinsey & Company (2020) highlights the importance of leveraging data analytics to assess the effectiveness of health and safety programs. Organisations should establish metrics and key performance indicators (KPIs) to monitor psychosocial safety.

3. ***Feedback Mechanisms:*** Implementing feedback mechanisms allows employees to voice their concerns and provide input on psychosocial safety initiatives. Anonymous feedback tools can encourage honest and constructive feedback. According to the Society for Human Resource Management (SHRM, 2020), employee feedback is essential for continuous improvement and employee engagement.

Sustaining a Psychosocially Safe Workplace

Maintaining a psychosocially safe workplace requires continuous effort, commitment, and adaptation to the evolving dynamics of the work environment. While implementing psychosocial safety policies is an important step, ensuring their sustainability is critical for long-term success. A sustained focus on psychosocial safety helps foster an environment where employees feel valued, supported, and empowered to speak up about their well-being without fear of retribution. However, it is not a one-time achievement but an ongoing process that demands reinforcement, leadership commitment, regular evaluation, and employee engagement.

1. Leadership Commitment and Role Modelling

Sustaining a psychosocially safe workplace begins at the top. Leadership must remain visibly committed to promoting a healthy and safe work environment by modelling psychosocial safety principles in their own behaviour. Leaders need to engage with employees regularly, actively listen to concerns, and take concrete steps to address challenges as they arise. In doing so, they reinforce the idea that psychosocial safety is a top priority within the organisation. Without ongoing leadership buy-in, efforts to maintain safety may falter, leading to a breakdown in communication, increased stress, and decreased trust among employees.

To support this, leadership training must be continuous, with an emphasis on emotional intelligence (EI), empathy, and trauma-informed communication. Leaders should also be held accountable for promoting psychosocial safety through regular reviews and performance evaluations, ensuring that their actions align with the organisation's safety goals.

2. Regular Evaluation and Feedback Loops

Organisations must regularly evaluate the effectiveness of their psychosocial safety measures. This can be achieved through anonymous employee surveys, focus groups, one-on-one interviews, and regular audits to identify new risks, concerns, or changes in the workplace culture that might impact psychosocial safety. Collecting this feedback allows for a proactive approach, where emerging issues are addressed before they become major problems.

Continuous monitoring and data collection can also help organisations understand the long-term impact of their psychosocial safety policies. By analysing trends in absenteeism, presenteeism, turnover, and employee engagement, companies can adjust their strategies to ensure they remain relevant and effective. Feedback loops should also allow employees to share their thoughts on the psychosocial safety measures in place, providing valuable insight into what's working and what requires improvement.

3. Adapting to Changing Work Environments

The modern workplace is constantly evolving due to technological advancements, remote work arrangements, shifting employee expectations, and global events. Organisations must remain agile and adaptable to these changes while sustaining psychosocial safety. For example, the rise of remote work has introduced new psychosocial hazards, such as feelings of isolation, lack of boundaries between work and personal life, and difficulties in communication. Addressing these challenges requires organisations to rethink how they support employees in remote or hybrid work setups.

Adapting to changes may also involve revisiting company policies and procedures, such as creating flexible work arrangements, enhancing mental health support, and building virtual spaces for open communication and collaboration. Organisations that are adaptable and responsive to these external factors are better positioned to maintain a safe and supportive environment for their employees.

4. Continuous Training and Development

Training is not a one-time event but a key component of sustaining a psychosocially safe workplace. Regular, ongoing training programs ensure that all employees—from frontline staff to senior management—are equipped with the knowledge and tools to promote and maintain psychosocial safety. These programs should cover topics like mental health awareness, conflict resolution, trauma-informed communication, and how to identify and respond to psychosocial hazards.

Moreover, as workplace dynamics evolve, training needs to be updated to reflect new challenges. For example, organisations may need to introduce specialised training on managing stress and maintaining boundaries in remote or hybrid work environments. By providing employees with continuous learning opportunities, organisations reinforce a culture of safety and adaptability.

5. Empowering Employees to Take Responsibility

Employees must feel empowered to contribute to the psycho-social safety of their workplace. This means creating an environment where employees are encouraged to speak up about concerns, offer solutions, and actively participate in creating a safe and supportive work culture. When employees feel ownership over their workplace safety, they are more likely to be vigilant in identifying risks and supporting their peers.

To foster this sense of ownership, organisations can create employee-led committees or working groups that focus on psychosocial safety initiatives. These groups can be responsible for monitoring workplace culture, raising awareness, and helping to implement new policies. Empowering employees to play an active role ensures that psychosocial safety is embedded into the day-to-day fabric of the organisation, rather than being seen as an external mandate.

6. Acknowledging Success and Celebrating Efforts

Sustaining a psychosocially safe workplace also involves recognising and celebrating successes. Acknowledging progress, whether it's a decrease in workplace stress, improved employee engagement, or higher retention rates, reinforces the importance of maintaining a safe work environment. Leaders should regularly celebrate employees who contribute to sustaining psychosocial safety, as recognition serves as motivation for continued efforts.

Organisations can also mark milestones in their psychosocial safety journey by sharing success stories, case studies, and testimonials from employees who have benefited from a supportive workplace culture. By highlighting these achievements, companies can build a sense of pride and ownership among employees while reinforcing the value of psychosocial safety to their long-term success.

7. Integration into Organisational Values and Practices

For psychosocial safety to be sustainable, it must be fully integrated into the organisation's core values and operational practices. Rather than treating it as a stand-alone initiative, psychosocial safety should be embedded into every aspect of the workplace, from onboarding new hires to evaluating performance and setting company goals. This integration ensures that every employee, from top leadership to entry-level staff, understands that maintaining a safe and supportive environment is a fundamental priority.

Organisations should also ensure that psychosocial safety is reflected in their policies and practices, including recruitment, promotion, and employee recognition programs. By making psychosocial safety an integral part of the company's values, organisations ensure that it remains a priority at every level of the business, creating a lasting and resilient work culture.

Sustaining a psychosocially safe workplace is an ongoing journey that requires continuous commitment from leadership and employees alike. By fostering a culture of accountability, continuous learning, and adaptability, organisations can create an environment where employees feel safe, valued, and supported. Ongoing evaluation, training, and engagement are critical to ensuring that psychosocial safety remains a central focus and evolves to meet the changing needs of the workplace. Ultimately, a sustained commitment to psychosocial safety leads to healthier employees, stronger organisational performance, and a more positive, inclusive work culture.

Case Studies: Celebrating Successes and Recognising Efforts

Case Study 1. Recognition Programs:

In a mid-sized financial services firm, the leadership team introduced a formal Psychosocial Safety Champion Recognition Program to motivate and reward employees who actively contribute to creating a safe and supportive work environment. Each quarter, employees who were nominated by their peers for going above and beyond in promoting mental health awareness, offering support to colleagues, or leading stress-reduction initiatives received recognition. For example, Maria, a team leader, was celebrated for organising weekly mindfulness sessions for her team and creating an open-door policy that encouraged her colleagues to voice concerns without fear of judgment. The recognition came with a small monetary bonus and a company-wide announcement highlighting her efforts. The recognition program not only motivated Maria but inspired others to prioritise psychosocial safety in their daily interactions. The Gallup Organisation (2016) found that recognition is a key driver of employee engagement, and in this case, it led to greater participation in well-being initiatives across the company.

Case Study 2. Celebrating Milestones:

In a large healthcare organisation, leadership made a concerted effort to celebrate milestones related to their psychosocial safety initiatives. After a year of implementing new mental health policies and completing extensive training for both managers and employees, the organisation held a Psychosocial Safety Celebration Day. The event marked significant achievements, including a 20% reduction in absenteeism and a notable improvement in employee satisfaction scores related to workplace well-being. The CEO recognised the human resources (HR) team and frontline workers who had played pivotal roles in implementing the initiatives, awarding them with plaques and public commendations. Additionally, an internal report was shared with the workforce, showcasing how these efforts had positively impacted overall productivity and team cohesion. This celebration reinforced the organisation's commitment to psychosocial safety and motivated employees to continue prioritising these values in their work environment.

Case Study 3. Communicating Success Stories:

In a global tech company, the HR department implemented a strategy to regularly communicate success stories related to psychosocial safety efforts. After completing a year-long program aimed at reducing stress and burnout among employees, the company began sharing Psychosocial Safety Success Stories in the monthly internal newsletter. One such story focused on a team in the customer service department, where a high-stress work environment had been drastically improved following the introduction of flexible working hours and additional mental health support. Employee testimonials detailed how the changes led to better work-life balance and significantly reduced burnout rates. Sharing these success stories not only showcased the effectiveness of the company's psychosocial safety initiatives but also helped employees across the organisation understand how these efforts contributed to a healthier and more supportive work culture. According to the International Labour Organization (ILO, 2019), such stories help build momentum and support for ongoing initiatives, and in this case, they helped maintain enthusiasm for future efforts.

Key Takeaways

Implementing and sustaining psychosocial safety in the workplace is a multifaceted process that requires a comprehensive approach. By integrating psychosocial safety principles into daily operations, encouraging collaboration and teamwork, and continuously monitoring and evaluating progress, organisations can create a supportive and inclusive work environment. Sustaining these efforts involves recognising and celebrating successes, maintaining open communication, and adapting to new challenges. Through ongoing commitment and adaptation, organisations can foster a culture of psychosocial safety that promotes employee well-being and organisational success.

References:

- Bernstein, E., & Turban, S. (2018). The impact of the 'open' workspace on human collaboration. *Philosophical Transactions of the Royal Society B: Biological Sciences*, *373*(1753).

- Chartered Institute of Personnel and Development (CIPD). (2020). Managing for sustainable employee engagement. Retrieved from https://www.cipd.co.uk/

- Gallup Organisation. (2016). Employee recognition: Low cost, high impact. Retrieved from https://www.gallup.com/

- Health and Safety Executive (HSE). (2017). Managing the causes of work-related stress: A step-by-step approach using the Management Standards. Retrieved from https://www.hse.gov.uk/

- International Labour Organization (ILO). (2019). Managing work-related psychosocial risks during the COVID-19 pandemic. Retrieved from https://www.ilo.org/

- Karasek, R., & Theorell, T. (1990). *Healthy work: Stress, productivity, and the reconstruction of working life*. Basic Books.

Klein, C., DiazGranados, D., Salas, E., Le, H., Burke, C. S., Lyons, R., & Goodwin, G. F. (2009). Does team building work? *Small Group Research*, *40*(2), 181-222.

Locke, E. A., & Latham, G. P. (2002). Building a practically useful theory of goal setting and task motivation: A 35-year odyssey. *American Psychologist*, *57*(9), 705-717.

McKinsey & Company. (2020). The future of workplace health and safety. Retrieved from https://www.mckinsey.com/

Society for Human Resource Management (SHRM). (2020). Employee feedback mechanisms. Retrieved from https://www.shrm.org/

World Economic Forum. (2021). Diversity, equity and inclusion 4.0: A toolkit for leaders to accelerate social progress in the future of work. Retrieved from https://www.weforum.org/

CHAPTER 17

Sustaining a Psychosocially Safe Workplace

Creating a psychosocially safe workplace is an ongoing commitment that requires continuous effort and adaptation. The journey does not end with the implementation of policies and training programs; it is sustained through constant evaluation, improvement, and reinforcement of safety practices.

Continuous Improvement and Adaptation

Maintaining a psychosocially safe workplace necessitates a culture of continuous improvement. This involves regularly reviewing and updating policies, procedures, and practices to ensure they remain effective and relevant.

Regular Assessments and Audits

1. *Periodic Audits:* Conducting regular audits of psychosocial safety policies and practices is essential. These audits should evaluate the effectiveness of current initiatives, identify gaps, and recommend improvements. According to the International Organization for Standardization (ISO, 2020), regular assessments are crucial for maintaining high standards of occupational health and safety (OHS).

2. *Employee Surveys and Feedback:* Gathering feedback from employees through surveys and focus groups can provide valuable insights into the workplace environment. A study by the SHRM (2019) found that employee

feedback is critical for identifying issues and improving workplace practices. Organisations should create channels for anonymous feedback to ensure employees feel safe to voice their concerns.

3. *Benchmarking and Best Practices:* Comparing psychosocial safety practices with industry standards and best practices can help organisations stay ahead. The HSE (2017) emphasises the importance of benchmarking against other organisations to identify areas for improvement and innovation.

Continuous Improvement and Adaptation

1. *Regular Assessments and Audits:* Conducting regular audits and assessments of psychosocial safety initiatives helps ensure that policies and practices remain effective and relevant. According to the ISO (2020), these evaluations are crucial for maintaining high standards of OHS.

2. *Employee Feedback:* Gathering feedback from employees through surveys and focus groups can provide valuable insights into the workplace environment. A study by the SHRM (2019) found that employee feedback is critical for identifying issues and improving workplace practices.

3. *Benchmarking:* Comparing psychosocial safety practices with industry standards and best practices can help organisations stay ahead. The HSE (2017) emphasises the importance of benchmarking against other organisations to identify areas for improvement and innovation.

Data-Driven Decision-Making

Scenario: Improving Employee Retention through Data-Driven Decision-Making

Company: FastGrowTech (Fictional Company)

Sector: Technology

Issue: High employee turnover in the software development department

Problem:

FastGrowTech, a fast-growing software development company, noticed that its employee turnover rate in the software development department had been steadily increasing over the past year. Despite offering competitive salaries and perks, the company found that highly skilled developers were leaving after only 1-2 years. The HR department initially speculated that the departures were due to industry competition but lacked concrete data to confirm the root causes. The leadership team decided to take a data-driven approach to resolve the issue.

Step 1: Collecting Data

FastGrowTech started by gathering quantitative and qualitative data to understand the underlying reasons for high turnover. This included:

- **Exit Interviews:** Collecting feedback from employees who had left, specifically asking about their reasons for leaving and suggestions for improvement.

- **Employee Engagement Surveys:** Conducting anonymous surveys to assess current employees' job satisfaction, workload, and team dynamics.

- **Performance Metrics:** Analysing developer performance and project completion rates to see if there was a correlation between high workload, burnout, and employee departure.

- **Workforce Analytics:** Evaluating demographic and tenure data to identify patterns, such as turnover rates by team, manager, or project type.

Step 2: Analysing the Data

Using the collected data, FastGrowTech's HR and data analytics teams identified three major trends:

1. **Workload and Burnout:** Developers who left the company consistently reported high levels of stress and excessive workloads. Data from project timelines showed that these employees were assigned to projects with tighter deadlines and more frequent overtime.

2. **Lack of Growth Opportunities:** Survey data revealed that many employees felt there was insufficient career development and mentorship within the company. Developers wanted more opportunities to learn new skills, receive promotions, and grow professionally.

3. **Managerial Impact:** Turnover was higher in teams managed by supervisors with low engagement scores, indicating that poor management was contributing to employees leaving.

Step 3: Implementing Solutions Based on Data

Based on these insights, FastGrowTech took the following data-driven actions:

- **Reducing Workload:** The company restructured project management by hiring more developers to distribute workloads evenly. They also implemented new work-life balance policies, limiting overtime and enforcing mandatory time off after project completion.

- **Career Development Programs:** FastGrowTech introduced a mentorship program and offered professional development budgets for developers to attend conferences, take courses, or pursue certifications. They also created clearer career progression paths for employees to advance within the company.

- **Manager Training:** Leadership recognised the impact of poor management on turnover rates. Managers with low engagement scores were required to undergo leadership training programs focused on communication, team building, and employee engagement.

Step 4: Monitoring and Measuring Success

To ensure these initiatives were effective, FastGrowTech set up KPIs to track:

- **Turnover Rates:** Monitoring turnover in the software development department after changes were made.

- **Employee Satisfaction Scores:** Repeating employee engagement surveys quarterly to measure improvements in job satisfaction, work-life balance, and manager relationships.

- **Productivity Metrics:** Tracking project delivery timelines and performance to ensure that workload distribution was balanced without negatively affecting project output.

Outcome:

Within six months, FastGrowTech saw a 30% decrease in turnover in the software development department. Employee engagement scores improved, especially in teams where workload was reduced, and leadership had taken action to develop employees' careers. Managers who participated in the training saw improved feedback from their teams, further reducing staff dissatisfaction. Overall, the company was able to retain top talent and improve organisational culture by using data-driven decision-making to identify and address the root causes of high turnover.

This scenario demonstrates how companies can use data to make informed decisions that directly address organisational issues.

In summary, to implement data-drive decision-making, companies should use:

1. *Metrics and KPIs:* Establishing KPIs and metrics to measure psychosocial safety initiatives is vital. These metrics can include employee well-being scores, turnover rates, absenteeism, and incident reports. According to McKinsey & Company (2020), data-driven decision-making enhances the effectiveness of workplace health and safety programs.

2. *Data Analysis:* Regular analysis of collected data can reveal trends and patterns that inform decision-making. Organisations should invest in data analytics tools to monitor and evaluate psychosocial safety initiatives. The use of dashboards and reports can help visualise progress and identify areas needing attention.

3. *Continuous Feedback Loops:* Creating continuous feedback loops between employees and management ensures ongoing dialogue and improvement. According to a report by Deloitte (2020), organisations with effective feedback mechanisms are better equipped to respond to challenges and maintain a positive work environment.

Maintaining a Culture of Safety

Creating and maintaining a culture of safety involves ongoing efforts to embed psychosocial safety principles into the organisational fabric. This requires commitment from leadership and active participation from all employees.

Leadership Commitment

1. *Role Modelling:* Leaders play a crucial role in setting the tone for a psychosocially safe workplace. They must model behaviours that promote safety, respect, and inclusivity. According to the Center for Creative Leadership (CCL, 2019), leaders who demonstrate commitment to safety and well-being positively influence organisational culture.

2. *Visible Support:* Leaders should visibly support psychosocial safety initiatives through participation and communication. Regularly discussing the importance of safety in meetings and communications reinforces its significance. A study by the Gallup Organisation (2018) found that visible leadership support is key to successful safety programs.

3. *Resource Allocation:* Providing adequate resources for psychosocial safety initiatives is essential. This includes funding for training programs, support services, and

necessary infrastructure. The World Health Organization (WHO, 2020) states that investing in workplace mental health and safety yields significant returns in productivity and employee well-being.

Celebrating Successes and Recognising Efforts

1. **Formal Recognition Programs**: Implementing formal recognition programs that celebrate contributions to psychosocial safety can motivate employees and reinforce the importance of safety. Awards, certificates, and public acknowledgments can highlight individual and team achievements. According to a report by the SHRM (2020), recognition programs are effective in promoting a positive workplace culture.

2. **Celebrating Milestones**: Marking significant milestones and achievements in psychosocial safety initiatives builds a sense of accomplishment and encourages continued efforts. Organisations can celebrate the completion of training programs, successful policy implementations, or notable improvements in employee well-being metrics. Celebrations can include events, awards ceremonies, and public acknowledgments.

3. **Communicating Success Stories**: Sharing success stories and case studies of psychosocial safety initiatives can inspire and educate employees. These stories can highlight the positive impact of initiatives on employee well-being and organisational outcomes. According to the International Labour Organization (ILO, 2019), communicating success stories can build momentum and support for ongoing efforts.

Real-World Examples: Leadership Commitment

Leadership Commitment to Mental Health and Psychosocial Safety

Sector: Government (New Zealand Defence Force)

Issue: High levels of stress and mental health challenges among military personnel

Leadership Commitment: In recent years, the New Zealand Defence Force (NZDF) made leadership commitment to mental health and psychosocial safety a priority. Leadership recognised that the demanding nature of military service, including deployment and high-stakes operations, contributed to significant stress, trauma, and burnout among personnel. Senior leadership took a proactive approach by launching a mental health strategy known as *Force4Families* in 2018, which focused on building resilience and providing psychological support to both service members and their families. Leaders were actively involved in promoting open discussions about mental health, ensuring resources were available, and fostering a culture where personnel felt safe seeking help without stigma.

Outcome: The leadership's visible commitment to psychosocial safety helped reduce stigma around mental health issues in the NZDF. Personnel reported feeling more supported, and the availability of mental health resources increased participation in well-being programs. The program led to a reduction in reported mental health issues and improved overall morale among troops. The NZDF's example shows how strong leadership commitment to mental health and psychosocial safety can lead to long-term improvements in employee well-being and organisational performance.

Reference:

- New Zealand Defence Force. (2018). Force4Families: Mental Health and Well-Being Strategy. Retrieved from https://www.nzdf.mil.nz

Leadership Commitment to Psychosocial Safety and Employee Well-Being

Sector: Technology (Microsoft)

Issue: Employee stress and work-life balance challenges

Leadership Commitment: Microsoft's CEO, Satya Nadella, made leadership commitment to employee well-being and psychosocial safety a key focus of his tenure, beginning in 2014. Under his leadership, Microsoft shifted its culture to prioritise empathy, mental health, and work-life balance. Nadella encouraged open discussions about employee well-being, and leadership took direct actions to implement policies promoting flexible working arrangements, access to mental health support, and enhanced Employee Assistance Programs (EAPs). Managers were trained to support employees facing stress or burnout, with an emphasis on creating a psychologically safe environment.

Outcome: Nadella's leadership commitment to psychosocial safety transformed Microsoft's culture, leading to higher employee satisfaction and retention rates. Employees reported feeling more empowered to manage their mental health and seek support when needed. The company also saw an increase in productivity and innovation as workers felt more secure in balancing their personal and professional lives. Microsoft's leadership model demonstrated that when top management actively promotes psychosocial safety, the entire organisation.

Reference:

- Harvard Business Review. (2017). *Satya Nadella's leadership and the rebirth of Microsoft's culture*. Retrieved from https://hbr.org

Leadership Commitment to Reducing Workplace Stress

Sector: Healthcare (UK National Health Service)

Issue: High levels of workplace stress and burnout among healthcare staff

Leadership Commitment: In response to rising levels of stress and burnout among healthcare professionals, the NHS launched the *Health and Wellbeing Framework* in 2019, with strong leadership backing from senior management across NHS trusts. The leadership recognised that the mental health and well-being of healthcare staff were critical to patient care quality and overall organisational performance. Senior leaders actively promoted the well-being framework, which included initiatives such as dedicated mental health resources, flexible working policies, stress management training, and regular well-being assessments. Leadership's involvement in advocating for these programs demonstrated their commitment to improving psychosocial safety across the NHS.

Outcome: The leadership commitment to psychosocial safety led to improvements in staff morale and a reduction in absenteeism due to stress and burnout. Healthcare staff reported feeling more supported by their managers and were more willing to access mental health services. The emphasis on leadership involvement in well-being initiatives also improved retention rates and patient care outcomes, as employees were better equipped to manage the emotional and psychological demands of their work.

Reference:

- National Health Service (NHS) England. (2019). NHS Health and Wellbeing Framework. Retrieved from https://www.england.nhs.uk/ Top of Form

Real-World Examples: Employee Engagement

Employee Engagement Enhancing Psychosocial Safety

Sector: Professional Services PricewaterhouseCoopers (PwC)

Issue: Employee burnout and stress in a high-pressure consulting environment

Employee Engagement Initiatives: PwC recognised that the fast-paced nature of their consulting services led to high levels of stress and burnout among employees. To address this, the company launched a series of employee engagement initiatives under its *Be Well, Work Well* program. Employees were encouraged to take an active role in managing their well-being by providing feedback through surveys, focus groups, and open discussions. PwC introduced flexible work arrangements, mental health resources, and regular check-ins between managers and their teams to address workplace stressors. Employees were also given the opportunity to participate in wellness programs tailored to their needs, including mindfulness sessions, physical fitness programs, and financial well-being workshops.

Outcome: Employee engagement played a key role in improving psychosocial safety at PwC. Workers reported feeling more empowered to manage their work-life balance, and the regular feedback loops helped the company identify stress points early and intervene before they escalated. As a result, PwC saw a significant reduction in burnout, improved retention rates, and an increase in employee satisfaction. Engaging employees in the conversation about their well-being fostered a culture of openness, where psychosocial safety became a shared responsibility between leadership and staff.

Reference:

- PricewaterhouseCoopers (PwC). (2019). Be well, work well: PwC's employee well-being strategy. Retrieved from https://www.pwc.com

Employee Engagement

1. *Empowerment and Participation:* Engaging employees in the development and implementation of safety initiatives fosters ownership and accountability. Employees should be encouraged to participate in safety committees, provide feedback, and contribute ideas. Research by the Harvard Business Review (HBR, 2019) shows that employee involvement leads to more effective and sustainable safety programs.

2. *Training and Development:* Ongoing training and development programs ensure that employees have the knowledge and skills to maintain a safe workplace. This includes refresher courses, workshops, and e-learning modules. The National Institute for Occupational Safety and Health (NIOSH, 2018) emphasises the importance of continuous learning in sustaining workplace safety.

3. *Recognition and Rewards:* Recognising and rewarding employees for their contributions to psychosocial safety reinforces positive behaviours and encourages ongoing participation. A study by Bersin & Associates (2017) found that recognition programs enhance employee engagement and commitment.

Employee Engagement Enhancing Psychosocial Safety

Sector: Consumer Goods (Unilever)

Issue: Work-related stress and psychosocial risks

Employee Engagement Initiatives: Unilever has long been a proponent of employee well-being and psychosocial safety. In 2014, the company launched its _Lamplighter_ program, a global initiative aimed at improving employee mental health and well-being. This program encouraged employees to engage with leadership to share their experiences of workplace stress, as well as their suggestions for improving the work environment. Employees were involved in designing and co-creating well-being initiatives, including mental health workshops, flexible work options, and stress-reduction programs. Unilever's leadership promoted a culture of listening and responding to employee feedback, ensuring that workers felt supported and included in decisions about their psychosocial safety.

Outcome: By actively engaging employees in well-being initiatives, Unilever significantly reduced absenteeism and presenteeism caused by workplace stress. Employees reported feeling more connected to the organisation and appreciated that their voices were heard and valued in shaping workplace policies. The company saw an improvement in overall employee morale and productivity, as well as a positive impact on their employer brand. Unilever's focus on employee engagement as a tool for enhancing psychosocial safety has made it a model for other large corporations.

Reference:

- Unilever. (2016). Lamplighter: Unilever's well-being program. Retrieved from https://www.unilever.com

Employee Engagement and Psychosocial Safety

Sector: Government (Victoria Police, Australia)

Issue: High levels of stress, PTSD, and psychological injuries among police officers

Employee Engagement Initiatives: Victoria Police launched the *Wellbeing Action Plan* in response to growing concerns about the mental health and well-being of its officers. As part of this initiative, police officers were encouraged to participate in regular mental health check-ins, engage in open conversations about stress and trauma, and provide feedback on their work environments through anonymous surveys. Officers were also invited to co-design the well-being resources offered by the organisation, including peer support networks, mental health training, and access to trauma-informed care. By engaging employees directly in the process, leadership aimed to reduce the stigma associated with seeking mental health support and increase the overall psychosocial safety of the workplace.

Outcome: The employee engagement strategies at Victoria Police led to a noticeable improvement in the psychosocial safety of the organisation. Officers reported feeling more supported in dealing with the psychological challenges of their jobs, and the regular check-ins provided early intervention for those at risk of burnout or PTSD. The initiative also helped improve trust between leadership and officers, fostering a more transparent and supportive workplace culture. As a result, Victoria Police saw a decrease in psychological injury claims and an improvement in job satisfaction and retention rates.

Reference:

- Victoria Police. (2020). Wellbeing Action Plan: Supporting the mental health of Victoria police officers. Retrieved from https://www.police.vic.gov.au

Key Takeaways

Implementing and sustaining psychosocial safety in the workplace is a multifaceted process that requires a comprehensive approach. By integrating psychosocial safety principles into daily operations, encouraging collaboration and teamwork, and continuously monitoring and evaluating progress, organisations can create a supportive and inclusive work environment. Sustaining these efforts involves recognising and celebrating successes, maintaining open communication, and adapting to new challenges. Through ongoing commitment and adaptation, organisations can foster a culture of psychosocial safety that promotes employee well-being and organisational success.

References:

- Bersin & Associates. (2017). The state of employee recognition in 2017. Retrieved from https://www.bersin.com/

- Center for Creative Leadership. (2019). The role of leadership in creating a safety culture. Retrieved from https://www.ccl.org/

- Chartered Institute of Personnel and Development (CIPD). (2020). Managing for sustainable employee engagement. Retrieved from https://www.cipd.co.uk/

- Deloitte. (2020). The importance of feedback in the workplace. Retrieved from https://www.deloitte.com/au/en.html

- Gallup Organisation. (2018). Employee engagement and workplace safety. Retrieved from https://www.gallup.com/

⏩ Harvard Business Review. (2019). The impact of employee involvement on workplace safety. Retrieved from https://hbr.org/

⏩ Health and Safety Executive (HSE). (2017). Managing the causes of work-related stress: A step-by-step approach using the Management Standards. Retrieved from https://www.hse.gov.uk/

⏩ International Labour Organization (ILO). (2019). Managing work-related psychosocial risks during the COVID-19 pandemic. Retrieved from https://www.ilo.org/

⏩ International Organization for Standardization (ISO). (2020). ISO 45001: Occupational health and safety management systems. Retrieved from https://www.iso.org/

⏩ McKinsey & Company. (2020). The future of workplace health and safety. Retrieved from https://www.mckinsey.com/

⏩ National Institute for Occupational Safety and Health (NIOSH). (2018). Total worker health. Retrieved from https://www.cdc.gov/niosh/twh/default.html

⏩ Society for Human Resource Management (SHRM). (2020). The importance of employee recognition. Retrieved from https://www.shrm.org/

⏩ World Health Organization (WHO). (2020). Mental health in the workplace. Retrieved from https://www.who.int/news-room/fact-sheets/detail/mental-health-in-the-workplace

PART 8

Bias in the Workplace

CHAPTER 18

Unconscious Bias in the Workplace

Introduction to Unconscious Bias

Unconscious bias refers to the automatic and often unintentional judgments, stereotypes, or attitudes that people hold about others based on characteristics such as race, gender, age, and appearance. Unlike explicit biases, which individuals are aware of and may consciously endorse, unconscious biases operate below the level of conscious awareness and can subtly influence behaviour and decision-making in the workplace. Understanding and addressing unconscious bias is critical to creating a psychosocially safe and inclusive workplace, as these biases can undermine efforts to promote diversity, equity, inclusion and fairness.

Unconscious bias is a pervasive issue that affects everyone, regardless of their intentions or beliefs. Research has shown that even individuals who strongly believe in equality and fairness can exhibit biased behaviours due to ingrained stereotypes and social conditioning. This chapter explores the nature of unconscious bias, its impact on workplace dynamics, and strategies for mitigating its effects to foster a more equitable and inclusive environment.

The Science Behind Unconscious Bias

The concept of unconscious bias is rooted in cognitive psychology and neuroscience. Our brains are wired to process vast amounts of information quickly, which often leads to the reliance on mental shortcuts or heuristics. These shortcuts help us make sense of the world but can also result in biased judgments and decisions.

One of the most influential theories explaining unconscious bias is *implicit social cognition*. According to this theory, our attitudes and stereotypes about social groups are formed through repeated exposure to cultural norms, media representations, and personal experiences. These associations become ingrained in our subconscious and influence our perceptions and interactions with others, even when we consciously reject these biases.

Implicit Association Tests (IATs), developed by researchers at Harvard University, are widely used to measure unconscious biases. These tests reveal the automatic associations individuals make between different social groups and positive or negative attributes. For example, an IAT might measure how quickly a person associates women with caregiving roles and men with leadership roles. The results often show that unconscious biases are widespread and can be surprisingly strong.

The Impact of Unconscious Bias in the Workplace

Unconscious bias can have far-reaching effects on various aspects of workplace dynamics, from hiring and promotion decisions to team interactions and leadership effectiveness. Some of the key areas where unconscious bias can manifest include:

1. *Hiring and Recruitment:* Unconscious bias can influence decisions about who gets hired, leading to a lack of diversity in the workforce. For example, research has shown that resumes with traditionally white-sounding names are more likely to receive callbacks than those

with traditionally ethnic-sounding names, even when the qualifications are identical. Gender bias can also result in women being overlooked for roles traditionally dominated by men.

2. *Performance Evaluations:* Biases can affect how employees' performance is evaluated, with certain groups receiving more favourable or harsher assessments based on stereotypes rather than actual performance. For instance, women may be judged more critically than men in leadership roles, and people of colour may face higher scrutiny in their work.

3. *Team Dynamics:* Unconscious bias can lead to the exclusion or marginalisation of certain employees within teams. This can create a hostile or unwelcoming environment for those who are perceived as different or less competent based on biased assumptions. These dynamics can hinder collaboration, reduce morale, and limit the effectiveness of the team.

4. *Promotion and Career Advancement:* Biases can also influence decisions about who gets promoted or offered leadership opportunities. Women and minorities often face barriers to advancement due to biased perceptions of their capabilities and leadership potential. This can result in a lack of diversity at the highest levels of an organisation.

5. *Everyday Interactions:* Unconscious bias can affect everyday workplace interactions, leading to microaggressions—subtle, often unintentional slights or insults that can be harmful to those on the receiving end. For example, consistently interrupting women in meetings or assuming that a person of colour is less qualified than their peers can contribute to a toxic work environment.

Addressing and Mitigating Unconscious Bias

To create a more inclusive and psychosocially safe workplace, it is essential to address and mitigate the effects of unconscious bias. Here are several strategies that organisations can implement:

1. *Awareness and Education:* The first step in addressing unconscious bias is raising awareness among employees and leaders. Training programs that educate employees about the nature of unconscious bias and its impact on workplace dynamics are crucial. These programs should include practical exercises that help individuals recognise their own biases and understand how they might influence their behaviour.

2. *Inclusive Hiring Practices:* To reduce bias in hiring, organisations can implement strategies such as blind recruitment, where identifying information (e.g., name, gender, age) is removed from resumes during the initial screening process. Additionally, using structured interviews with standardised questions can help ensure that all candidates are evaluated based on the same criteria.

3. *Bias Interruption Techniques:* Bias interruption techniques are proactive measures that individuals can use to counteract their own biases in real-time. For example, before making a decision, an individual might pause to reflect on whether their judgement is being influenced by stereotypes or assumptions. Encouraging employees to use these techniques can help reduce the impact of unconscious bias on decision-making.

4. *Diverse Leadership and Mentorship Programs:* Promoting diversity in leadership positions and creating mentorship programs for underrepresented groups can

help counteract the effects of unconscious bias. When employees see diverse leaders in positions of power, it challenges stereotypes and creates a more inclusive environment.

5. *Regular Bias Audits:* Conducting regular bias audits can help organisations identify areas where unconscious bias may be affecting workplace dynamics. These audits can include reviewing hiring and promotion data, analysing employee feedback, and assessing team interactions. The findings from these audits can inform targeted interventions to address bias.

6. *Accountability and Transparency:* Holding individuals and teams accountable for their actions and decisions is essential in addressing unconscious bias. Organisations should establish clear policies and procedures for addressing bias-related issues and ensure that all employees understand their role in creating an inclusive workplace. Transparency in decision-making processes, such as promotions and performance evaluations, can also help reduce the influence of bias.

7. *Creating a Culture of Inclusion:* Ultimately, addressing unconscious bias requires a cultural shift within the organisation. Leaders must model inclusive behaviours and demonstrate a commitment to diversity, equity, and inclusion (DE&I). This includes actively seeking out diverse perspectives, encouraging open dialogue about bias and discrimination, and fostering an environment where all employees feel valued and respected.

Real-World Examples

Unconscious Bias Impacting Hiring Decisions

Sector: Technology (Google)

Issue: Unconscious bias affecting diversity in recruitment and hiring

Unconscious Bias in Decision Making: In 2014, Google publicly shared its workforce diversity data, revealing that its workforce was predominantly white and male, particularly in technical roles. Further internal reviews identified that unconscious bias during the recruitment process played a significant role in these outcomes. Despite efforts to increase diversity, hiring managers tended to favour candidates who were similar to themselves in terms of background, education, and gender—an example of affinity bias. This unconscious bias led to a lack of diversity in Google's talent pipeline, particularly in leadership and technical roles, despite a large pool of qualified candidates from under-represented groups.

Impact on the Workplace: Google's failure to address unconscious bias in hiring contributed to a homogenous workforce, which affected innovation and the company's ability to tap into diverse perspectives. In response, Google launched unconscious bias training programs for all employees, particularly for hiring managers and leaders, to address these biases and encourage more inclusive hiring practices. Over time, Google made strides toward improving diversity in its workforce, but the initial impact of unconscious bias slowed the company's progress and drew public criticism. The company also recognised that diverse teams drive innovation and better problem-solving, so addressing this bias became key to its success.

Reference:

- Google Diversity Report. (2014). Google's commitment to diversity. Retrieved from https://www.google.com

Unconscious Bias Leading to Discriminatory Decision-Making

Sector: Retail and Hospitality (Starbucks)

Issue: Unconscious racial bias affecting customer service decisions

Unconscious Bias in Decision Making: In 2018, two African American men were arrested at a Philadelphia Starbucks while waiting for a business meeting, leading to widespread outrage and allegations of racial profiling. The incident highlighted how unconscious racial bias influenced the store manager's decision to call the police. Although the men were simply waiting for their meeting, the manager's implicit bias led to discriminatory behaviour, with significant negative consequences for Starbucks' reputation. This event exposed how unconscious bias in customer service decisions can lead to unequal treatment and harm both individuals and the organisation.

Impact on the Workplace: The incident prompted Starbucks to close all of its U.S. stores for a day to conduct mandatory racial bias training for 175,000 employees. The training aimed to raise awareness about unconscious biases and provide tools to help employees make fair and equitable decisions when serving customers. This incident forced Starbucks to confront the broader issue of unconscious bias in its organisational culture and decision-making processes. The company's response was praised, but the incident itself led to financial losses, reputational damage, and strained relationships with customers, particularly in communities of colour.

Reference:

- The New York Times. (2018). *Starbucks closes 8,000 stores for racial bias training*. Retrieved from https://www.nytimes.com

Unconscious Gender Bias in Promotion Decisions

Sector: Banking (HSBC)

Issue: Unconscious gender bias limiting women's advancement into leadership positions

Unconscious Bias in Decision Making: HSBC, one of the world's largest banks, conducted an internal review of its promotion practices and discovered that unconscious gender bias was playing a role in limiting the advancement of women into senior leadership positions. Although women made up a significant portion of the workforce, they were underrepresented in top executive roles. The review found that performance evaluations and promotion decisions were influenced by unconscious gender stereotypes, with women being overlooked for leadership positions despite having equal or superior qualifications compared to their male counterparts.

Impact on the Workplace: This unconscious bias created a glass ceiling for women, leading to a lack of gender diversity in the bank's leadership. HSBC responded by introducing initiatives to mitigate bias in its promotion processes, including blind reviews of performance evaluations, mandatory unconscious bias training for managers, and specific targets for increasing female representation in leadership roles. While the bias initially slowed the career progression of many talented women at the bank, HSBC's efforts to address the issue resulted in more equitable promotion practices and a gradual increase in the number of women in senior leadership roles. The bank also benefited from the diverse perspectives that come with a more inclusive leadership team.

Reference:

- ⊗ Financial Times. (2019). *HSBC sets gender targets amid unconscious bias concerns*. Retrieved from https://www.ft.com

Key Takeaways

Addressing unconscious bias is not a one-time effort but an ongoing journey that requires continuous learning, reflection, and action. Organisations must remain vigilant in their efforts to identify and mitigate bias, recognising that unconscious biases can evolve and change over time. By fostering a culture of inclusion and implementing targeted strategies to address bias, organisations can create a psychosocially safe workplace where all employees have the opportunity to thrive.

Resources:

- ⊗ Banaji, M.R. & Greenwald, A.G. (2013). *Blindspot: Hidden biases of good people*. Random House.

  ▸ A book that explores the science of unconscious bias and its impact on behaviour.

- ⊗ Google's Unbiasing Initiative: https://rework.withgoogle.com/guides/unbiasing/

  ▸ Google's approach to addressing unconscious bias in the workplace.

- PricewaterhouseCoopers' (PwC's) Diversity and Inclusion Efforts: https://www.pwc.com/gx/en/about/diversity-and-inclusion.html

- Project Implicit: https://implicit.harvard.edu/implicit/

  - A resource for learning more about implicit bias and taking the Implicit Association Test (IAT).

  - Information on PwC's strategies for promoting diversity and inclusion.

- Ross, H.J. (2014). *Everyday bias: Identifying and navigating unconscious judgments in our daily lives.* Rowman & Littlefield.

  - A book that provides practical advice on recognising and addressing unconscious bias in various contexts, including the workplace.

CHAPTER 19

Conscious Bias in the Workplace

While much attention is given to unconscious bias in workplace discussions, conscious bias—deliberate, intentional prejudices that individuals hold and act upon—can be just as harmful, if not more so, when left unmanaged. Conscious bias occurs when individuals knowingly make decisions or behave in ways that discriminate against others based on race, gender, age, disability, or other protected characteristics. Unlike unconscious bias, which operates below the surface of awareness, conscious bias is a clear and overt form of discrimination that can create toxic workplace environments, diminish employee morale, and severely impact organisational performance.

This chapter will explore the nature of conscious bias, its impact on the workplace, and how organisations can address and manage this form of discrimination to foster a more inclusive and productive environment.

What is Conscious Bias?

Conscious bias refers to the explicit and intentional prejudices or stereotypes that individuals hold and act upon. Unlike unconscious bias, which operates below conscious awareness, conscious bias involves deliberate decisions or actions based on discriminatory beliefs or attitudes. Individuals with conscious biases may knowingly treat certain groups of people unfairly, and these biases can manifest in hiring practices, promotions, project assignments, and everyday workplace interactions.

Examples of Conscious Bias in the Workplace:

> A manager may refuse to hire a qualified candidate because of their race, gender, or sexual orientation.

> An employee may consistently exclude colleagues of a different cultural background from team activities or important meetings.

> Leadership may purposefully overlook women or people of colour for promotions, even when they are more qualified than their counterparts.

Conscious bias can manifest in various ways, from overt discrimination to more subtle actions that undermine certain groups. When allowed to persist, it creates a hostile work environment and undermines diversity and inclusion efforts.

The Impact of Conscious Bias

1. Decreased Employee Morale

One of the most immediate effects of conscious bias in the workplace is the significant decrease in employee morale. When employees perceive or experience bias, it creates a sense of exclusion, frustration, and even fear. Employees who are targets of conscious bias may feel unwelcome, undervalued, and unsupported. Over time, this leads to decreased motivation, lower job satisfaction, and disengagement from their work.

Example: In a healthcare organisation, a nurse of Middle Eastern descent experienced frequent discriminatory comments from colleagues, including inappropriate jokes and exclusion from social activities. The nurse reported feeling isolated and demoralised, which impacted her job performance and emotional well-being. Despite raising concerns with HR, no action was taken, further reinforcing the belief that the organisation tolerated bias. This ultimately led to her resignation, highlighting the harmful effects of unchecked conscious bias.

2. Increased Employee Turnover

When conscious bias goes unmanaged, employees who are subjected to discrimination or harassment are more likely to leave the organisation. High turnover not only affects the individuals who experience bias but also creates significant costs for the organisation. The recruitment, onboarding, and training of new employees require time and resources, and high turnover can disrupt team dynamics and productivity.

Example: A prominent financial services firm experienced high turnover among its female employees due to a pervasive culture of gender bias. Female employees were frequently passed over for promotions in favour of less qualified male colleagues, despite excelling in their roles. Exit interviews revealed that many women left because they felt there was a lack of equal opportunity and that leadership was complicit in perpetuating the bias. This high turnover led to substantial financial losses for the firm due to the constant need to recruit and train new talent.

3. Decreased Productivity and Innovation

Workplace environments where conscious bias exists are often less productive and innovative. Employees who feel discriminated against or marginalised are less likely to contribute ideas, collaborate with colleagues, or take initiative. Fear of being judged or dismissed can stifle creativity and reduce problem-solving within teams. Moreover, bias often leads to a lack of diversity in decision-making, as the same voices are prioritised over diverse perspectives.

Example: A technology company had a predominantly male leadership team that exhibited conscious bias in decision-making processes. When female engineers proposed new ideas or solutions, they were often ignored or dismissed without consideration. This created a toxic work culture where women felt discouraged from contributing to meetings or projects. As a result, the company missed out on innovative solutions that could have been developed through more inclusive collaboration.

4. Reputation Damage

Organisations that allow conscious bias to go unchecked risk damaging their reputation both internally and externally. Employees are increasingly vocal about workplace discrimination, and negative stories about bias or discrimination can spread quickly through social media or media coverage. This can deter top talent from joining the organisation and impact relationships with clients, customers, and stakeholders who value diversity and inclusion.

Example: In 2018, H&M faced a public relations crisis after an employee posted a viral video describing the conscious racial bias she experienced at the hands of her manager. The employee detailed instances of being denied promotions, being excluded from important projects, and enduring inappropriate comments about her race. The viral video prompted public backlash, and the retailer faced calls for a boycott, leading to a significant dip in sales and lasting reputational damage. The company was forced to implement widespread anti-bias training and overhaul its leadership team to regain public trust.

5. Legal and Financial Consequences

Conscious bias can also lead to legal ramifications for organisations, particularly when discriminatory actions violate employment laws. Discrimination based on race, gender, age, disability, religion, or other protected characteristics is illegal in many countries, and organisations that allow conscious bias to flourish may face lawsuits, legal fees, and hefty settlements. Beyond the financial costs of litigation, the long-term damage to employee trust and morale can be even more significant.

Example: In 2021, Tesla Inc faced a class-action lawsuit from employees who had been systematically discriminated against based on their ethnicity. The company's management had consistently refused to promote employees of colour to leadership positions, despite their qualifications. After a lengthy legal battle, the company was ordered to pay millions in damages and implement mandatory diversity training for all employees. The lawsuit not only resulted in financial loss but also damaged the company's reputation as an employer of choice.

Addressing and Managing Conscious Bias

1. Leadership Commitment to Diversity and Inclusion

The first step in addressing conscious bias is securing leadership's commitment to fostering a diverse and inclusive workplace. Leaders must actively promote a zero-tolerance policy for discriminatory behaviours and ensure that diversity and inclusion are embedded into the organisation's values and goals. Without strong leadership, efforts to address bias may be ineffective.

Example: PricewaterhouseCoopers (PwC) took a stand against conscious bias by launching a comprehensive diversity and inclusion initiative led by its CEO. The initiative included mandatory training for all employees, accountability measures for managers, and specific goals to increase representation of underrepresented groups in leadership roles. The firm's leadership commitment to diversity not only improved internal culture but also strengthened its reputation with clients and partners.

2. Implementing Anti-Discrimination Policies

Organisations must have clear anti-discrimination policies that outline unacceptable behaviours and the consequences of engaging in discriminatory practices. These policies should be communicated regularly and reinforced through training programs, employee handbooks, and onboarding processes. Employees need to understand that conscious bias will not be tolerated and that there are consequences for discriminatory actions.

3. Bias Awareness and Training Programs

Training programs that raise awareness of both conscious and unconscious bias are essential in helping employees recognise and address their own prejudices. These programs should include real-world examples of bias in the workplace and strategies for mitigating its impact. Importantly, training should not be a one-off event but part of an ongoing effort to maintain an inclusive workplace.

4. Inclusive Hiring and Promotion Practices

To reduce conscious bias in hiring and promotions, organisations should adopt structured processes that prioritise diversity and fairness. This can include using diverse hiring panels, removing identifying information from resumes, and establishing clear, objective criteria for promotions. Regular audits of hiring and promotion practices can help identify and address patterns of bias.

Real-World Examples

1. Conscious Bias in Client Allocation

Sector: Legal (Baker McKenzie)

Issue: Conscious bias in client allocation favouring senior male partners

Conscious Bias in Decision Making: At Baker McKenzie, an internal analysis revealed a conscious bias in how client accounts were assigned, with senior male partners often receiving high-profile cases over their female counterparts. Despite having highly qualified female partners with successful case histories, the firm's leadership consciously believed that male partners were better suited to handle key clients due to perceived client preferences. This bias was rooted in longstanding traditions and assumptions about gender roles in high-stakes legal representation.

Impact on the Workplace: This practice limited female partners' opportunities for career advancement and reduced their visibility within the firm. In response, Baker McKenzie launched a comprehensive client allocation review process, implemented more transparent criteria for assigning high-profile cases, and introduced leadership workshops focusing on gender bias. These changes led to a more equitable distribution of client work, improved morale among female attorneys, and greater gender balance in client-facing leadership roles.

Reference: Law Society Gazette. Reports on gender bias in legal practices and measures to improve gender equity in client assignments. https://www.lawgazette.co.uk/

2. Conscious Bias in Tech Hiring Practices

Sector: Technology (Google)

Issue: Conscious bias in hiring practices favoring candidates from elite universities

Conscious Bias in Decision Making: At Google, an internal review highlighted a conscious bias in its hiring practices, with a preference for candidates from prestigious universities such as Stanford, MIT, and Harvard. Hiring managers believed these schools produced the top talent, leading them to consciously favour graduates from these institutions over equally skilled candidates from less recognized schools. This created a homogeneous workforce and overlooked the potential contributions of individuals from more diverse educational backgrounds.

Impact on the Workplace: This bias limited the diversity of thought and innovation within teams, leading to criticism from employees and industry watchdogs. Google responded by broadening its recruitment criteria, placing more emphasis on skills and practical experience rather than the prestige of a candidate's alma mater. This shift contributed to a more diverse talent pool, enriched team collaboration, and an overall boost in creative problem-solving within the company.

Reference:

- Harvard Business Review. Analysis on hiring bias in tech companies. https://hbr.org/

3. Conscious Bias in Project Leadership Assignments

Sector: Manufacturing (John Deere)

Issue: Conscious bias in project leadership assignments based on age

Conscious Bias in Decision Making: At John Deere, a leading manufacturer, conscious bias emerged in project leadership assignments, with younger employees often being chosen over older, more experienced team members. Management believed that younger employees were more familiar with modern technology and practices, consciously favouring them for leading innovation-focused projects. This left seasoned employees feeling undervalued and excluded from contributing their expertise.

Impact on the Workplace: This bias led to dissatisfaction among experienced employees, decreased engagement, and missed opportunities for projects that could have benefited from a mix of experience and new perspectives. Recognizing the impact, John Deere introduced age inclusivity training and a new project assignment policy that considered both experience and adaptability. The initiative improved team morale, utilised the strengths of a more diverse range of employees, and enhanced the overall effectiveness of project outcomes.

Reference:

- Forbes. Articles on age bias in the workplace. https://www.forbes.com/

- Society for Human Resource Management (SHRM). Reports on age inclusivity in leadership assignments. https://www.shrm.org/

Key Takeaways

Conscious bias is a serious issue that, when left unmanaged, can have devastating effects on both individual employees and the organisation as a whole. From decreased morale and productivity to legal and financial consequences, the impact of conscious bias can be long-lasting. Organisations must take a proactive approach by promoting leadership commitment, implementing strong anti-discrimination policies, providing ongoing bias training, and fostering a culture of inclusion. By addressing conscious bias head-on, businesses can create healthier, more productive workplaces where diversity is celebrated, and everyone has an equal opportunity to succeed.

References:

Anthony, S. D. (2016). *Kodak's Downfall Wasn't About Technology*. Harvard Business Review.

BBC News. (2018). *H&M apologises for 'racist' ad*. Retrieved from https://www.bbc.com/news/world-africa-42635624

CNBC. (2021). *Tesla hit with lawsuit alleging widespread racism at its Fremont factory*. Retrieved from https://www.cnbc.com/2021/07/01/tesla-hit-with-lawsuit-alleging-widespread-racism-at-its-fremont-factory.html

Financial Times. (2021). *How PwC and other firms are approaching diversity and inclusion*. Retrieved from https://www.ft.com/content/7e8c9c8e-c6b2-11e9-a1f4-3669401ba76f

Paluck, E. L., & Green, D. P. (2009). Prejudice reduction: What works? A review and assessment of research and practice. *Annual Review of Psychology*, 60, 339-367.

PricewaterhouseCoopers (PwC). (2024). Diversity and inclusion. Retrieved from https://www.pwc.com/gx/en/about/diversity-inclusion.html

The Guardian. 2018). *H&M faces backlash over 'coolest monkey in the jungle' hoodie ad* https://www.theguardian.com/fashion/2018/jan/08/hm-faces-backlash-over-coolest-monkey-in-the-jungle-hoodie-ad

U.S. Chemical Safety Board. (2011). BP Deepwater Horizon Accident Investigation Report. Retrieved from https://www.csb.gov/

CHAPTER 20

Affinity Bias in the Workplace

Affinity bias, also known as similarity bias, occurs when people gravitate toward others who are similar to them in terms of background, interests, or beliefs. This unconscious preference often leads individuals to favour people who look like them, share similar experiences, or hold comparable values. In the workplace, this bias can subtly influence decision-making in recruitment, promotions, team-building, and everyday interactions. While seemingly innocuous, affinity bias can significantly undermine diversity, inclusion, and organisational success, as it hinders equitable opportunities and fosters homogeneity in leadership and culture. This chapter explores the origins, impact, and strategies for addressing affinity bias, with a focus on creating more inclusive and equitable workplaces.

What is Affinity Bias?

Affinity bias is the unconscious tendency to prefer people who are similar to ourselves in various ways, such as shared race, gender, age, socioeconomic background, interests, or experiences. It is a natural human instinct to seek familiarity and comfort, often manifesting in the workplace through decisions made about hiring, promotions, mentoring, and forming social connections. For instance, a manager might feel a stronger connection with a candidate who shares their alma mater, or a leader might give more opportunities to someone who reminds them of their younger self. While this bias may seem harmless, it creates a barrier to diversity and inclusion, as it excludes individuals who may be equally or more qualified but do not share these similarities.

Affinity bias stems from the psychological principle of in-group favouritism, which suggests that people tend to favour those within their own social group and view them as more competent or trustworthy. This bias is reinforced by the social dynamics of most workplaces, where senior leaders or influential employees tend to be surrounded by like-minded or similar individuals. The result is often a homogenous culture, with underrepresented groups facing greater obstacles to advancement and success.

The Impact of Affinity Bias on Recruitment and Promotions

Affinity bias has a profound impact on recruitment and promotions. In recruitment, hiring managers may unconsciously select candidates who share commonalities with them—whether it's the same educational background, similar hobbies, or shared social identities. This can lead to a lack of diversity in the workforce and perpetuate exclusionary hiring practices. Even when organisations have strong diversity initiatives, affinity bias can undermine these efforts by consistently favouring a narrow pool of candidates.

Case Study 1: Recruitment Bias at a Consulting Firm

In a large consulting firm, it was found that managers consistently hired employees from a select group of prestigious universities, leading to a homogenous team composition. Most of the new hires shared the same socioeconomic background, and many had been involved in similar extracurricular activities, such as sports teams or fraternities. Over time, the company realised that their recruitment strategy, driven by affinity bias, was limiting the diversity of thought and perspective within their teams. As a result, the firm restructured its recruitment process to include blind resume reviews, diverse hiring panels, and unconscious bias training for hiring managers.

In promotions, affinity bias often plays a similar role. Managers may give more opportunities for advancement to those they feel an inherent connection with, often without realising it. This can result in certain employees being overlooked or marginalised, even if they possess the skills and qualifications needed for promotion.

Affinity Bias and Its Impact on Team Dynamics

Beyond hiring and promotions, affinity bias also affects day-to-day interactions in the workplace. Teams that are built around shared similarities may find themselves in an "echo chamber", where diverse perspectives are limited, and innovation is stifled. Employees may unconsciously form social cliques, leading to the exclusion of those who are different from the majority. Over time, this can create a workplace culture that is less inclusive and more resistant to change.

Case Study 2: Lack of Diversity in Leadership Teams

A tech company found that its leadership team, made up predominantly of men from similar educational and professional backgrounds, was struggling to innovate in response to a rapidly changing market. Despite attempts to introduce diversity into the team, affinity bias led to promotions of individuals who fit the existing mould. As a result, the team lacked gender and racial diversity, as well as diversity of thought. By introducing policies that required more inclusive decision-making processes and diverse candidate slates for leadership positions, the company saw improved innovation and a broader range of ideas.

Affinity bias can also affect how employees are assigned to projects or teams. Managers may choose individuals who remind them of themselves or with whom they feel a stronger personal connection. This can create disparities in opportunity, as some employees consistently receive more challenging or visible projects, while others are sidelined.

Addressing Affinity Bias: Strategies for Change

To combat the effects of affinity bias, organisations need to adopt intentional strategies that promote diversity and inclusion while raising awareness of unconscious bias. Here are key steps that organisations can take to address affinity bias:

Unconscious Bias Training

Training programs that educate employees and managers about unconscious bias are a critical first step in addressing affinity bias. These training sessions help individuals recognise their biases, understand how those biases impact decision-making, and learn strategies to mitigate their effects. However, research shows that training alone is not enough—it must be followed by actionable changes in policies and practices.

Structured and Standardised Hiring and Promotion Processes

Implementing structured and standardised hiring and promotion processes can reduce the influence of affinity bias. This includes using blind resume reviews, diverse hiring panels, and data-driven performance evaluations. By focusing on objective criteria and ensuring that decisions are made by multiple stakeholders, organisations can minimise the impact of personal preferences.

Diverse Teams and Leadership

Encouraging diverse leadership and ensuring that hiring and promotion panels include people from different backgrounds can also help mitigate affinity bias. When decision-makers come from a range of perspectives, they are less likely to default to familiar or similar individuals and are more likely to consider diverse candidates.

Mentorship and Sponsorship Programs

Affinity bias often affects access to mentorship and sponsorship, as people tend to mentor individuals who remind them of their younger selves. To counteract this, organisations should create formalised mentorship and sponsorship programs that pair diverse employees with senior leaders, ensuring that opportunities are evenly distributed.

The Long-Term Benefits of Reducing Affinity Bias

Reducing affinity bias in the workplace has significant long-term benefits for organisations. It leads to greater diversity in leadership, which in turn fosters more innovation and adaptability in the face of change. Diverse teams are more likely to approach problems from multiple perspectives, leading to more creative and effective solutions. Moreover, organisations that prioritise diversity and inclusion tend to attract and retain top talent, as employees are more likely to feel valued and respected.

Case Study 1: Enhancing Team Collaboration through Reduced Affinity Bias in a Tech Startup

A tech startup specialising in software development identified that affinity bias was influencing team formation and project leadership. Managers often selected team leads and members who shared similar educational backgrounds and personal interests, resulting in homogenous teams. This practice limited the range of perspectives in problem-solving and stifled creativity.

Measures Taken: To address this, the company implemented targeted training programs on recognizing and mitigating affinity bias, as well as anonymous project leader selection processes based on skills and past performance rather than personal connections. They also promoted cross-functional team collaboration to encourage diverse working relationships.

Outcome: Within a year, the startup reported higher levels of innovation and collaboration. Teams that were more diverse in background and thought outperformed homogenous groups in terms of problem-solving efficiency and customer satisfaction ratings. This change not only improved team dynamics but also boosted the company's reputation as an inclusive and forward-thinking workplace.

Case Study 2: Reducing Affinity Bias in Recruitment for a Financial Services Firm

A well-established financial services firm realised that affinity bias was affecting its recruitment process. Hiring managers tended to favour candidates who shared similar professional backgrounds, alma maters, or personal interests, leading to a workforce that lacked diversity in experiences and perspectives. This narrowed the talent pool and reduced the firm's ability to innovate and adapt to market changes.

Measures Taken: The firm restructured its hiring process to focus on skill-based assessments and blind resume screening. It also mandated diverse interview panels to minimise affinity bias in decision-making. Training workshops were conducted for hiring managers to make them aware of unconscious affinity preferences and their impact on the company.

Outcome: After implementing these measures, the firm saw a significant increase in hires from different backgrounds and educational institutions. The new hires brought fresh perspectives and problem-solving approaches, which enhanced team performance and strategic planning. The company noted that teams with members from varied backgrounds were more agile and better equipped to handle complex financial projects. This shift ultimately contributed to stronger client relationships and a 15% increase in project success rates.

Case Study 3: Increased Innovation through Diverse Leadership at a Global Corporation

A global manufacturing company recognized that affinity bias was impacting its leadership structure and stifling innovation. Leaders were often promoted based on shared backgrounds and interests, leading to a lack of diversity at the decision-making level.

Measures Taken: The company implemented several key measures to address affinity bias. These included diversifying promotion criteria to prioritise skills and performance over personal connections, introducing training programs focused on bias awareness for senior management, and establishing mentorship programs that paired employees across different backgrounds to foster varied perspectives.

Outcome: After implementing these measures, the company saw a significant increase in the number of patents filed and innovative solutions developed. The diverse leadership team brought different perspectives and experiences to the table, resulting in more creative approaches to product development and customer engagement. This diversity-led innovation translated into an improved financial performance, demonstrating the tangible benefits of reducing affinity bias. The company's culture also became more inclusive, leading to higher employee satisfaction and retention rates.

Key Takeaways

Affinity bias is a powerful but often overlooked force in the workplace. While it is human nature to seek out similarities, organisations that allow affinity bias to dictate decision-making risk undermining diversity, innovation, and inclusivity. By implementing unconscious bias training, structured hiring processes, and fostering diverse teams, organisations can create an environment where all employees have equal opportunities to succeed. As the case studies demonstrate, addressing affinity bias not only benefits individual employees but also contributes to stronger organisational performance and competitiveness in the long run.

References:

● Brewer, M. B. (1999). The psychology of prejudice: In-group love and outgroup hate? *Journal of Social Issues*, 55(3), 429-444.

● Castilla, E. J. (2016). Achieving meritocracy in the workplace. *MIT Sloan Management Review*, 57(4), 35-41.

● Phillips, K. W. (2014). How diversity makes us smarter. *Scientific American*, 311(4), 42-47.

● Chang, E. H., Milkman, K. L., Chugh, D., & Akinola, M. (2019). Diversity thresholds: How social norms, visibility, and scrutiny relate to group composition. *Academy of Management Journal*, 62(3), 864-881.

● Ibarra, H., Carter, N. M., & Silva, C. (2010). Why men still get more promotions than women. *Harvard Business Review*, 88(9), 80-85.

● Hunt, V., Layton, D., & Prince, S. (2015). *Diversity Matters*. McKinsey & Company. Retrieved from https://www.mckinsey.com

CHAPTER 21

Uncertainty Bias in the Workplace

Introduction to Uncertainty Bias

Uncertainty bias is a cognitive phenomenon where individuals tend to favour certain or familiar outcomes over uncertain or unfamiliar ones, even when the uncertain option might offer a greater reward. This bias can significantly influence decision-making in the workplace, affecting everything from hiring practices and leadership decisions to strategic planning and innovation. Understanding and addressing uncertainty bias is essential for creating a dynamic and adaptive workplace that can thrive in a rapidly changing environment.

Uncertainty bias is closely linked to the human brain's natural aversion to ambiguity and the unknown. In the face of uncertainty, people often default to known quantities and past experiences, leading to a preference for the status quo. While this can provide a sense of security, it can also hinder growth, innovation, and the ability to respond effectively to new challenges. This chapter explores the nature of uncertainty bias, its impact on workplace dynamics, and strategies for overcoming it to foster a more open and adaptable organisational culture.

The Science Behind Uncertainty Bias

The concept of uncertainty bias is rooted in behavioural economics and psychology. It is closely related to prospect theory, developed by psychologists Daniel Kahneman and Amos Tversky, which describes how people make decisions involving risk and uncertainty. According to prospect theory, individuals tend to overvalue certain outcomes and undervalue uncertain ones, even when the expected value of the uncertain option is higher. This is because the fear of loss often outweighs the potential for gain, leading to risk-averse behaviour.

One of the key cognitive mechanisms underlying uncertainty bias is ambiguity aversion. This is the tendency to avoid options with unknown probabilities or outcomes, preferring those with clear and certain prospects. For example, in a hiring context, managers may prefer candidates with familiar backgrounds or qualifications over those with more diverse or unconventional experiences, even if the latter group could bring new perspectives and skills to the team.

Another related concept is status quo bias, which refers to the preference for maintaining current conditions rather than embracing change. This bias can lead to resistance to innovation, as individuals may be reluctant to adopt new technologies, processes, or strategies that involve uncertainty. In organisational settings, uncertainty bias can result in missed opportunities for growth and improvement, as well as a lack of DE&I.

The Impact of Uncertainty Bias

Uncertainty bias can manifest in various aspects of workplace dynamics, often leading to suboptimal decision-making and limiting the organisation's potential for success. Some of the key areas where uncertainty bias can have an impact include:

1. *Hiring and Recruitment:* Uncertainty bias can influence hiring decisions by leading managers to favour candidates with traditional or familiar qualifications over those with more diverse or unconventional back-

grounds. This can manifest as a lack of diversity in the workforce, as well as missed opportunities to bring in fresh perspectives and innovative ideas.

2. *Leadership and Decision-Making:* Leaders who are influenced by uncertainty bias may be more likely to stick with the status quo rather than pursuing new initiatives or strategies that involve risk. This can hinder the organisation's ability to adapt to changing market conditions, respond to emerging trends, and stay competitive.

3. *Innovation and Change Management:* Opportunities and can limit its long-term growth potential Uncertainty bias can stifle innovation by causing resistance to new ideas, technologies, and processes. Employees and leaders alike may be hesitant to embrace change, leading to a culture of complacency and a reluctance to take calculated risks. This can prevent the organisation from capitalising on new opportunities.

4. *Performance Evaluations:* Uncertainty bias can also affect how employees are evaluated and rewarded. For example, managers may be more likely to favour employees who conform to established norms and expectations, rather than those who take risks or challenge the status quo. This can discourage creativity and initiative, as employees may feel that taking risks is not valued or rewarded.

5. *Strategic Planning:* In strategic planning, uncertainty bias can lead to a preference for short-term, low-risk goals over long-term, high-reward strategies. This can result in a lack of investment in innovation and growth, as well as a failure to anticipate and prepare for future challenges. Organisations that are overly focused on avoiding uncer-

tainty may find themselves unprepared for disruptions or unable to seize emerging opportunities.

Addressing and Mitigating Uncertainty Bias

To create a more dynamic and adaptive workplace, it is essential to address and mitigate the effects of uncertainty bias. Here are several strategies that organisations can implement:

1. *Promoting a Growth Mindset:* One of the most effective ways to combat uncertainty bias is by fostering a growth mindset within the organisation. A growth mindset encourages individuals to embrace challenges, take risks, and view failures as opportunities for learning and development. By promoting a culture that values experimentation and continuous improvement, organisations can reduce the fear of uncertainty and encourage more innovative thinking.

2. *Encouraging DE&I:* DE&I are critical to overcoming uncertainty bias, as they expose employees to a wider range of perspectives, ideas, and experiences. Organisations can promote diversity by implementing inclusive hiring practices, providing diversity training, and creating a culture where different viewpoints are valued and respected. This can help reduce the tendency to favour familiar or conventional options and encourage more open-minded decision-making.

3. *Leadership Development and Training:* Leaders play a crucial role in shaping organisational culture and decision-making processes. Providing leadership development and training focused on recognising and overcoming uncertainty bias can help leaders become more effective at navigating ambiguity and making informed

decisions. This training can include techniques for evaluating risks, considering alternative perspectives, and fostering a culture of innovation.

4. *Implementing Decision-Making Frameworks:* Decision-making frameworks, such as scenario planning and risk analysis, can help organisations systematically evaluate options and consider the potential outcomes of different courses of action. By using these frameworks, organisations can reduce the influence of uncertainty bias and make more informed decisions. For example, scenario planning can help leaders anticipate and prepare for a range of possible futures, rather than relying on familiar or certain outcomes.

5. *Encouraging Risk-Taking and Experimentation:* To overcome uncertainty bias, organisations should encourage employees to take calculated risks and experiment with new ideas. This can be achieved by creating a supportive environment where failure is viewed as a natural part of the learning process. Leaders can set the tone by recognising and rewarding employees who take initiative and innovate, even if their efforts do not always succeed.

6. *Providing Psychological Safety:* Psychological safety is the belief that one can speak up, share ideas, and take risks without fear of negative consequences. Creating a psychologically safe work environment can help reduce uncertainty bias by encouraging employees to voice their opinions and contribute to decision-making processes. This can lead to more diverse and innovative solutions, as employees feel empowered to challenge the status quo and propose new ideas.

7. *Using Data and Analytics:* Leveraging data and analytics can help organisations make more objective and informed decisions, reducing the influence of uncertainty bias. By collecting and analysing data on various aspects of the business, organisations can gain insights into trends, risks, and opportunities that may not be immediately apparent. This can help leaders make more informed decisions and reduce the reliance on gut feelings or intuition.

Embracing Uncertainty for Long-Term Success

Uncertainty bias is a natural human tendency, but it can limit an organisation's potential for growth and innovation. By recognising and addressing this bias, organisations can create a more dynamic and adaptive workplace that is better equipped to navigate the complexities of the modern business environment.

The journey to overcoming uncertainty bias requires a cultural shift, where risk-taking and experimentation are valued, DE&I are prioritised, and leaders are equipped with the tools and mindset to make informed decisions in the face of ambiguity. By embracing uncertainty, organisations can unlock new opportunities for success and position themselves for long-term growth and resilience.

Real-World Examples

Case Study 1: Mitigating Uncertainty Bias through AI Ethics at IBM

Sector: Technology (IBM)

Conscious Bias in Decision Making: IBM, a leader in technology and innovation, recognized that uncertainty bias was influencing decision-making processes, particularly in the development and implementation of AI tools. This type of bias occurs when decisions are skewed due to a preference for familiar or predictable outcomes, potentially impacting fairness and inclusivity.

Measures Taken: To mitigate this, IBM established an AI Ethics Board dedicated to ensuring that AI and decision-making tools are designed to minimise bias, including uncertainty bias. The board oversees the development and implementation of AI technologies to ensure equitable decision-making. Additionally, IBM invested in training programs for employees to understand and address uncertainty bias in their work.

Outcome: IBM's proactive measures resulted in more transparent and inclusive decision-making processes, both internally and externally. The company's commitment to addressing bias strengthened its reputation as an ethical leader in AI, fostering trust among clients and partners. Employee engagement also increased as teams became more aware of bias and how to counteract it effectively.

Reference:

- IBM Research – AI Ethics Overview. https://www.research.ibm.com/ai-ethics/

Case Study 2: Implementing Bias Interruption Techniques at PwC

Sector: Professional Services (PwC)

Issue: Reducing uncertainty bias in consulting practices and client recommendations

Conscious Bias in Decision Making: PwC identified that uncertainty bias was affecting its consulting practices, leading to decision-making that favoured more predictable, less risky recommendations. This impacted the firm's ability to provide the most innovative and tailored solutions for their clients.

Measures Taken: To address this, PwC implemented bias interruption techniques such as structured decision-making processes and comprehensive diversity training programs. These measures encouraged consultants to be more aware of their biases and approach client recommendations with a more balanced perspective.

Outcome: The structured decision-making processes and training programs led to a reduction in uncertainty bias, allowing for more innovative and customised client solutions. As a result, PwC's consulting practices became more dynamic and responsive, enhancing client satisfaction and fostering a culture of continuous improvement within the firm.

Reference:

> PwC – Diversity and Inclusion. https://www.pwc.com/gx/en/about/diversity-inclusion.html

Case Study 3: Using Advanced Analytics to Mitigate Bias at Accenture

Sector: Consulting (Accenture)

Issue: Addressing unconscious biases, including uncertainty bias, in decision-making

Conscious Bias in Decision Making: Accenture recognized that unconscious biases, including uncertainty bias, were present in their global decision-making processes. This bias influenced hiring practices, promotions, and client engagements, leading to potential inequities and missed opportunities for diverse input.

Measures Taken: Accenture implemented an "Inclusion and Diversity" strategy that leveraged advanced analytics to identify and mitigate biases in decision-making processes. The company also launched specific initiatives aimed at promoting bias awareness and training employees to recognize and counteract uncertainty bias.

Outcome: The advanced analytics and targeted initiatives improved equity and inclusivity across Accenture's global workforce. The company reported more balanced decision-making and increased representation of diverse perspectives in leadership and project teams. These efforts enhanced the overall inclusiveness of the workplace, strengthened client relationships, and reinforced Accenture's standing as a leader in diversity and inclusion practices.

Reference:

- Accenture – Inclusion and Diversity. https://www.accenture.com/us-en/about/inclusion-diversity

Key Takeaways

Uncertainty bias causes individuals tend to avoid or undervalue unknown or unpredictable situations this can negatively impact decision-making, innovation, and diversity. When uncertainty bias goes unchecked, leaders may stick to familiar ideas, people, and processes, limiting creativity and the ability to embrace change. This bias can prevent organisations from exploring new opportunities, hiring diverse talent, or adapting to evolving markets. Addressing uncertainty bias involves fostering a culture of openness, encouraging calculated risk-taking, and promoting inclusivity in decision-making, which helps organisations thrive in dynamic and competitive environments.

References and Resources:

- Christensen, C.M. (1997). *The innovator's dilemma*. Harvard Business Review Press.

- A book that examines how companies can navigate uncertainty and disruption by embracing innovation and challenging the status quo.

⊙ Edmondson, A. C. (1999). Psychological safety and learning behaviour in work teams. *Administrative Science Quarterly*, *44*(2), 350-383.

- This paper discusses the concept of psychological safety and its impact on team learning and decision-making.

⊙ Heath, C., & Heath, D. (2013*). Decisive: How to make better choices in life and work*. Crown Business.

- A book that explores decision-making strategies and provides practical advice for overcoming cognitive biases, including uncertainty bias.

⊙ Kahneman, D., & Tversky, A. (1979). Prospect theory: An analysis of decision under risk. *Econometrica*, *47*(2), 263-291.

- This seminal paper introduces prospect theory and explains how people make decisions involving risk and uncertainty.

⊙ Kahneman, D. (2011). *Thinking, fast and slow*. Farrar, Straus and Giroux.

- A comprehensive exploration of cognitive biases and decision-making processes, including insights into uncertainty bias and risk aversion.

CHAPTER 22

Confirmation Bias in the Workplace

Introduction to Confirmation Bias

Confirmation bias is a psychological phenomenon in which individuals tend to seek, interpret, and remember information in a way that confirms their pre-existing beliefs or theories. This bias prevents individuals from objectively evaluating information and often leads to distorted judgments and decision-making. In the workplace, confirmation bias can have far-reaching implications, impacting everything from hiring decisions to leadership effectiveness, collaboration, and overall company culture.

Understanding confirmation bias is essential for creating an inclusive, fair, and objective work environment. This chapter explores the origins and mechanisms of confirmation bias, its manifestations in the workplace, and strategies to mitigate its impact on organisational processes. Additionally, this chapter will include examples and case studies to illustrate how confirmation bias can hinder both individual and organisational growth.

The Psychology of Confirmation Bias

Confirmation bias is deeply rooted in human cognitive processing. People tend to prefer information that supports their existing viewpoints while dismissing or ignoring information that contradicts those beliefs. According to Nickerson (1998), confirmation bias results from the inherent desire for cognitive consistency—people prefer to avoid the discomfort of holding contradictory beliefs or information. Therefore, they uncon-sciously seek out data that reinforces their existing worldview and dismiss anything that challenges it.

Cognitive Dissonance and Motivated Reasoning

Cognitive dissonance, a related concept, refers to the discom-fort people experience when confronted with contradictory be-liefs or information. To reduce this discomfort, individuals often engage in motivated reasoning, selectively processing informa-tion that aligns with their pre-existing beliefs and dismissing or devaluing information that contradicts those beliefs (Festinger, 1957). This motivated reasoning underpins confirmation bias in the workplace, affecting decision-making, communication, and team dynamics.

Manifestations of Confirmation Bias

Confirmation bias can manifest in various ways in the work-place, and its effects are often subtle but pervasive. The fol-lowing sections detail how confirmation bias influences critical areas of organisational life, such as hiring practices, leadership decision-making, workplace conflict, and innovation.

1. Confirmation Bias in Hiring Practices

Confirmation bias can significantly distort hiring decisions by in-fluencing how recruiters and managers interpret candidate in-formation. For example, if a recruiter holds a belief that a certain university produces the best candidates, they may unconscious-ly give more weight to a candidate's resume from that institu-tion, ignoring other candidates' merits. Similarly, if a manager has a preconceived notion about the personality traits of a suc-cessful employee, they may select candidates based on those traits without considering alternative perspectives.

According to a study by Bertrand and Mullainathan (2004), hiring biases, including confirmation bias, are prevalent across industries, leading to discriminatory practices. In their study, resumes with stereotypically African American names received fewer callbacks than identical resumes with stereotypically white names. This study highlights how confirmation bias can lead to biased assumptions about candidates' capabilities and experiences, contributing to systemic inequality in the workplace.

2. Confirmation Bias in Leadership and Decision-Making

Leaders are particularly vulnerable to confirmation bias because of their role in shaping organisational direction and culture. When leaders seek out information that aligns with their strategies or perspectives, they may overlook valuable insights that could challenge their thinking and generate more innovative solutions. This selective perception can result in poor decision-making and missed opportunities for growth.

For instance, a CEO who strongly believes in a particular marketing strategy may only consult data or opinions that support that strategy, ignoring alternative approaches or criticisms. Over time, this tunnel vision can lead to stagnation, as the company fails to adapt to changing market conditions. A well-known case of confirmation bias in leadership occurred at Blockbuster, where executives dismissed the growing trend of digital streaming services. Their reluctance to consider the emerging Netflix model, due to their entrenched belief in physical rental stores, ultimately contributed to the company's downfall (Kumar, 2012).

3. Confirmation Bias in Workplace Conflicts

In workplace conflicts, confirmation bias often fuels misunderstandings and escalates tensions. When individuals are involved in a dispute, they are likely to focus on evidence that supports their position while ignoring information that could validate the

other party's perspective. This selective interpretation can pro-
long conflicts and prevent resolutions, as neither party is willing
to consider alternative viewpoints.

Confirmation bias also contributes to "groupthink" in teams,
where members of a group reinforce each other's ideas without
critical evaluation. This phenomenon occurs when individuals
are unwilling to challenge the prevailing opinion within the
group because they seek cohesion or fear standing out. Groupthink, fuelled by confirmation bias, can stifle creativity and prevent teams from exploring innovative solutions.

4. Confirmation Bias and Innovation

Innovation thrives in environments where diverse perspectives
are encouraged and explored. However, confirmation bias can
hinder this process by narrowing the range of ideas that are
considered. When leaders and teams favour familiar solutions
or approaches, they may dismiss novel ideas that challenge the
status quo, even when those ideas could prompt breakthroughs.

An example of confirmation bias stifling innovation can be found
in the case of Kodak. Despite being a pioneer in the development of digital photography, Kodak's leadership clung to their
belief that film would remain the dominant medium. As a result, they failed to fully embrace the digital revolution, allowing
competitors to overtake them in the market. This reluctance to
consider alternative possibilities, fuelled by confirmation bias,
ultimately led to Kodak's decline (Lucas & Goh, 2009).

Strategies for Overcoming Confirmation Bias

Overcoming confirmation bias in the workplace requires intentional effort from individuals and organisations to foster a culture of openness, critical thinking, and continuous learning. The

following strategies can help mitigate the impact of confirmation bias in the workplace:

1. Promote Diverse Perspectives

Encouraging diversity in thought, background, and experience can help counteract confirmation bias. When teams are composed of individuals with varied perspectives, they are more likely to challenge each other's assumptions and explore alternative ideas. Research by Page (2007) shows that diverse teams are more innovative and effective at problem-solving because they bring a broader range of viewpoints to the table.

Leaders should actively seek out input from employees at all levels of the organisation, creating opportunities for candid discussions that challenge conventional thinking.

2. Foster a Culture of Curiosity and Inquiry

Organisations should foster a culture that encourages curiosity and critical thinking. Leaders can model this behaviour by asking open-ended questions, seeking feedback, and demonstrating a willingness to reconsider their assumptions. Encouraging employees to engage in constructive debates and explore alternative solutions can help create a more dynamic and innovative work environment.

3. Utilise Data-Driven Decision-Making

Data-driven decision-making can help mitigate confirmation bias by providing objective evidence to support or refute assumptions. By relying on data rather than personal beliefs or intuition, organisations can make more informed decisions. It is crucial, however, that data is interpreted fairly and not selectively cherry-picked to fit preconceived notions.

Implementing standardised metrics and decision-making frameworks can also reduce the influence of confirmation bias in key processes such as hiring, promotions, and project evaluations.

4. Encourage Regular Feedback and Reflection

Regular feedback loops are essential for combating confirmation bias. Leaders and employees should be encouraged to reflect on their decisions and consider whether confirmation bias may have influenced their judgments. Peer feedback, 360-degree reviews, and mentoring programs can help individuals gain insights into how their biases may be affecting their work.

Real-World Examples

Confirmation Bias Leading to Business Decline

Sector: Photography and Imaging (Kodak)

Issue: Refusal to adapt to digital photography due to confirmation bias

Impact: Kodak, once a dominant force in the photography industry, failed to embrace digital photography despite having developed the first digital camera in the 1970s. The company's leadership clung to their belief that film would remain the preferred medium, ignoring market data that indicated a growing demand for digital technology. Confirmation bias led executives to selectively interpret information in a way that supported their existing view of the industry, causing Kodak to miss out on the digital photography revolution. As a result, Kodak filed for bankruptcy in 2012, having been overtaken by more adaptable competitors like Canon and Sony. The company's reluctance to confront new realities and adapt to technological changes became a cautionary tale of confirmation bias in business.

Reference:

⬙ Anthony, S. D. (2016). Kodak's downfall wasn't about technology. Harvard Business Review.

Confirmation Bias in Risk Assessment

Sector: Oil and Gas (BP)

Issue: Overconfidence in safety protocols and dismissal of potential risks due to confirmation bias

Impact: In 2010, BP experienced one of the largest environmental disasters in history when the Deepwater Horizon oil rig exploded, causing a massive oil spill in the Gulf of Mexico. Leading up to the disaster, BP's management team exhibited confirmation bias by overestimating the reliability of their safety systems and disregarding warning signs that suggested potential vulnerabilities in their drilling operations. Internal reports and safety assessments were ignored or downplayed in favour of maintaining high productivity. BP's confirmation bias prevented the company from fully addressing safety risks, leading to catastrophic environmental damage, legal liabilities, and a total cost exceeding $60 billion.

Reference:

⬙ U.S. Chemical Safety Board. (2011). BP Deepwater Horizon Accident Investigation Report.

Confirmation Bias in Ignoring Streaming Services

Sector: Entertainment (Blockbuster Video)

Issue: Failure to adapt to the rise of streaming services due to confirmation bias

Impact: Blockbuster, once the largest video rental chain in the world, fell victim to confirmation bias by assuming that its physical rental model would continue to thrive, even as streaming services like Netflix gained popularity. Executives ignored data and market trends that pointed toward the growing dominance of digital content and on-demand video services. This led them to reject opportunities to pivot or acquire Netflix when the chance arose. Confirmation bias caused Blockbuster to overlook the threat posed by technological shifts in consumer preferences, ultimately leading to the company's bankruptcy in 2010, while Netflix became a global leader in streaming entertainment.

Reference:

- Tryon, D. (2020). *The rise and fall of Blockbuster*. Business Insider.

Key Takeaways

Confirmation bias is a pervasive challenge that affects decision-making, collaboration, and innovation in the workplace. Left unchecked, it can lead to poor decisions, missed opportunities, and a lack of diversity in thought. However, by recognising and addressing confirmation bias, organisations can foster a more open, inclusive, and dynamic work environment. Promoting diverse perspectives, fostering curiosity, relying on data, and encouraging feedback are essential strategies for overcoming confirmation bias and creating a culture that values critical thinking and continuous improvement.

References and Resources:

- Bertrand, M., & Mullainathan, S. (2004). Are Emily and Greg more employable than Lakisha and Jamal? A field experiment on labour market discrimination. *American Economic Review*, *94*(4), 991-1013.

⊙ Festinger, L. (1957). *A theory of cognitive dissonance*. Stanford University Press.

⊙ Kumar, V. (2012). Blockbuster's fatal flaw wasn't one of intelligence, it was one of insight. *Forbes*. Retrieved from https://www.forbes.com

⊙ Lucas, H. C., & Goh, J. M. (2009). Disruptive technology: How Kodak missed the digital photography revolution. *Journal of Strategic Information Systems*, *18*(1), 46-55.

⊙ Nickerson, R. S. (1998). Confirmation bias: A ubiquitous phenomenon in many guises. *Review of General Psychology*, *2*(2), 175-220.

⊙ Page, S. E. (2007). *The difference: How the power of diversity creates better groups, firms, schools, and societies*. Princeton University Press.

PART 9

Special Topics

CHAPTER 23

Addressing DFV in the Workplace

Understanding the Impact of DFV on Employees

DFV (domestic and family violence) can have profound and far-reaching impacts on employees, affecting their physical and mental health, productivity, and overall well-being. This violence often extends into the workplace, leading to absenteeism, reduced productivity, and higher turnover rates.

Physical and Mental Health Impacts

1. *Physical Health:* Victims of DFV often suffer from injuries and chronic health conditions. According to the World Health Organization (WHO), physical violence by a partner is associated with an increased risk of various health problems, including injuries, chronic pain, autoimmune diseases, gastrointestinal disorders, and gynaecological problems (WHO, 2013).

2. *Mental Health:* The psychological effects of DFV can be severe, leading to conditions such as depression, anxiety, and post-traumatic stress disorder (PTSD). The American Psychological Association (APA) notes that victims of DFV are at a higher risk of developing mental health issues and may experience long-term emotional distress (APA, 2019).

3. *Workplace Performance:* The impacts on health directly translate to diminished workplace performance. The Centers for Disease Control and Prevention (CDC) es-

timate that DFV costs U.S. workplaces around $8.3 billion annually in lost productivity and health care costs (CDC, 2003). In Australia, the economic impact of DFV on workplaces is significant. A report by PricewaterhouseCoopers (PwC, 2015) estimates that DFV costs Australian businesses approximately **$1.9 billion annually** in lost productivity, absenteeism, and staff turnover. This includes direct and indirect costs, highlighting the need for workplace policies that address and mitigate the impact of DFV on employees.

Economic and Workplace Impacts

1. *Absenteeism and Presenteeism:* Victims of DFV are more likely to miss work due to injuries, court dates, or psychological distress. Presenteeism, where employees are physically present but not fully functioning due to mental distress, is also a significant issue (Reeves & O'Leary-Kelly, 2007).

2. *Turnover and Recruitment Costs:* Higher turnover rates among victims of DFV lead to increased recruitment and training costs for employers. The costs associated with replacing employees can be substantial, ranging from 50% to 200% of an employee's annual salary (Boushey & Glynn, 2012).

3. *Workplace Safety:* DFV can sometimes extend into the workplace, with abusers harassing or stalking their victims at work, creating safety risks for the entire workforce. A report by the U.S. Department of Labor indicates that about 25% of workplace violence incidents are related to DFV (U.S. Department of Labor, 2016).

Developing Supportive Policies and Procedures

To effectively address DFV in the workplace, organisations need to develop comprehensive policies and procedures that provide support to victims, ensure their safety, and create an environment that does not tolerate abuse.

Policy Development

1. *Zero-Tolerance Policy:* Implementing a zero-tolerance policy toward DFV sends a clear message that such behaviour will not be tolerated. This policy should outline the consequences for perpetrators and the support available to victims.

2. *Supportive Leave Policies:* Offering flexible leave policies, such as paid leave for medical, legal, or counselling appointments, can provide victims with the time they need to address their situation without fear of losing their job. Research by the Australian Institute of Health and Welfare (AIHW) suggests that supportive workplace policies can significantly reduce the stress and financial burden on victims (AIHW, 2019).

3. *Confidentiality and Privacy:* Ensuring confidentiality is crucial for the safety and well-being of victims. Policies should include measures to protect the privacy of those who disclose violence, and information should only be shared on a need-to-know basis.

Implementing Procedures

1. *Employee Assistance Programs (EAPs):* EAPs can provide confidential counselling and support services to employees experiencing DFV. Studies have shown that

EAPs can effectively reduce the symptoms of stress and improve mental health outcomes for employees (Attridge, 2010).

2. *Safety Planning:* Developing safety plans for employees who are victims of DFV can help mitigate risks. This may include changing work schedules, providing secure parking, or implementing other security measures. The Corporate Alliance to End Partner Violence (CAEPV) provides guidelines for creating effective workplace safety plans (CAEPV, 2017).

3. *Training and Awareness Programs:* Regular training for employees and managers on recognising the signs of DFV and understanding the resources available is essential. According to a report by the Society for Human Resource Management (SHRM), well-designed training programs can increase awareness and help create a supportive workplace culture (SHRM, 2017).

DFV Policy Example Template

There are a number of elements that DFV policies should include. The following is a template that outlines the key areas that a standard DFV policy should include.

- **Purpose and Scope**
    - **Objective:** Outline the policy's purpose, emphasising the commitment to creating a safe, supportive workplace for all employees impacted by domestic and family violence (DFV).
    - **Scope:** Define who the policy applies to (e.g., all employees, contractors) and in what situations (e.g., during work hours, at work events).

Definition of DFV

- ▶ **Clear Definitions:** Provide clear definitions of DFV, including physical, emotional, psychological, financial, and sexual abuse. Clarify that the policy covers violence from intimate partners, family members, or anyone living in the same household.

Support for Affected Employees

- ▶ **Leave Entitlements:** Detail leave entitlements for employees experiencing DFV, such as paid or unpaid leave for attending court appearances, seeking medical treatment, or relocating.

- ▶ **Flexible Work Arrangements:** Outline options for flexible work arrangements, including altered hours, remote work, or temporary changes to work location.

- ▶ **Confidentiality:** Stress the importance of maintaining confidentiality when an employee discloses their situation, ensuring their privacy and safety are prioritised.

Reporting and Response Procedures

- ▶ **Reporting Mechanisms:** Provide clear guidance on how employees can report DFV, including internal contacts (e.g., HR, a designated DFV contact person/s) and external resources (e.g., hotlines, shelters).

- ▶ **Response Plan:** Outline the organisation's response plan, including assessing risks, providing immediate support, and referring to external services where necessary.

- **Training and Awareness**

  ▸ **Employee Training:** Ensure that all employees receive training on DFV awareness, recognising signs of abuse, and understanding the support available.

  ▸ **Management Responsibilities:** Specify that managers and HR personnel receive specialised training to handle disclosures sensitively and effectively.

- **Safety Planning**

  ▸ **Risk Assessment:** Implement procedures for assessing and managing risks associated with DFV, including safety planning for affected employees.

  ▸ **Workplace Safety Measures:** Describe any workplace safety measures that may be taken, such as changes to work schedules, security enhancements, or escort services.

- **External Resources and Partnerships**

  ▸ **Community Resources:** Provide information on external DFV resources, such as hotlines, counselling services, and legal support.

  ▸ **Partnerships:** Mention any partnerships with local DFV organisations that can provide additional support.

- **Monitoring and Review**

  ▸ **Policy Review:** Set a timeline for regularly reviewing and updating the policy to ensure it remains effective and relevant.

- > **Feedback Mechanisms:** Encourage feedback from employees on the policy's effectiveness and any areas for improvement.

- ◈ **Legal Compliance**

- > **Legislation Compliance:** Ensure the policy complies with relevant laws and regulations, such as those related to employment rights, discrimination, and occupational health and safety (OHS).

- ◈ **Commitment to a Safe Workplace**

- ◈ **Organisational Statement:** Conclude with a strong statement from leadership reaffirming the organisation's commitment to providing a safe and supportive environment for all employees.

Training Employees to Respond to DFV Disclosures

Training employees to respond appropriately to disclosures of DFV is critical in creating a supportive and safe work environment. Effective training programs should equip employees with the skills and knowledge to handle disclosures sensitively and confidently.

Creating Safe Spaces for Disclosure

1. *Trust and Rapport:* Employees should be trained to build trust and rapport with colleagues, creating an environment where victims feel safe to disclose abuse. According to the National DFV Hotline, establishing trust is key to encouraging victims to seek help (NDVH, 2020).

2. *Active Listening:* Training on active listening techniques can help employees respond empathetically and supportively to disclosures. Active listening involves giving full attention to the speaker, acknowledging their feelings, and avoiding judgement or unsolicited advice.

3. *Non-Judgmental Support:* Employees should be taught to provide non-judgmental support and avoid victim-blaming. The Australian Human Rights Commission (AHRC) emphasises the importance of an empathetic and supportive response to disclosures of abuse (AHRC, 2014).

Providing Information and Resources

1. *Resource Availability:* Employees should be informed about the resources available both within the organisation and in the community. This includes EAPs, local shelters, hotlines, and legal services.

2. *Referral Procedures:* Clear referral procedures should be established so that employees know how to connect victims with the appropriate support services. According to the DFV Prevention Centre, having a structured referral process ensures that victims receive timely and appropriate help (DVPC, 2018).

3. *Confidentiality Protocols:* Training should include information on maintaining confidentiality and understanding the legal and ethical considerations related to disclosure. The International Labour Organization (ILO) highlights the importance of confidentiality in protecting the safety and privacy of victims (ILO, 2016).

Real-World Examples

Case Study 1: Comprehensive DFV Policy Implementation at Vodafone

Sector: Telecommunications (Vodafone)

Issue: Addressing Domestic and Family Violence (DFV) to support employees

DFV Policy Implementation: Vodafone recognized the impact of DFV on employees' well-being and productivity. The company implemented a comprehensive DFV policy that included paid leave for victims, flexible working arrangements, and access to counselling and support services. The policy aimed to create a safe and supportive environment for employees experiencing DFV.

Measures Taken: Vodafone provided mandatory training for managers to recognize signs of DFV and respond with empathy and discretion. The company also partnered with local support organisations to offer additional resources and assistance to affected employees.

Outcome: The policy led to increased trust and openness within the company, allowing employees to feel more secure in seeking support. This proactive approach improved staff retention and demonstrated Vodafone's commitment to employee well-being and safety. The initiative was widely recognized and became a benchmark for other organisations looking to implement similar measures.

Reference:

- Vodafone Group – Domestic Violence and Abuse Policy. https://www.vodafone.com/news/digital-society/domestic-violence-abuse-policy

Case Study 2: Creating a Safe Support Network at NAB (National Australia Bank)

Sector: Banking and Finance (National Australia Bank)

Issue: Addressing DFV to support employees and promote workplace safety

DFV Policy Implementation: National Australia Bank (NAB) launched a comprehensive approach to supporting employees facing DFV. This included 10 days of paid leave for victims, flexible work options, and tailored financial assistance. NAB's policy aimed to reduce the stress and impact DFV had on employees' professional and personal lives.

Measures Taken: NAB incorporated DFV awareness training for staff and leaders, focusing on how to identify signs and provide support without breaching privacy. The bank also established partnerships with external DFV support organisations to provide expert assistance and counselling services to employees.

Outcome: The DFV initiatives at NAB strengthened the company's culture of care and demonstrated its commitment to employee safety and well-being. Employees reported feeling more supported and valued, which enhanced workplace morale and engagement. The policy also set an example in the financial sector, encouraging other banks to adopt similar practices.

Reference:

> NAB Corporate Social Responsibility – DFV Support. https://www.nab.com.au/about-us/social-impact/domestic-and-family-violence-support

Case Study 3: Developing DFV Awareness and Response Training at PwC Australia

Sector: Professional Services (PwC Australia)

Issue: Enhancing the workplace response to DFV and ensuring support structures are in place

DFV Policy Implementation: PwC Australia recognized the need to go beyond standard HR policies by embedding DFV support into their culture. This included developing specialised training programs for managers to identify and respond to DFV situations effectively and empathetically. The company offered paid DFV leave and confidential access to counselling and support networks.

Measures Taken: PwC rolled out a DFV training program aimed at equipping managers and HR personnel with the tools to handle disclosures of DFV sensitively and ensure that affected employees received appropriate support. The company also partnered with local DFV advocacy groups to provide ongoing education and resources.

Outcome: PwC's DFV training and support initiatives led to increased awareness and a safer work environment. Employees felt reassured that the company was committed to their safety and well-being, fostering loyalty and trust. This move also positioned PwC as a leader in corporate responsibility, influencing other organisations to prioritise DFV awareness.

Reference:

- PwC Australia – DFV Support Initiatives. https://www.pwc.com.au/about-us/social-impact/domestic-family-ly-violence.html

Key Takeaways

It is the essential role organisations play in supporting employees affected by DFV. By acknowledging the impact of DFV on employee well-being, mental health, and workplace performance, companies can implement policies, training and support systems that create a safe and supportive environment. This includes offering confidential resources, such as Employee Assistance Programs (EAPs), flexible work arrangements, and clear reporting procedures. Addressing DFV proactively not only protects vulnerable employees but also fosters a culture of empathy, reduces absenteeism, and enhances overall organisational resilience.

References:

- American Psychological Association (APA). (2019). The impact of DFV on mental health. Retrieved from https://www.apa.org/

- Australian Human Rights Commission (AHRC). (2014). Supporting employees experiencing DFV. Retrieved from https://www.humanrights.gov.au/

- Australian Institute of Health and Welfare (AIHW). (2019). Family, domestic and sexual violence in Australia. Retrieved from https://www.aihw.gov.au/

- Australian National Research Organisation for Women's Safety (ANROWS). (2016). Workplace responses to DFV: A toolkit for employers. Retrieved from https://www.anrows.org.au/

- Attridge, M. (2010). Employee Assistance Programs: Evidence and current trends. ResearchGate. Retrieved from https://www.researchgate.net/

- Boushey, H., & Glynn, S. J. (2012). There are significant business costs to replacing employees. Center for American Progress. Retrieved from https://www.american-progress.org/

- Centers for Disease Control and Prevention (CDC). (2003). Costs of intimate partner violence against women in the United States. Retrieved from https://www.cdc.gov/

- Commonwealth Bank of Australia (CBA). (2018). DFV Emergency Assistance Program. Retrieved from https://www.commbank.com.au/

- Corporate Alliance to End Partner Violence (CAEPV). (2017). Guidelines for creating effective workplace safety plans. Retrieved from https://www.caepv.org/

- Domestic Violence Prevention Centre (DVPC). (2018). Workplace strategies for responding to domestic violence. Retrieved from https://www.dvpc.org.au/

- International Labour Organization (ILO). (2016). Ending violence and harassment against women and men in the world of work. Retrieved from https://www.ilo.org/

- National Domestic Violence Hotline (NDVH). (2020). Building trust with victims of domestic violence. Retrieved from https://www.thehotline.org/

- PricewaterhouseCoopers (PwC). (2015). A high price to pay: The economic case for preventing violence against women. Retrieved from https://www.pwc.com/gx/en/psrc/publications/assets/high-price-to-pay.pdf

⊘ Reeves, C., & O'Leary-Kelly, A. (2007). The effects and costs of intimate partner violence for work organisations. *Journal of Interpersonal Violence, 22*(3), 327-344.

⊘ Society for Human Resource Management (SHRM). (2017). Workplace training on domestic violence. Retrieved from https://www.shrm.org/

⊘ U.S. Department of Labor. (2016). Domestic violence and the workplace. Retrieved from https://www.dol.gov/

⊘ Vodafone. (2019). Global policy on domestic violence and violence. Retrieved from https://www.vodafone.com/

CHAPTER 24

Mental Health and Well-Being Initiatives

Promoting Mental Health Awareness

Promoting mental health awareness within the workplace is a critical component of fostering a psychosocially safe environment. Understanding the importance of mental health and implementing strategies to support it can significantly improve overall employee well-being and productivity.

The Importance of Mental Health Awareness

Mental health issues are prevalent in the workplace, with one in five adults experiencing mental health problems each year, according to the WHO (2020). Mental health conditions, such as depression and anxiety, can have a significant impact on an individual's ability to work effectively. The WHO estimates that depression and anxiety disorders cost the global economy $1 trillion per year in lost productivity (WHO, 2017). These statistics highlight the need for employers to prioritise mental health awareness and support within their organisations.

Strategies for Promoting Mental Health Awareness

Promoting mental health awareness can be achieved through various strategies, including education, communication, and creating a supportive environment. According to the Mental Health Foundation (2021), employers should provide training to employees and managers on mental health issues, how to recognise the signs of mental health problems, and how to support colleagues who may be struggling. Additionally, organisations should promote open communication about mental health, encouraging employees to speak up and seek help when needed.

Providing Resources and Support

Providing resources and support for mental health is essential for creating a supportive and inclusive workplace. Employers must ensure that employees have access to the necessary tools and services to maintain their mental well-being.

Employee Assistance Programs (EAPs)

EAPs are a valuable resource for supporting employee mental health. EAPs offer confidential counselling and support services to employees dealing with personal or work-related issues. According to a study by the Employee Assistance Professional Association (EAPA), employees who use EAP services report improved mental health, increased productivity, and reduced absenteeism (EAPA, 2015). Employers should promote the availability of EAPs and encourage employees to take advantage of these services.

Mental Health Benefits

Providing comprehensive mental health benefits is another way to support employee well-being. This includes offering mental health coverage as part of employee health insurance plans, providing access to mental health professionals, and covering the cost of mental health services. According to the National Alliance on Mental Illness (NAMI), employees who have access to mental health benefits are more likely to seek help and receive the necessary treatment (NAMI, 2019). Employers should ensure that their health benefits include robust mental health coverage and communicate this information to employees.

Wellness Programs

Implementing wellness programs that focus on mental health can also support employee well-being. Wellness programs can include activities such as mindfulness training, stress management workshops, and mental health seminars. A study by the American Psychological Association (APA) found that employees who participate in wellness programs report higher levels of job satisfaction and overall well-being (APA, 2019). Employers should consider offering a variety of wellness programs to address different aspects of mental health.

Creating a Stigma-Free Environment

Creating a stigma-free environment is crucial for encouraging employees to seek help and support for mental health issues. Stigma surrounding mental health can prevent individuals from speaking up and accessing the resources they need.

Reducing Stigma

Reducing stigma involves challenging negative perceptions and stereotypes about mental health. According to the Mental Health Commission of Canada (MHCC), employers can reduce stigma by promoting positive messages about mental health, sharing stories of recovery, and providing education on mental health issues (MHCC, 2013). Employers should also encourage open discussions about mental health and create a culture where employees feel comfortable seeking help.

Supporting Employees

Supporting employees who disclose mental health issues is essential for creating a stigma-free environment. Employers should provide accommodations and support for employees dealing with mental health problems, such as flexible work arrangements, reduced workloads, and access to mental health resources. The Job Accommodation Network (JAN) states that providing accommodations for employees with mental health conditions can lead to increased productivity, reduced absenteeism, and improved employee retention (JAN, 2017). Employers should work with employees to identify and implement appropriate accommodations.

Leadership Commitment

Leadership commitment to mental health is crucial for creating a supportive and inclusive workplace. Leaders should model positive behaviours, promote mental health initiatives, and demonstrate a commitment to supporting employee well-being. According to a report by Business in the Community (BITC), organisations with strong leadership commitment to mental health see higher levels of employee engagement and overall well-being (BITC, 2019). Leaders should actively participate in mental health initiatives and communicate their support to employees.

Real-World Examples

Mental Health and Well-Being Initiatives
Improving Workplace Culture

Sector: Banking (Lloyds Banking Group, UK)

Issue: High stress levels and mental health challenges among employees

Mental Health and Well-Being Initiatives Implemented: In response to growing concerns about workplace stress and mental health challenges among its employees, Lloyds Banking Group launched a comprehensive mental health and well-being program in 2018. The initiative included the appointment of mental health champions across the organisation, confidential counselling services through EAPs, and the introduction of Mental Health First Aid (MHFA) training. Lloyds also launched well-being workshops and online mental health resources to help employees manage stress, build resilience, and maintain work-life balance.

Outcome: The implementation of these mental health and well-being initiatives had a transformative effect on employee well-being and workplace culture. Employee engagement surveys showed a significant increase in job satisfaction and a decrease in stress-related absenteeism. The introduction of mental health champions fostered a supportive environment where employees felt more comfortable discussing mental health issues openly. The well-being workshops also helped employees develop better coping strategies, improving productivity and reducing burnout. As a result, Lloyds Banking Group saw higher retention rates and enhanced overall morale, positioning the company as a leader in employee well-being within the banking sector.

Reference:

- ❯ Lloyds Banking Group. (2018). Mental health and well-being initiatives: Supporting employee well-being. Retrieved from https://www.lloydsbankinggroup.com

Mental Health and Well-Being Initiatives Reducing Turnover

Sector: Logistics (DHL Express)

Issue: High turnover and burnout among front-line workers

Mental Health and Well-Being Initiatives Implemented: DHL Express recognised that the fast-paced nature of the logistics industry contributed to high stress levels and burnout, particularly among front-line workers. In 2019, the company implemented a global well-being program aimed at addressing employee mental health through a combination of initiatives. These included offering mindfulness and stress management workshops, providing access to mental health counsellors through EAP, and incorporating flexible working arrangements to support work-life balance. The program also focused on raising awareness about mental health, reducing stigma, and promoting open conversations about well-being among staff.

Outcome: After the implementation of these initiatives, DHL Express saw a marked improvement in employee well-being and retention. Employee surveys indicated that workers felt more supported, with a notable decrease in burnout and stress-related illnesses. Turnover rates, which had previously been high, significantly decreased as employees found it easier to manage the pressures of the job with access to mental health resources and flexible work options. Additionally, DHL's focus on mental health awareness improved team cohesion and productivity, as employees reported feeling more engaged and valued by the organisation. This proactive approach to well-being enhanced the company's reputation as an employer of choice in the logistics industry.

Reference:

- DHL Express. (2019). Global well-being program: Supporting employee mental health. Retrieved from https://www.dhl.com

Mental Health and Well-Being Initiatives
for Healthcare Workers

Sector: Government (New South Wales Health, Australia)

Issue: High levels of stress and mental health challenges among healthcare workers

Mental Health and Well-Being Initiatives Implemented: In 2020, NSW Health introduced a targeted mental health and well-being initiative for healthcare workers who were under immense pressure, particularly during the COVID-19 pandemic. The initiative included access to 24/7 confidential mental health support through EAP, well-being coaching, resilience-building workshops, and MHFA training for supervisors and team leaders. The program also focused on creating a culture of well-being, encouraging open dialogue about mental health challenges and offering flexible working arrangements for staff where possible.

Outcome: The mental health and well-being initiative had a significant positive impact on both employee well-being and the overall workplace culture within NSW Health. Healthcare workers reported feeling more supported and were more likely to seek help when experiencing mental health challenges. Absenteeism due to stress-related illnesses decreased, and overall morale improved as employees were provided with the tools and resources to manage their mental well-being effectively. The program's success was particularly evident during the pandemic, as it helped staff remain resilient and focused, contributing to better patient care and enhanced staff retention rates. The initiative has since become a key part of NSW Health's long-term workforce strategy.

Reference:

- NSW Health. (2021). Mental health and well-being program for healthcare workers. Retrieved from https://www.health.nsw.gov.au

Key Takeaways

Implementing mental health and well-being initiatives is essential for creating a psychosocially safe workplace. By promoting mental health awareness, providing resources and support, and creating a stigma-free environment, employers can support employee well-being and improve overall productivity. Prioritising mental health in the workplace not only benefits employees but also contributes to the success and sustainability of the organisation.

References:

⬦ American Psychological Association (APA). (2019). The benefits of a wellness program. Retrieved from https://www.apa.org/helpcenter/workplace-wellness

⬦ Business in the Community (BITC). (2019). Mental health at work 2019: Time to take ownership. Retrieved from https://www.bitc.org.uk

⬦ Employee Assistance Professional Association (EAPA). (2015). The EAP and mental health: An overview. Retrieved from https://www.eapassn.org/

⬦ Job Accommodation Network (JAN). (2017). Workplace accommodations: Low cost, high impact. Retrieved from https://askjan.org/

⬦ Mental Health Commission of Canada (MHCC). (2013). Opening minds interim report. Retrieved from https://mentalhealthcommission.ca/

⬦ Mental Health Foundation. (2021). How to support mental health at work. Retrieved from https://www.mental-health.org.uk/

⬦ National Alliance on Mental Illness (NAMI). (2019). Mental Health Benefits: Cost and Coverage. Retrieved from https://www.nami.org/

- World Health Organization (WHO). (2017). Mental health in the workplace. Retrieved from https://www.who.int/mental_health/in_the_workplace/en/

- World Health Organization (WHO). (2020). Mental health and substance use. Retrieved from https://www.who.int/teams/mental-health-and-substance-use

CHAPTER 25

Handling Difficult Personalities and Toxic Behaviours

Identifying and Addressing Toxic Behaviours

Toxic behaviours in the workplace can significantly impact employee morale, productivity, and overall workplace culture. Understanding and addressing these behaviours is crucial for maintaining a healthy work environment. According to a study by Gallup (2017), about 75% of employees who leave their jobs do so because of their managers, indicating that leadership and management play a significant role in workplace toxicity.

Recognising Toxic Behaviours

Toxic behaviours can manifest in various forms, including bullying, manipulation, passive-aggressiveness, and undermining others (see Chapter 7). These behaviours create a hostile work environment and can lead to increased stress, absenteeism, and turnover. A survey conducted by the Workplace Bullying Institute (WBI) in 2021 found that 30% of workers in the U.S. have experienced bullying at work, highlighting the prevalence of this issue (WBI, 2021).

Recognising these behaviours involves paying attention to patterns of conduct that consistently harm others. Common signs of toxic behaviour include:

1. *Bullying and Harassment:* Repeated, unwanted actions intended to intimidate or harm an individual.

2. *Manipulation:* Using deceit or coercion to influence others for personal gain.

3. *Passive-Aggressiveness:* Indirect resistance and avoidance of direct communication.

4. *Undermining:* Deliberately sabotaging or diminishing the efforts of others.

It is important to remember however that many of these toxic behaviours are covert in nature and this means they often go unrecognised and undetected.

Addressing Toxic Behaviours

Addressing toxic behaviours requires a proactive approach from both management and employees. According to the SHRM, implementing a zero-tolerance policy for bullying and harassment is essential (SHRM, 2019). This policy should outline the consequences of such behaviours and provide clear procedures for reporting and addressing incidents.

Effective strategies for addressing toxic behaviours include:

1. *Establishing Clear Policies:* Develop and enforce policies that define unacceptable behaviours and outline the steps for reporting and addressing them.

2. *Training and Education:* Provide training programs that educate employees and managers on recognising and addressing toxic behaviours.

3. *Support Systems:* Create support systems, such as EAPs, that offer counselling and resources for affected employees.

4. *Mediation and Conflict Resolution:* Implement mediation and conflict resolution processes to address and resolve conflicts between employees.

Conflict Resolution and Mediation

Conflict is inevitable in any workplace, but how it is managed can significantly impact the work environment. Effective conflict resolution and mediation are crucial for maintaining a harmonious and productive workplace. According to the American Management Association (AMA), organisations that effectively manage conflict see a 28% increase in productivity (AMA, 2019).

Effective Conflict Resolution Strategies

Conflict resolution involves identifying the underlying issues, facilitating open communication, and finding mutually agreeable solutions. Key strategies for effective conflict resolution include:

1. *Active Listening:* Encourage active listening to ensure that all parties feel heard and understood.

2. *Open Communication:* Promote open and honest communication to address issues directly and constructively.

3. *Empathy and Understanding:* Foster empathy and understanding by encouraging employees to consider each other's perspectives.

4. *Problem-Solving:* Focus on finding solutions rather than assigning blame.

The Role of Mediation

Mediation is a structured process in which a neutral third party helps facilitate the resolution of conflicts. According to the Harvard Law School's Program on Negotiation, mediation is effective because it allows parties to explore solutions collaboratively and maintain control over the outcome (Harvard PON, 2020).

The benefits of mediation include:

1. *Impartiality:* A neutral mediator can provide an unbiased perspective and help facilitate fair resolutions.

2. *Confidentiality:* Mediation is typically a confidential process, which can encourage open and honest communication.

3. *Collaboration:* Mediation encourages collaborative problem-solving and helps preserve working relationships.

4. *Efficiency:* Mediation can often resolve conflicts more quickly than formal grievance procedures or litigation.

Fostering Respect and Inclusivity

Creating a respectful and inclusive workplace culture is essential for preventing and addressing toxic behaviours. According to a report by McKinsey & Company (2020), organisations with diverse, equitable and inclusive cultures are 35% more likely to outperform their competitors.

Promoting Respect

Promoting respect involves fostering an environment where all employees feel valued and respected. Key strategies for promoting respect include:

1. *Setting Expectations:* Clearly communicate expectations for respectful behaviour and hold employees accountable.

2. *Leading by Example:* Encourage leaders and managers to model respectful behaviour.

3. *Recognition and Appreciation:* Regularly recognise and appreciate employees' contributions and efforts.

Encouraging Inclusivity

Encouraging inclusivity involves creating an environment where all employees feel included and valued, regardless of their background or identity. According to a study by Deloitte (2018), inclusive workplaces are more likely to attract and retain top talent.

Key strategies for encouraging inclusivity include:

1. *Diversity Training:* Provide diversity training to educate employees about the importance of inclusivity and how to foster an inclusive environment.

2. *Inclusive Policies:* Develop and enforce policies that promote inclusivity and prevent discrimination.

3. *Employee Resource Groups:* Support the formation of employee resource groups (ERGs) that provide a platform for underrepresented groups to connect and support each other.

4. *Inclusive Leadership:* Encourage leaders to adopt inclusive leadership practices, such as soliciting diverse perspectives and creating opportunities for all employees.

Real-World Examples

Mishandling Toxic Behaviour Leading to Bankruptcy

Sector: Entertainment (Weinstein Company)

Issue: Failure to address toxic behaviour and harassment within the company

Financial Cost: The Weinstein Company faced severe financial consequences due to its mishandling of the toxic behaviour and abusive conduct of its co-founder, Harvey Weinstein. Allegations of sexual harassment and misconduct, which had been ongoing for years, were largely ignored by the company's leadership, leading to a toxic work environment. As the #MeToo movement gained momentum and Weinstein's actions became public, the company faced multiple lawsuits, reputational damage, and the loss of business partnerships. Major actors, directors, and studios severed ties with the Weinstein Company, leading to a sharp decline in revenue and market share.

Outcome: The fallout from Weinstein's actions and the company's failure to act resulted in its bankruptcy in 2018. The company was forced to sell its assets at a loss, and it faced over **$47 million** in financial liabilities related to lawsuits and settlements. The cost of ignoring toxic behaviour at the leadership level ultimately led to the company's collapse.

Reference:

- BBC News. (2018). *Weinstein Company files for bankruptcy following harassment scandal.* Retrieved from https://www.bbc.com

Financial Fallout Due to Toxic Workplace Culture

Sector: Ride-Sharing (Uber)

Issue: Failure to address toxic behaviours, bullying, and harassment

Financial Cost: In 2017, Uber was rocked by a series of scandals involving toxic workplace behaviours, including harassment, bullying, and discrimination, particularly against women and minorities. Reports surfaced of rampant inappropriate behaviour from managers, and employees felt unsafe reporting these issues due to fear of retaliation. The company's leadership failed to take swift action, which resulted in public backlash, multiple lawsuits, and a #DeleteUber campaign that significantly damaged its brand reputation.

Outcome: Uber's mishandling of toxic behaviours led to the resignation of its CEO, the firing of over 20 employees, and a series of costly legal settlements. The company had to invest millions in overhauling its workplace culture and implementing new policies to prevent harassment and discrimination. In addition to legal costs, Uber's valuation dropped by billions during the crisis, delaying its IPO and causing long-term financial harm.

Reference:

⊙ The New York Times. (2017). *Uber fires 20 employees after sexual harassment investigation*. Retrieved from https://www.nytimes.com

Financial Losses from Mishandling Workplace Harassment

Sector: Media (Fox News)

Issue: Toxic behaviour, including sexual harassment, ignored by leadership

Financial Cost: Fox News faced a major financial and reputational crisis after failing to address persistent allegations of sexual harassment by senior executives, including former CEO Roger Ailes and anchor Bill O'Reilly. Both men were accused of creating a toxic work environment for female employees. Leadership at Fox News initially ignored or downplayed the allegations, leading to widespread criticism of the company's handling of workplace misconduct. As more women came forward with accusations, the company faced lawsuits, settlements, and loss of major advertisers.

Outcome: Fox News had to pay millions in settlements, including **$45 million** to settle claims related to harassment. Bill O'Reilly's ousting alone led to an advertiser boycott, costing the company millions in lost revenue. Additionally, the damage to Fox News' brand and reputation resulted in leadership changes and ongoing legal expenses. The mishandling of toxic behaviours caused long-lasting financial repercussions for the network.

Reference:

CNN Business. (2017). *Fox News' $45 million in harassment settlements revealed*. Retrieved from https://www.cnn.com

Key Takeaways

Handling difficult personalities and toxic behaviours is crucial for maintaining a healthy and productive work environment. By recognising and addressing toxic behaviours, implementing effective conflict resolution and mediation strategies, and fostering respect and inclusivity, organisations can create a workplace where all employees feel valued and supported. Promoting a positive workplace culture not only benefits employees but also contributes to the overall success and sustainability of the organisation.

References:

- American Management Association (AMA). (2019). The benefits of effective conflict management. Retrieved from https://www.amanet.org/

- Deloitte. (2018). The inclusion imperative: How organisations can drive business success by fostering an inclusive culture. Retrieved from https://www.deloitte.com/au/en.html

- Gallup. (2017). State of the American manager: Analytics and advice for leaders. Retrieved from https://www.gallup.com/

- Harvard Law School Program on Negotiation (PON). (2020). The benefits of mediation in conflict resolution. Retrieved from https://www.pon.harvard.edu/

- McKinsey & Company. (2020). Diversity wins: How inclusion matters. Retrieved from https://www.mckinsey.com/

- Society for Human Resource Management (SHRM). (2019). Bullying and harassment in the workplace: What HR needs to know. Retrieved from https://www.shrm.org/

- Workplace Bullying Institute (WBI). (2021). 2021 WBI U.S. workplace bullying survey. Retrieved from https://workplacebullying.org/

CHAPTER 26

Upward Bullying in the Workplace

Bullying is often viewed as a top-down issue, with managers or supervisors exerting inappropriate control or power over their subordinates. However, an equally damaging yet less discussed form of bullying is upward bullying, where subordinates bully those in positions of authority, such as managers, team leaders, or supervisors. Upward bullying can disrupt workplace harmony, lower productivity, and significantly impact the psychosocial safety of both leaders and employees. It can undermine leadership and organisational culture and, if left unchecked, cause long-term damage to the organisation's structure and reputation.

This chapter will explore the dynamics of upward bullying, the various forms it can take, its impact on the workplace, and how organisations can identify and mitigate this destructive behaviour.

What is Upward Bullying?

Upward bullying occurs when an employee or a group of employees targets a supervisor or manager with inappropriate, aggressive, or coercive behaviour. It can manifest in various ways, including insubordination, undermining authority, and more subtle actions, such as gossip or sabotage. The key characteristic of upward bullying is the use of coercive tactics to destabilise or harm those in leadership positions.

Unlike traditional forms of workplace bullying, upward bullying is often more difficult to detect because it subverts the traditional power dynamics. A subordinate might engage in behaviours that are disguised as mere disagreements or conflicts, making it difficult for managers to recognise the behaviour as bullying without fearing accusations of retaliation.

According to the Workplace Bullying Institute (WBI, 2021), bullying is typically defined as a pattern of abusive behaviour that humiliates or intimidates the target. In upward bullying, the roles are reversed, but the impact is just as harmful—if not more so, given that leaders are often less equipped or supported to handle such harassment from subordinates.

Forms of Upward Bullying

Upward bullying can take many forms, ranging from overt aggression to more subtle psychological tactics. Some common behaviours include:

- ❯ *Insubordination and Defiance:* Refusing to follow instructions or deliberately ignoring directives from supervisors, creating chaos and undermining leadership.

- ❯ *Gossip and Character Assassination:* Spreading malicious rumours about the leader to undermine their reputation or credibility among peers or senior management.

- ❯ *Sabotage:* Deliberately performing poorly on tasks or failing to meet deadlines to make the leader appear incompetent or unfit for their role.

- ❯ *Undermining:* Consistently questioning the manager's decisions, withholding important information, or challenging their authority in front of others.

- *Passive-Aggression:* Using non-verbal cues, such as eye-rolling or body language, to disrespect the leader in meetings or team interactions.

- **Exclusion**: Intentionally leaving the leader out from important discussions or events, isolating them and creating a toxic environment.

These behaviours create an environment where leaders feel isolated, disrespected, and ineffective, which can severely damage their confidence and decision-making abilities. In extreme cases, upward bullying may lead to managerial burnout, resignation, or even legal action.

Why Does Upward Bullying Occur?

The causes of upward bullying are multifaceted and can stem from various workplace dynamics. In many cases, it is a reaction to power struggles, perceived unfairness, or frustration within the team. Some potential factors contributing to upward bullying include:

- *Resentment of Authority:* Employees who feel overlooked for promotions or opportunities may take out their frustration on their supervisors.

- *Cultural Dynamics:* In organisations with poor communication or unclear hierarchies, employees may feel emboldened to challenge leadership, especially when there is a lack of support for managers.

- *Leadership Style:* Managers with a more collaborative or lenient style may inadvertently create an environment where boundaries are blurred, making it easier for subordinates to take advantage of the situation.

- *Perceived Incompetence:* When employees perceive that their leader lacks the necessary skills or expertise to manage the team, they may engage in behaviour designed to expose these perceived weaknesses.

According to research conducted by Branch, Ramsay, and Barker (2013), the rise of more participative management styles and flatter organisational structures has provided more room for upward bullying, as employees often feel they are on equal footing with their supervisors. This shift in traditional power dynamics can make it more difficult for managers to assert their authority without encountering resistance or sabotage.

Impact on the Workplace

The impact of upward bullying is not limited to the individuals involved; it can permeate throughout the organisation and create a toxic work environment. Some of the most significant consequences include:

- *Loss of Managerial Confidence:* Being the target of bullying can significantly erode a manager's confidence in their leadership abilities, leading to poor decision-making and increased stress.

- *Decreased Productivity:* The energy spent managing the bullying behaviour, along with the emotional toll it takes on the leader, can result in decreased productivity and inefficiencies.

- *High Staff Turnover:* Leaders who are bullied may leave the organisation due to the stress and strain, causing high turnover rates that can be costly for the company.

- *Team Fragmentation:* Upward bullying often divides teams, with some employees aligning with the bullies and others siding with the manager. This fragmentation can hinder collaboration and negatively impact morale.

- ⊙ *Reputation Damage:* When upward bullying is left unchecked, it can harm the reputation of the company, making it a less attractive place to work for future talent.

Additionally, upward bullying has a direct impact on the psychosocial safety of the workplace. Psychosocial hazards are those that relate to how work is organised, the relationships among employees, and the work environment itself. The presence of bullying—whether upward, lateral, or downward—creates a psychologically unsafe environment, increasing the risk of stress, absenteeism, and mental health issues among both leaders and their teams.

Addressing and Preventing Upward Bullying

Preventing and addressing upward bullying requires both proactive measures and reactive strategies. Leadership buy-in, clear policies, and an organisational culture that fosters respect and accountability are essential. Here are some steps organisations can take:

- ⊙ *Leadership Training:* Equip managers with the tools and training needed to recognise and address upward bullying, as well as strategies for asserting their authority in a healthy and productive manner.

- ⊙ *Clear Policies:* Ensure that anti-bullying policies explicitly mention upward bullying and provide clear steps for addressing and reporting such behaviour. All employees, regardless of their position, should be held accountable for their actions.

- *Open Communication:* Foster an open and transparent culture where both leaders and employees can voice concerns without fear of retaliation. Encouraging feedback from all levels of the organisation can prevent resentment from festering.

- *Mediation and Conflict Resolution:* Implement conflict resolution strategies, such as mediation, to address tensions between leaders and their teams before they escalate into bullying behaviour. Third-party mediators can help facilitate discussions and foster understanding.

- *Employee Assistance Programs (EAPs):* Promote the use of EAPs for both leaders and employees as a resource for coping with stress, resolving conflict, and addressing bullying issues in a confidential and supportive manner.

Organisations that address upward bullying are not only protecting their leadership but also preserving the overall health of the workplace. As bullying in any form is a psychosocial hazard, leaders and HR professionals must take action to mitigate its harmful effects. By promoting a culture of respect and support, companies can ensure that all employees, including managers, feel valued and safe.

Upward bullying is a serious yet under-recognised issue in many workplaces. It has far-reaching consequences that go beyond the individual manager or team leader being targeted. By understanding the dynamics of upward bullying and implementing strategies to address it, organisations can create healthier, more productive environments where both leaders and employees can thrive.

In the broader context of psychosocial safety, upward bullying is one of many hazards that needs to be addressed to ensure the well-being of all employees. A proactive approach to identifying and mitigating upward bullying can contribute to a more harmonious and resilient workplace.

Real-World Examples

Upward Bullying in Healthcare Management

Sector: Healthcare (UK National Health Service - NHS)

Issue: Upward bullying by staff toward senior management

Negative Impact: Within the NHS, reports surfaced that senior doctors and consultants were subject to upward bullying by junior staff and other colleagues. Senior managers experienced intimidation, undermining, and passive-aggressive behaviour from staff, particularly during periods of organisational change or restructuring. The bullying took the form of excessive complaints, refusal to cooperate with new policies, and deliberately sabotaging management initiatives. This led to a breakdown in leadership confidence and morale, as senior staff felt pressured to appease those engaging in bullying behaviour, which in turn, stalled important reforms and affected patient care.

Outcome: The impact of upward bullying was severe, resulting in delays to key organisational changes, strained working relationships, and a toxic atmosphere within some NHS departments. It also led to increased absenteeism and turnover among senior management, as individuals chose to leave rather than continue working in an environment where they felt disrespected and undermined. In some cases, upward bullying led to legal disputes, further damaging the NHS's reputation and costing the organisation significant financial resources in litigation and staff replacement.

Reference:

⊙ National Health Service (NHS) England. (2015). *The health and well-being of NHS Staff: Bullying in the workplace*. Retrieved from https://www.england.nhs.uk

Upward Bullying in Corporate Finance

Sector: Banking and Finance (Deutsche Bank)

Issue: Upward bullying by mid-level employees towards senior managers

Negative Impact: In the aftermath of the 2008 financial crisis, Deutsche Bank experienced significant internal pressure as it tried to rebuild its reputation and implement structural reforms. During this period, senior managers found themselves targets of upward bullying by mid-level executives and traders who resisted changes to compensation structures, transparency initiatives, and risk management practices. Mid-level employees used collective pressure, passive resistance, and even attempts to publicly discredit senior managers to maintain the status quo. The senior leadership faced intimidation and pushback whenever they attempted to implement reforms that were unpopular with influential internal factions.

Outcome: The internal conflict caused by upward bullying delayed much-needed reforms at Deutsche Bank and contributed to an extended period of instability. The bank faced financial losses due to delays in implementing risk management practices and was also subject to regulatory fines for failing to act swiftly enough. Leadership changes became frequent, as many senior managers resigned or were replaced, further disrupting organisational cohesion. Upward bullying also harmed Deutsche Bank's reputation, as reports of internal conflicts and dysfunction became public.

Reference:

- Reuters. (2016). *Deutsche Bank faces internal resistance to post-crisis reforms*. Retrieved from https://www.reuters.com

Upward Bullying in Government Departments

Sector: Government (Australian Public Service - APS)

Issue: Upward bullying from junior staff towards senior public servants

Negative Impact: In several APS departments, upward bullying emerged as a significant issue, particularly during times of departmental restructuring and policy changes. Senior managers reported being bullied by their subordinates, who would undermine their authority by spreading rumours, openly challenging decisions in meetings, and using formal complaint processes as a means of exerting pressure. In one high-profile case within the Department of Human Services, senior public servants found it difficult to implement necessary policy changes due to constant resistance and sabotage from their teams, leading to a toxic and unproductive work environment.

Outcome: Upward bullying in the APS contributed to a toxic work culture where senior leaders felt isolated and unsupported. It led to decreased morale among senior staff, higher turnover rates, and an inability to effectively manage policy implementation. In several instances, public service departments faced delays in delivering key services to the public due to internal conflicts, resulting in poor public perception and scrutiny from government oversight bodies. The long-term impact was not only organisational dysfunction but also financial losses from high turnover, legal battles, and delays in service delivery.

Reference:

⊘ Australian Public Service Commission. (2018). *Managing bullying in the public service: A guide to workplace culture*. Retrieved from https://www.apsc.gov.au

Upward Bullying in Healthcare Management

Sector: Healthcare (UK National Health Service - NHS)

Issue: Upward bullying by staff toward senior management

Negative Impact: Within the NHS, reports surfaced that senior doctors and consultants were subject to upward bullying by junior staff and other colleagues. Senior managers experienced intimidation, undermining, and passive-aggressive behaviour from staff, particularly during periods of organisational change or restructuring. The bullying took the form of excessive complaints, refusal to cooperate with new policies, and deliberately sabotaging management initiatives. This led to a breakdown in leadership confidence and morale, as senior staff felt pressured to appease those engaging in bullying behaviour, which in turn, stalled important reforms and affected patient care.

Outcome: The impact of upward bullying was severe, resulting in delays to key organisational changes, strained working relationships, and a toxic atmosphere within some NHS departments. It also led to increased absenteeism and turnover among senior management, as individuals chose to leave rather than continue working in an environment where they felt disrespected and undermined. In some cases, upward bullying led to legal disputes, further damaging the NHS's reputation and costing the organisation significant financial resources in litigation and staff replacement.

Reference:

- National Health Service (NHS) England. (2015). The health and well-being of NHS Staff: Bullying in the workplace. Retrieved from https://www.england.nhs.uk

Upward Bullying in Corporate Finance

Sector: Banking and Finance (Deutsche Bank)

Issue: Upward bullying by mid-level employees towards senior managers

Negative Impact: In the aftermath of the 2008 financial crisis, Deutsche Bank experienced significant internal pressure as it tried to rebuild its reputation and implement structural reforms. During this period, senior managers found themselves targets of upward bullying by mid-level executives and traders who resisted changes to compensation structures, transparency initiatives, and risk management practices. Mid-level employees used collective pressure, passive resistance, and even attempts to publicly discredit senior managers to maintain the status quo. The senior leadership faced intimidation and pushback whenever they attempted to implement reforms that were unpopular with influential internal factions.

Outcome: The internal conflict caused by upward bullying delayed much-needed reforms at Deutsche Bank and contributed to an extended period of instability. The bank faced financial losses due to delays in implementing risk management practices and was also subject to regulatory fines for failing to act swiftly enough. Leadership changes became frequent, as many senior managers resigned or were replaced, further disrupting organisational cohesion. Upward bullying also harmed Deutsche Bank's reputation, as reports of internal conflicts and dysfunction became public.

Reference:

- Reuters. (2016). *Deutsche Bank faces internal resistance to post-crisis reforms*. Retrieved from https://www.reuters.com

Upward Bullying in Government Departments

Sector: Government (Australian Public Service - APS)

Issue: Upward bullying from junior staff towards senior public servants

Negative Impact: In several APS departments, upward bullying emerged as a significant issue, particularly during times of departmental restructuring and policy changes. Senior managers reported being bullied by their subordinates, who would undermine their authority by spreading rumours, openly challenging decisions in meetings, and using formal complaint processes as a means of exerting pressure. In one high-profile case within the Department of Human Services, senior public servants found it difficult to implement necessary policy changes due to constant resistance and sabotage from their teams, leading to a toxic and unproductive work environment.

Outcome: Upward bullying in the APS contributed to a toxic work culture where senior leaders felt isolated and unsupported. It led to decreased morale among senior staff, higher turnover rates, and an inability to effectively manage policy implementation. In several instances, public service departments faced delays in delivering key services to the public due to internal conflicts, resulting in poor public perception and scrutiny from government oversight bodies. The long-term impact was not only organisational dysfunction but also financial losses from high turnover, legal battles, and delays in service delivery.

Reference:

- Australian Public Service Commission. (2018). Managing bullying in the public service: A guide to workplace culture. Retrieved from https://www.apsc.gov.au

Key Takeaways

Upward bullying creates a hostile environment where managers may struggle to assert authority or make critical decisions, leading to decreased morale, poor team cohesion, and reduced productivity. This form of bullying can also foster a toxic culture of disrespect and undermine leadership credibility. If managers are forced out of their roles due to such bullying, it creates an environment of fear, making it nearly impossible for anyone stepping into that position to manage effectively, as they inherit an atmosphere of distrust and instability. Addressing upward bullying requires clear policies, leadership training, and an organisational commitment to maintaining respect and accountability at all levels.

References and Resources:

- Kyne emphasises that upward bullying is often not conducted by a single individual but rather through a group or "mob" that may not even realise they are being manipulated. This collective approach can make it particularly challenging for managers to address https://www.hrmonline.com.au/harassment/spot-an-upward-bully/

- Branch, S., Ramsay, S., & Barker, M. (2013). Workplace bullying, mobbing, and general harassment: A review. *Journal of Management & Organisation*, *19*(5), 541-561.

Lisa McAdams | 355

Workplace Bullying Institute (WBI). (2021). What is workplace bullying? Retrieved from https://www.workplace-bullying.org/individuals/problem/definition/

PART 10

Financial Analysis and Future Direction

Proactive vs. Reactive Approaches to Psychosocial Safety—A Financial Analysis

In today's corporate landscape, the emphasis on psychosocial safety is paramount. Ensuring a safe, supportive, and inclusive work environment is not just a moral imperative but also a financial one. Organisations face a crucial decision: invest proactively in psychosocial safety or continue reacting to issues as they arise. This chapter delves into the financial implications of both approaches, highlighting the cost-effectiveness of proactive strategies and the potential financial pitfalls of a reactive stance.

The Cost of Proactive Investment in Psychosocial Safety

Proactive investment in psychosocial safety involves implementing comprehensive programs and policies designed to prevent psychosocial risks, support employee well-being, and foster a positive workplace culture. While there are upfront costs associated with these initiatives, the long-term financial benefits significantly outweigh these initial expenses.

1. **Initial Investment Costs**

    ▸ **Training Programs**: Developing and conducting training sessions for employees, managers, and leaders on psychosocial safety, mental health awareness, and handling difficult personalities can cost between $200 and $1,000 per employee per year (not accounting for inflation), depending on the program's depth and complexity (SHRM, 2020).

- **Policy Development**: Crafting and implementing comprehensive psychosocial safety policies might require consultation fees ranging from $5,000 to $50,000, depending on the organisation's size and complexity (Deloitte, 2018).

- **Support Systems**: Establishing support systems such as Employee Assistance Programs (EAPs), peer support networks, and mental health resources can cost approximately $20 to $60 per employee per month (EAPA, 2021).

2. **Ongoing Maintenance Costs**

- **Continuous Training**: Providing ongoing training and development to keep employees informed about best practices and emerging trends in psychosocial safety.

- **Program Evaluation**: Regularly assessing the effectiveness of psychosocial safety programs and making necessary adjustments. This might involve additional consultation fees or the allocation of internal resources.

- **Employee Support Services**: Maintaining support services like EAPs and mental health resources.

3. **Long-Term Financial Benefits**

- **Reduced Absenteeism and Turnover**: Organisations with robust psychosocial safety programs report a 25% reduction in absenteeism and a 40% reduction in employee turnover (Gallup, 2017). The costs associated with recruiting, hiring, and training new employees are significantly lower in such organisations.

▸ **Increased Productivity**: Employees who feel safe and supported are more engaged and productive. Studies show a 20% increase in productivity in workplaces with strong psychosocial safety measures (Deloitte, 2019).

▸ **Lower Healthcare Costs**: Proactively addressing mental health and psychosocial risks can lead to a 15% reduction in healthcare costs due to fewer stress-related illnesses and injuries (WHO, 2019).

The Cost of Delaying Action and Being Reactive

In contrast, a reactive approach to psychosocial safety involves addressing issues only as they arise, often resulting in higher long-term costs and more severe organisational impacts.

1. **Crisis Management Costs**

   ▸ **Legal Fees**: Reacting to incidents of workplace harassment, bullying, or mental health crises often involves significant legal expenses. Lawsuits related to workplace misconduct can cost organisations anywhere from $100,000 to several million dollars in settlements and legal fees (Equal Employment Opportunity Commission, 2020).

   ▸ **Damage Control**: Managing public relations crises and reputational damage following incidents of workplace misconduct requires substantial financial resources. This can include hiring PR firms, running damage control campaigns, and offering compensation to affected employees.

2. **Higher Turnover and Absenteeism**

   ▸ **Increased Recruitment Costs**: High turnover rates necessitate constant recruitment efforts. The cost of replacing an employee is estimated to be 20% of their annual salary for mid-range positions and up to 213% for highly specialised roles (SHRM, 2021).

   ▸ **Lost Productivity:** Frequent absenteeism and high turnover disrupt workflow, leading to decreased productivity. Studies show that organisations with poor psychosocial safety experience up to a 30% reduction in productivity (Harvard Business Review, 2018).

3. **Employee Health and Well-Being**

   ▸ **Higher Healthcare Costs**: Reacting to psychosocial issues rather than preventing them leads to higher healthcare costs due to stress-related illnesses, mental health issues, and workplace injuries. Organisations with inadequate psychosocial safety measures report 50% higher healthcare costs (APA, 2019).

   ▸ **Increased Workers' Compensation Claims**: Stress-related workers' compensation claims can be costly, averaging $70,000 per claim. Organisations with poor psychosocial safety measures see a higher incidence of such claims (NIOSH, 2020).

4. **Impact on Organisational Culture**

   ▸ **Decreased Employee Morale**: A reactive approach can erode employee morale, leading to disengagement, dissatisfaction, and a toxic workplace culture. This can have long-lasting effects on employee loyalty and overall workplace harmony.

> ▸ **Reputation and Brand Damage**: Incidents of workplace misconduct and poor psychosocial safety can severely damage an organisation's reputation. This can affect customer trust, investor confidence, and the ability to attract top talent.

Real-World Examples and Research Findings

To illustrate the financial impact of proactive versus reactive approaches, let's examine a few real-world examples and research findings.

Johnson & Johnson

Johnson & Johnson has been a leader in promoting employee well-being and psychosocial safety. Their comprehensive health and wellness programs, including mental health support and stress management, have resulted in a 15% reduction in healthcare costs and a 20% increase in employee productivity over five years (Harvard Business Review, 2018).

Google

Google's emphasis on creating a supportive and inclusive workplace culture has led to high employee engagement and low turnover rates. Their proactive investment in employee well-being programs, including psychosocial safety initiatives, has contributed to a 37% increase in employee satisfaction and a significant reduction in absenteeism (Deloitte, 2019).

World Health Organization (WHO)

According to the WHO, for every $1 invested in scaling up treatment for common mental health disorders, there is a return of

$4 in improved health and productivity. This highlights the financial benefits of proactive investment in mental health and psychosocial safety (WHO, 2019).

The Long-Term Return on Investment: Proactive Measures Pay Off

Taking a proactive stance on psychosocial safety isn't just about mitigating risks—it's a strategic investment that delivers substantial returns over time. Companies that prioritise proactive measures in their psychosocial safety strategies often see a significant boost in both employee well-being and overall organisational performance.

Enhanced Employee Engagement and Productivity

When employees feel safe, supported, and valued, their engagement levels soar. This increase in engagement translates into higher productivity, better job performance, and a more innovative workforce. By fostering a psychosocially safe environment, organisations can harness the full potential of their employees, driving growth and competitive advantage.

Reduced Costs Associated with Turnover

High turnover rates are a common consequence of poor workplace culture and inadequate psychosocial safety measures. The cost of replacing employees, which includes recruitment, onboarding, and training, can be staggering. Proactively addressing psychosocial hazards can significantly reduce turnover, saving the organisation both time and money.

Attracting Top Talent

A strong commitment to psychosocial safety is a powerful draw for top talent. In today's competitive job market, candidates are increasingly seeking employers who prioritise mental health, well-being, and a positive work culture. By investing in proactive psychosocial safety measures, your organisation becomes a more attractive destination for high-performing professionals.

Minimised Legal Risks and Associated Costs

Proactively implementing comprehensive psychosocial safety programs can help organisations avoid costly legal battles and settlements. By addressing issues before they escalate, companies can protect themselves from potential lawsuits related to workplace bullying, harassment, or mental health concerns.

The Hidden Costs of Reactive Measures: Too Little, Too Late

While it may seem easier or more cost-effective to take a reactive approach to psychosocial safety, the reality is that waiting until issues arise often leads to far greater expenses—both financially and in terms of organisational culture.

Damage to Company Reputation

Reacting to crises rather than preventing them can severely damage a company's reputation. News of workplace issues such as harassment or mental health crises can quickly spread, leading to public backlash and a loss of customer trust. Rebuilding a damaged reputation can be costly and time-consuming, with no guarantee of full recovery.

Increased Employee Turnover and Lost Productivity

When organisations only address psychosocial safety issues after they have occurred, the damage to employee morale can be irreversible. Disengaged employees are more likely to leave, and those who remain may struggle with decreased productivity. The long-term impact on team dynamics and overall performance can be profound.

Escalating Legal and Compliance Costs

Reacting to psychosocial safety issues after they arise often involves navigating complex legal challenges. The costs associated with defending against lawsuits, settling claims, and paying fines can quickly add up, draining resources that could have been better spent on proactive measures.

The Psychological Toll on Employees

Waiting to address psychosocial safety concerns can have severe psychological impacts on employees. This can lead to an increase in absenteeism, presenteeism, and long-term health issues. The emotional and mental toll on employees not only affects their personal lives but also diminishes their ability to contribute effectively to the organisation.

Real-World Examples

Cost Savings from Implementing Psychosocial Safety Measures

Sector: Government (Australian Public Service - APS)

Cost Analysis: The APS launched an initiative in 2018 to improve psychosocial safety within its departments, focusing on mental health support, workplace bullying prevention, and training programs to build a healthier organisational culture. Prior to the initiative, the APS was losing approximately **AUD $10 million** annually due to absenteeism, presenteeism, and high turnover rates caused by workplace stress and bullying.

After implementing comprehensive psychosocial safety measures, including EAPs, mandatory mental health training, and a formal process for addressing workplace bullying, the APS saw a significant reduction in absenteeism by 25% within the first year. This translated into cost savings of nearly **AUD $3.5 million annually**. Turnover also decreased by 15%, reducing recruitment and training costs by an additional **AUD $2 million**. In total, the APS saved over AUD 5.5 million annually by investing in psychosocial safety, proving that a proactive approach to employee well-being has long-term cost-saving benefits.

Reference:

- Australian Public Service Commission. (2019). *Psychosocial Safety in the Workplace: A Government Strategy*. Retrieved from https://www.apsc.gov.au

Financial Benefits of Mental Health and Well-Being Initiatives

Sector: Retail (Marks & Spencer)

Cost Analysis: Marks & Spencer, a leading British retailer, implemented a company-wide mental health and well-being initiative in 2017 after internal data revealed that workplace stress and burnout were costing the company over **£20 million annually** in lost productivity and increased absenteeism. As part of their initiative, Marks & Spencer introduced mental health training for managers, rolled out EAPs, and launched wellness programs to help employees manage stress.

Within two years of launching these programs, Marks & Spencer saw a 30% reduction in absenteeism, resulting in savings of approximately **£6 million per year**. Presenteeism (where employees come to work but are not fully productive) also decreased by 15%, leading to an additional **productivity boost valued at £3 million**. Moreover, the initiative improved employee retention, **reducing recruitment and training costs by £2 million annually**. Overall, Marks & Spencer experienced annual **savings of nearly £11 million**, demonstrating that investing in psychosocial safety was a cost-effective strategy.

Reference:

- Marks & Spencer. (2018). *Employee well-being and mental health report*. Retrieved from https://www.marksandspencer.com

*Financial Impact of Psychosocial Safety
Measures on Operations*

Sector: Aviation (Heathrow Airport, UK)

Cost Analysis: Heathrow Airport experienced operational challenges related to high stress levels and workplace bullying, especially among frontline staff such as security and baggage handling teams. Prior to implementing psychosocial safety measures, absenteeism was **costing Heathrow approximately £5 million annually**, and turnover among these key positions was high, leading to increased recruitment and training costs.

In 2019, Heathrow introduced a comprehensive psychosocial safety program that included mental health training, stress management workshops, and a zero-tolerance policy on workplace bullying. Within 18 months, absenteeism had decreased by 20%, saving the airport £1 million annually. Turnover rates among frontline staff dropped by 12%, leading to recruitment and training **cost savings of £800,000 per year.** Additionally, overall productivity and employee morale improved, which had an indirect positive impact on customer service ratings and operational efficiency. Heathrow estimated that the psychosocial safety measures saved the company a total of **£1.8 million annually,** far exceeding the initial investment in the well-being programs.

Reference:

- Heathrow Airport. (2020). *Heathrow workplace well-being and psychosocial safety initiative report*. Retrieved from https://www.heathrow.com

Key Takeaways

In today's fast-paced and increasingly complex workplace environment, the importance of proactive psychosocial safety measures cannot be overstated. The cost of inaction or delayed action can be far greater than the upfront investment required to create and maintain a safe, supportive, and positive work environment.

Proactive approaches to psychosocial safety are not just a cost—they are an investment in your organisation's future. By prioritising employee well-being, companies can build a resilient workforce, reduce turnover, enhance productivity, and ultimately, secure their long-term success.

The choice is clear: Act now to protect your employees and your business, or risk the far-reaching consequences of reactive, crisis-driven measures. Your organisation will end up paying twice: first, to address the consequences of reactive measures, and then again to implement proactive strategies to prevent further issues.

The financial analysis clearly demonstrates that a proactive approach to psychosocial safety in the workplace is not only beneficial for employee well-being but also for an organisation's bottom line. Investing in comprehensive training programs, supportive policies, and robust support systems can lead to significant cost savings in the long run, including reduced turnover and absenteeism, lower healthcare costs, and increased productivity.

Conversely, a reactive approach, while seemingly less costly initially, often results in higher long-term expenses due to crisis management, legal fees, high turnover, and healthcare costs. The damage to organisational culture and reputation can also have far-reaching financial implications.

By prioritising psychosocial safety, organisations can create a healthier, more productive, and more supportive work environment, ultimately leading to greater financial stability and success.

References:

- American Psychological Association (APA). (2019). Workplace stress and health. Retrieved from https://www.apa.org/

- Deloitte. (2018). The ROI of mental health programs: Good for people, good for business. Retrieved from https://www.deloitte.com/au/en.html

- Deloitte. (2019). The impact of mental health on workplaces. Retrieved from https://www.deloitte.com/au/en.html

- Equal Employment Opportunity Commission. (2020). Workplace harassment statistics. Retrieved from https://www.eeoc.gov/

- Gallup. (2017). State of the American workplace. Retrieved from https://www.gallup.com/home.aspx

- Harvard Business Review. (2018). The financial benefits of employee well-being. Retrieved from https://hbr.org/

- National Institute for Occupational Safety and Health (NIOSH). (2020). Stress at work. Retrieved from https://www.cdc.gov/niosh/index.html

- Society for Human Resource Management (SHRM). (2020). Cost of training and development. Retrieved from https://www.shrm.org/

◉ Society for Human Resource Management (SHRM). (2021). Employee turnover and retention. Retrieved from https://www.shrm.org/

◉ World Health Organization (WHO). (2019). Investing in mental health: Evidence for action. Retrieved from https://www.who.int/

CHAPTER 28

The Future of Psychosocial Safety in Workplaces

As we look ahead to the future of workplaces, psychosocial safety emerges as a crucial factor in shaping productive, inclusive, and resilient organisations. The importance of fostering an environment where employees feel psychologically and socially safe cannot be overstated. Looking at the evolving landscape of psychosocial safety, highlighting emerging trends, innovative practices, and the imperative for organisations to commit to long-term strategies that prioritise the well-being of their workforce. By understanding the future directions of psychosocial safety, organisations can better prepare to create environments that not only support their employees but also drive organisational success.

The Evolving Landscape of Psychosocial Safety

The concept of psychosocial safety is continually evolving, driven by changes in societal attitudes, workplace dynamics, and regulatory frameworks. Understanding these changes is essential for organisations aiming to stay ahead of the curve.

1. **Increased Awareness and Advocacy**

    ▸   Over the past decade, there has been a significant increase in awareness around mental health and psychosocial safety in the workplace. Advocacy from mental health organisations, employee groups, and government bodies has brought these issues to the forefront, leading to a greater emphasis on creating safe and supportive work environments.

2. **Regulatory Developments**

   ▸ Governments and regulatory bodies are increasingly recognising the importance of psychosocial safety. For instance, in Australia, the *Work Health and Safety (WHS) Act* emphasises the need for employers to manage psychosocial risks alongside physical risks. This trend is expected to continue globally, with more stringent regulations and guidelines being implemented to ensure workplaces prioritise psychosocial safety.

3. **Technological Advancements**

   ▸ Technology plays a critical role in shaping the future of psychosocial safety. Digital tools and platforms are being developed to help organisations monitor, assess, and improve the psychosocial environment. For example, employee wellness apps and anonymous reporting systems enable real-time feedback and support, fostering a safer workplace culture.

Emerging Trends in Psychosocial Safety

Several key trends are shaping the future of psychosocial safety, providing organisations with new opportunities to enhance their practices and policies.

1. **Holistic Well-Being Programs**

   ▸ Organisations are increasingly adopting holistic approaches to employee well-being, recognising that psychosocial safety is interlinked with physical health, mental health, and overall life satisfaction. Comprehensive well-being programs that address all these aspects are becoming more common, promoting a more balanced and supportive work environment.

2. **Proactive Risk Management**

   ▶ Rather than reacting to issues as they arise, forward-thinking organisations are adopting proactive risk management strategies. This involves regularly assessing psychosocial risks, implementing preventive measures, and fostering a culture of continuous improvement. By identifying potential issues early, organisations can mitigate risks before they escalate.

3. **Inclusive and Diverse Workplaces**

   ▶ Diversity, equity and inclusion (DE&I) are integral to psychosocial safety. As organisations strive to create more inclusive workplaces, they must also address the unique psychosocial needs of diverse employee groups. Tailoring support and resources to meet these needs is essential for fostering an environment where everyone feels valued and safe.

4. **Remote and Hybrid Work Models**

   ▶ The shift toward remote and hybrid work models, accelerated by the COVID-19 pandemic, has significant implications for psychosocial safety. Organisations must adapt their strategies to ensure that remote employees receive the same level of support and protection as those working on-site. This includes fostering virtual team cohesion, providing remote mental health resources, and ensuring clear communication channels.

Innovative Practices in Psychosocial Safety

To stay ahead in the evolving landscape of psychosocial safety, organisations must embrace innovative practices that go beyond traditional approaches.

1. **Psychosocial Safety Leadership Training**

   ▸ Leadership plays a crucial role in shaping workplace culture. Providing leaders with specialised training on psychosocial safety equips them with the skills and knowledge to create supportive and inclusive environments. This training should cover topics such as active listening, empathy, conflict resolution, and fostering open communication.

2. **Employee-Led Initiatives**

   ▸ Empowering employees to take an active role in promoting psychosocial safety can lead to more effective and sustainable outcomes. Employee-led initiatives, such as peer support networks and wellness committees, encourage a sense of ownership and collective responsibility for creating a safe workplace.

3. Data-Driven Approaches

   ▸ Leveraging data and analytics allows organisations to gain deeper insights into the psychosocial environment and identify areas for improvement. Regular surveys, feedback mechanisms, and predictive analytics can help organisations track progress, measure the impact of interventions, and make informed decisions.

The Imperative for Long-Term Commitment

Creating a psychosocially safe workplace requires a sustained and long-term commitment from organisations. This commitment involves integrating psychosocial safety into all aspects of the organisation, from strategic planning to daily operations.

1. **Integrating Psychosocial Safety into Organisational Strategy**

   ▶ Psychosocial safety should be a core component of an organisation's strategic plan. This involves setting clear goals and objectives, allocating resources, and establishing metrics to measure progress. By embedding psychosocial safety into the organisational strategy, leaders demonstrate their commitment to prioritising employee well-being.

2. **Continuous Improvement and Adaptation**

   ▶ The journey toward a psychosocially safe workplace is ongoing. Organisations must continually assess their practices, gather feedback, and adapt to changing circumstances. This approach ensures that psychosocial safety remains a dynamic and evolving aspect of the workplace.

3. **Celebrating Successes and Recognising Efforts**

   ▶ Recognising and celebrating achievements in psychosocial safety can motivate employees and reinforce positive behaviours. Regularly highlighting success stories, acknowledging the efforts of individuals and teams, and sharing best practices create a culture of appreciation and continuous improvement.

The Role of External Partnerships and Collaboration

Organisations do not have to navigate the journey toward psychosocial safety alone. Partnering with external experts, industry peers, and community organisations can provide valuable insights, resources, and support.

1. **Engaging with Industry Experts**

   ▸ Collaborating with experts in psychosocial safety, mental health, DFV support and organisational behaviour can help organisations develop and implement effective strategies. These experts bring specialised knowledge and experience, enabling organisations to address complex challenges more effectively.

2. **Building Networks and Communities of Practice**

   ▸ Participating in networks and communities of practice allows organisations to share experiences, learn from others, and stay updated on the latest trends and best practices. These collaborative spaces foster a sense of community and collective responsibility for advancing psychosocial safety.

3. **Leveraging Community Resources**

   ▸ Community organisations, such as mental health nonprofits and advocacy groups, offer valuable resources and support for promoting psychosocial safety. Partnering with these organisations can enhance the impact of workplace initiatives and provide employees with access to additional resources.

The Future of Psychosocial Safety: A Call to Action

The future of psychosocial safety in workplaces hinges on the collective efforts of organisations, leaders, and employees. By embracing the evolving landscape, adopting innovative practices, and committing to long-term strategies, organisations can create environments where everyone feels safe, supported, and empowered to thrive.

1. **Encouraging a Long-Term Commitment to Psychosocial Safety**

   ▶ The journey toward a psychosocially safe workplace is ongoing. Organisations must commit to continuous improvement, adapting to new challenges and opportunities as they arise. This long-term commitment is essential for creating a sustainable and resilient workplace culture.

2. **Call to Action**

   ▶ It is clear that psychosocial safety is not just a buzzword but a fundamental aspect of a healthy and productive workplace. The benefits of prioritising psychosocial safety extend beyond individual well-being, impacting organisational performance, employee engagement, and overall success. It is no longer a nice to have in Australia and many other countries globally but written into legislation. The time to act is now.

Key Takeaways

The increasing importance of embedding psychosocial safety as a core organisational value to meet the evolving needs of modern work environments. As mental health awareness grows and employees demand safer, more supportive workplaces, organisations must prioritise ongoing psychosocial safety initiatives to remain competitive. This includes integrating mental health resources, fostering open communication, and maintaining inclusive leadership practices. The future of psychosocial safety lies in a proactive, preventative approach that not only reduces risks but also enhances employee well-being, productivity, and organizational resilience in the face of emerging challenges.

Resources and References:

- Safe Work Australia. (2021). Model code of practice: Managing psychosocial hazards at work. Retrieved from https://www.safeworkaustralia.gov.au/

- World Health Organization (WHO). (2020). Mental health at work: Policy brief. Retrieved from https://www.who.int/

- Harvard Business Review. (2019). The case for psychological safety in the workplace. Retrieved from https://hbr.org/

- Australian Human Rights Commission (AHRC). (2020). Respect@Work: Sexual harassment national inquiry report. Retrieved from https://humanrights.gov.au/

- Beyond Blue. (2021). Heads up: Creating mentally healthy workplaces. Retrieved from https://www.beyondblue.org.au/

The Evolution of Psychosocial Safety in Workplaces

Encouraging a Long-Term Commitment to Psychosocial Safety

The journey toward creating psychosocially safe workplaces is ongoing and requires sustained commitment from all levels of an organisation. As we look to the future, it is essential to understand that psychosocial safety is not a one-time initiative but a continuous effort that evolves with the changing dynamics of the workplace. Here are key aspects to consider for fostering a long-term commitment to psychosocial safety.

Embedding Psychosocial Safety into Organisational Culture

For psychosocial safety to be genuinely effective, it must become an integral part of the organisation's culture. This involves:

- **Leadership Commitment:** Leaders must consistently demonstrate their commitment to psychosocial safety. This can be achieved by integrating psychosocial safety into the organisation's vision, mission, and values. Leaders should model the desired behaviours and provide the necessary resources to support psychosocial safety initiatives. Leadership commitment also involves recognising and addressing any psychosocial hazards that may arise, thus setting the tone for a culture that prioritises employee well-being.

- **Continuous Education and Training:** Regular training programs should be implemented to keep employees

informed about psychosocial safety practices and updates. This helps maintain awareness and equips employees with the skills needed to foster a safe and supportive work environment. Ongoing education ensures
that all employees, from new hires to seasoned professionals, remain aligned with the organisation's commitment to psychosocial safety.

- ❯ *Policy and Procedure Reviews:* Regularly reviewing and
  updating policies and procedures ensures they remain
  relevant and effective. This includes incorporating feedback from employees and adapting to new challenges
  and opportunities. An iterative approach to policy review helps organisations stay proactive in addressing
  emerging psychosocial risks and continuously improving their safety strategies.

Building a Supportive Infrastructure

Creating a supportive infrastructure is crucial for sustaining psychosocial safety in the workplace. This includes:

- ❯ *Support Systems:* Establishing support systems such as
  EAPs, mental health resources, and peer support networks provides employees with access to help when
  needed. These systems should be easily accessible and
  confidential to encourage employees to seek support
  without fear of stigma. Effective support systems also
  involve providing training for managers and supervisors
  on how to recognise and respond to signs of distress
  among employees.

- ❯ *Open Communication Channels:* Encouraging open communication channels where employees can voice their
  concerns and suggestions helps identify potential issues

early and fosters a culture of transparency and trust. Regular surveys, feedback sessions, and anonymous reporting mechanisms can facilitate this. Open communication not only helps in addressing immediate concerns but also promotes a culture of continuous improvement where employee input is valued and acted upon.

- *Monitoring and Evaluation:* Implementing robust monitoring and evaluation mechanisms allows organisations to track the progress of their psychosocial safety initiatives. This involves setting clear metrics, conducting regular assessments, and using the data collected to make informed decisions and improvements. By regularly measuring the impact of psychosocial safety efforts, organisations can identify areas for enhancement and ensure that their initiatives remain effective and relevant.

Promoting Employee Engagement and Ownership

Engaging employees in the process of creating and maintaining a psychosocially safe workplace is vital for long-term success. This can be achieved by:

- *Empowering Employees:* Encouraging employees to take an active role in promoting psychosocial safety fosters a sense of ownership and responsibility. This can be done through initiatives such as employee-led safety committees, suggestion programs, and involvement in policy development. Empowered employees are more likely to advocate for a safe and supportive work environment and to hold themselves and their peers accountable for maintaining high standards of conduct.

➤ *Recognising and Rewarding Efforts:* Acknowledging and rewarding employees who contribute to psychosocial safety initiatives reinforces the importance of these efforts and motivates others to participate. Recognition can take various forms, including awards, public acknowledgment, and incentives. Celebrating successes not only boosts morale but also highlights the tangible benefits of psychosocial safety initiatives, encouraging broader participation and commitment.

The Imperative for Psychosocial Safety

In today's rapidly evolving work environment, the need for psychosocial safety has never been more pressing. The challenges posed by globalisation, technological advancements, and changing workforce demographics necessitate a proactive approach to workplace safety and well-being. Psychosocial safety addresses these challenges by fostering a culture of respect, inclusivity, and support.

Moreover, the benefits of a psychosocially safe workplace extend beyond the individual employee to the organisation as a whole. Research has consistently shown that organisations that prioritise psychosocial safety experience higher levels of employee engagement, productivity, and retention. They also enjoy a positive reputation, which attracts top talent and enhances their competitive edge. Furthermore, a psychosocially safe workplace can significantly reduce the costs associated with turnover, absenteeism, and workplace conflicts, leading to substantial financial savings and improved organisational performance.

Taking Action

Creating a psychosocially safe workplace requires collective effort and unwavering commitment. Here are actionable steps that organisations can take to embark on this journey:

1. *Assess Your Current State:* Begin by conducting a comprehensive psychosocial safety audit to understand the existing strengths and areas for improvement. This involves gathering feedback from employees, reviewing policies and practices, and analysing workplace culture. An in-depth assessment provides a clear baseline from which to develop targeted and effective psychosocial safety strategies.

2. *Develop a Clear Strategy:* Based on the audit results, develop a clear and actionable psychosocial safety strategy. This strategy should include specific goals, objectives, and timelines. It should also outline the roles and responsibilities of various stakeholders. A well-defined strategy ensures that efforts are coordinated and that all members of the organisation are aligned with the goals of promoting psychosocial safety.

3. *Engage and Educate:* Engage all employees in the process by providing education and training on psychosocial safety. Ensure that everyone understands the importance of these initiatives and how they can contribute to a safe and supportive work environment. Comprehensive training programs should be tailored to different roles within the organisation, ensuring that everyone has the knowledge and skills necessary to uphold psychosocial safety standards.

4. *Implement and Monitor:* Implement the strategies and monitor progress regularly. Use the data collected to make necessary adjustments and improvements. Celebrate successes and learn from challenges to continuously enhance the effectiveness of psychosocial safety initiatives. Regular monitoring and evaluation help to ensure that initiatives are achieving their intended outcomes and that any issues are promptly addressed.

5. *Foster a Culture of Continuous Improvement:* Recognise that psychosocial safety is an ongoing process that requires continuous improvement. Stay informed about emerging trends and best practices. Be open to adopting new approaches that enhance workplace safety and well-being. A commitment to continuous improvement ensures that psychosocial safety initiatives remain relevant and effective in the face of changing workplace dynamics.

The Broader Impact of Psychosocial Safety

The benefits of psychosocial safety extend beyond the confines of individual organisations. When companies, organisations and Government Departments commit to fostering psychosocially safe environments, they contribute to broader societal well-being. Here are several ways in which this impact can be felt:

Enhancing Community Well-Being

Workplaces that prioritise psychosocial safety create a ripple effect that extends into the wider community. Employees who feel valued and supported are likely to bring these positive experiences into their personal lives, fostering healthier relationships and contributing to the well-being of their communities. Additionally, businesses that uphold high standards of psychosocial safety can inspire other organisations to follow suit, leading to a more widespread culture of care and support across industries.

Promoting Economic Stability

Psychosocially safe workplaces contribute to economic stability by reducing the costs associated with workplace-related stress and mental health issues. High levels of absenteeism, turnover, and healthcare expenses can place a significant financial burden on organisations and, by extension, on the economy. By addressing these issues proactively, companies can enhance their financial performance and contribute to a more stable and resilient economy.

Driving Innovation and Growth

A work environment that prioritises psychosocial safety fosters creativity, innovation, and growth. When employees feel safe to express their ideas and take risks without fear of negative repercussions, they are more likely to contribute innovative solutions and drive the company forward. This culture of openness and support can lead to breakthroughs in products, services, and processes, positioning the organisation as a leader in its field.

Strengthening Corporate Reputation

Organisations that demonstrate a genuine commitment to psychosocial safety can enhance their reputation among stakeholders, including customers, investors, and the general public. A positive reputation for prioritising employee well-being can attract top talent, foster customer loyalty, and build investor confidence. As more consumers and investors prioritise corporate social responsibility, companies that lead in psychosocial safety will have a competitive advantage.

Contributing to Public Health

By promoting psychosocial safety, organisations can play a vital role in supporting public health initiatives. Workplaces that prioritise mental health and well-being can help reduce the prevalence of stress-related illnesses and mental health disorders. This, in turn, alleviates the pressure on public health systems and contributes to overall societal health and well-being.

Looking Ahead: The Future of Work and Psychosocial Safety

As we look to the future, it is clear that psychosocial safety will continue to play a crucial role in shaping the workplace of tomorrow. Several emerging trends and developments are likely to influence the evolution of psychosocial safety practices:

The Rise of Remote and Hybrid Work

The COVID-19 pandemic has accelerated the adoption of remote and hybrid work models. While these arrangements offer flexibility and convenience, they also present unique challenges to psychosocial safety. Organisations will need to develop strategies to support the well-being of remote and hybrid workers, addressing issues such as social isolation, work-life balance, and the blurring of boundaries between work and personal life.

Advancements in Technology

Technological advancements, including artificial intelligence (AI) and machine learning, are transforming the workplace. These technologies have the potential to enhance psychosocial safety by enabling more effective monitoring and analysis of employee well-being. However, they also raise ethical considerations around privacy and data security. Organisations will need to navigate these complexities to leverage technology in ways that support, rather than undermine, psychosocial safety.

The Importance of Diversity, Equity and Inclusion

DE&I are integral components of psychosocial safety. As organisations become more diverse, they must create environments where all employees feel valued and included. This involves addressing systemic biases, promoting inclusive leadership, and ensuring that D&I principles are embedded in all aspects of organisational culture and practice.

A Focus on Sustainable Work Practices

Sustainability is becoming a key consideration for organisations worldwide. Psychosocial safety aligns with this focus by promoting sustainable work practices that prioritise the long-term well-being of employees. Sustainable work practices include fostering work-life balance, providing opportunities for continuous learning and development, and creating supportive and flexible work environments.

The Role of Leadership

Effective leadership is critical to the success of psychosocial safety initiatives. Future leaders will need to be adept at fostering a culture of care and support, demonstrating empathy, and leading by example. Leadership development programs should emphasise the importance of psychosocial safety and equip leaders with the skills needed to navigate the complexities of the modern workplace.

A Commitment to a Better Future

The journey toward creating psychosocially safe workplaces is an ongoing and evolving process that requires a collective commitment from all stakeholders. By embedding psychosocial safety into organisational culture, building a supportive infrastructure, and promoting employee engagement and ownership, organisations can create environments where employees thrive.

The broader impact of psychosocial safety extends beyond individual organisations, contributing to community well-being, economic stability, innovation, and public health. As we look to the future, it is clear that psychosocial safety will continue to play a crucial role in shaping the workplace of tomorrow.

By prioritising psychosocial safety, we not only enhance the quality of work life for employees but also drive organisational success and contribute to a better, more inclusive, and sustainable future. This commitment to psychosocial safety is not just a strategic imperative; it is a moral obligation that reflects our shared responsibility to care for one another and to create workplaces that are safe, supportive, and thriving for all.

Organisations are encouraged to take the insights and strategies shared in this book and apply them to their unique contexts. By doing so, they can create workplaces where employees feel valued, respected, and empowered to contribute their best.

As we move forward, let us reaffirm our commitment to psychosocial safety and take concrete steps to foster environments where everyone can flourish. Together, we can build a future where psychosocial safety is the foundation of every workplace, ensuring that all employees are valued, respected, and empowered to reach their full potential.

Comprehensive Psychosocial Safety Assessment Questionnaire

Is Your Workplace Psychosocially Safe?

Take the Assessment and Protect Your Organisation Now!

In today's complex and ever-changing work environment, the importance of psychosocial safety cannot be overstated. A safe workplace is not just about physical well-being; it's about fostering an environment where employees feel respected, valued, and supported. However, many organisations overlook critical aspects of psychosocial safety, leaving themselves vulnerable to toxic behaviours, increased turnover, and costly legal challenges.

Are you confident that your workplace policies and culture are truly safeguarding your employees?

Do you have the right strategies in place to address domestic and family violence, mental health issues, and other psychosocial hazards?

If you're uncertain, it's time to take action. Start by assessing your current state with our **Psychosocial Safety Assessment**. This comprehensive evaluation will help you identify gaps, weaknesses, and areas for improvement within your organisation.

Why Take the Assessment?

- ❱ **Protect Your People:** Ensure that your employees are working in an environment free from bullying, harassment, and other toxic behaviours.

- ❱ **Reduce Risk:** Address potential legal and financial risks by proactively implementing effective policies and procedures.

- ❱ **Enhance Reputation:** Build a positive company culture that attracts top talent and retains your best employees.

- ❱ **Boost Productivity:** Increase engagement, productivity, and overall business success.

What Does the Assessment Cover?

- ❱ **Existing Policies and Practices:** We'll help you identify what's working and where you may be falling short.

- ❱ **Employee Feedback:** Understand how your team really feels about their work environment.

- ❱ **Workplace Culture Analysis:** Dive deep into the underlying culture that may be contributing to hidden problems.

- ❱ **Domestic and Family Violence:** Evaluate the effectiveness of your support systems and procedures for dealing with DFV.

- ❱ **Mental Health Initiatives:** Assess your current efforts to support employee mental health and well-being.

Act Now – Don't Wait for a Crisis to Hit

The time to address psychosocial safety is before a crisis arises, not after. Waiting until an issue surfaces can lead to severe consequences, including employee burnout, increased absenteeism, and even costly litigation.

Take the first step toward creating a truly safe and supportive workplace.

Book a Consultation Today to discuss your assessment results and explore how our tailored services can help you build a resilient, thriving organisation.

Don't leave your workplace's psychosocial safety to chance. Be proactive, be prepared, and protect what matters most—your people and your company's future.

Scan the QR and complete the Safe Space Workplace Psychosocial Safety Assessment. Once completed, you'll receive a detailed report highlighting your priorities and key areas of focus to ensure a safe, compliant, and supportive environment within 48-hours.

Section 1: Organisational Culture and Leadership

1. **Leadership Commitment:**

    ❯ How would you rate your organisation's leadership commitment to promoting psychosocial safety?

    - Strongly Committed

    - Somewhat Committed

    - Neutral

    - Somewhat Uncommitted

    - Strongly Uncommitted

2. **Communication of Values:**

    ❯ How effectively does your leadership communicate the importance of psychosocial safety to all employees?

    - Very Effectively

    - Effectively

    - Neutral

    - Ineffectively

    - Very Ineffectively

3. **Role Modelling:**

    ❯ Do your leaders and managers model behaviours that support a psychosocially safe workplace?

    - Always

- ▸ Frequently

- ▸ Sometimes

- ▸ Rarely

- ▸ Never

4. **Inclusivity:**

   ❯ How inclusive is your organisation's culture in promoting diversity, equity, and inclusion?

   - ▸ Highly Inclusive

   - ▸ Somewhat Inclusive

   - ▸ Neutral

   - ▸ Somewhat Exclusive

   - ▸ Highly Exclusive

Section 2: Policies and Procedures

5. **Existing Policies:**

   ❯ Does your organisation have formal policies in place that address psychosocial safety?

   - ▸ Yes, comprehensive policies

   - ▸ Yes, basic policies

   - ▸ Yes, but need reviewing and updating

   - ▸ No, but we are planning to develop them

   - ▸ No, we do not have any

6. **Policy Awareness:**

⊙ Are employees aware of the existing policies related to psychosocial safety?

▸ Yes, all employees are aware

▸ Most employees are aware

▸ Some employees are aware

▸ Few employees are aware

▸ No, employees are not aware

7. **Confidentiality:**

⊙ How well do your policies ensure confidentiality for employees seeking support for psychosocial issues?

▸ Very Well

▸ Well

▸ Neutral

▸ Poorly

▸ Very Poorly

8. **Policy Effectiveness:**

⊙ How effective are your current policies in preventing and addressing psychosocial hazards?

▸ Very Effective

▸ Effective

▸ Neutral

- ▶ Ineffective

- ▶ Very Ineffective

Section 3: Employee Well-Being and Support

9. **Mental Health Resources:**

   ◉ Does your organisation provide adequate mental health resources and support for employees?

   - ▶ Yes, comprehensive resources

   - ▶ Yes, some resources

   - ▶ No, but we are planning to provide them

   - ▶ No, we do not provide any resources

10. **Support Systems:**

    ◉ How accessible are support systems (e.g., Employee Assistance Programs, counselling) to employees?

    - ▶ Very Accessible

    - ▶ Accessible

    - ▶ Neutral

    - ▶ Inaccessible

    - ▶ Very Inaccessible

11. **Work-Life Balance:**

    ◉ How would you rate your organisation's support for employees maintaining a healthy work-life balance?

- ‣ Excellent

- ‣ Good

- ‣ Neutral

- ‣ Poor

- ‣ Very Poor

12. **Stress Management:**

   ❯ How effective are your organisation's efforts in helping employees manage work-related stress?

   - ‣ Very Effective

   - ‣ Effective

   - ‣ Neutral

   - ‣ Ineffective

   - ‣ Very Ineffective

Section 4: Workplace Relationships and Dynamics

13. **Team Collaboration:**

   ❯ How well does your organisation promote teamwork and collaboration among employees?

   - ‣ Excellent

   - ‣ Good

   - ‣ Neutral

- ▹ Poor

- ▹ Very Poor

14. **Conflict Resolution:**

   ❯ How effective are your organisation's conflict resolution mechanisms?

   - ▹ Very Effective

   - ▹ Effective

   - ▹ Neutral

   - ▹ Ineffective

   - ▹ Very Ineffective

15. **Addressing Toxic Behaviour:**

   ❯ How effectively does your organisation address toxic behaviour and difficult personalities?

   - ▹ Very Effectively

   - ▹ Effectively

   - ▹ Neutral

   - ▹ Ineffectively

   - ▹ Very Ineffectively

16. **Respect and Inclusivity:**

   ❯ How would you rate the level of respect and inclusivity within your organisation?

   - ▹ Very High

- ▸ High

- ▸ Neutral

- ▸ Low

- ▸ Very Low

Section 5: Training and Development

17. Leadership Training:

◉ Does your organisation provide training for leaders on psychosocial safety and related topics?

- ▸ Yes, comprehensive training

- ▸ Yes, some training

- ▸ Yes, but not specialised training

- ▸ No, but we are planning to provide it

- ▸ No, we do not provide any training

18. Employee Training:

◉ How well are employees trained on recognising and addressing psychosocial hazards?

- ▸ Very Well

- ▸ Well

- ▸ Neutral

- ▸ Poorly

- ▸ Very Poorly

19. **Ongoing Development:**

 ▶ Does your organisation offer ongoing training and development programs related to psychosocial safety?

  ▸ Yes, regularly

  ▸ Occasionally

  ▸ No, but we are planning to start

  ▸ No, we do not offer any

20. **Awareness Campaigns:**

 ▶ How frequently does your organisation conduct awareness campaigns on mental health, DFV, and other psychosocial issues?

  ▸ Regularly

  ▸ Occasionally

  ▸ Rarely

  ▸ Never

Section 6: Evaluation and Continuous Improvement

21. **Monitoring Progress:**

 ▶ How regularly does your organisation monitor and evaluate the effectiveness of its psychosocial safety measures?

  ▸ Very Regularly

- ▸ Regularly

- ▸ Occasionally

- ▸ Rarely

- ▸ Never

22. **Feedback Mechanisms:**

⊙ How accessible are feedback mechanisms for employees to voice concerns or suggestions about psychosocial safety?

- ▸ Very Accessible

- ▸ Accessible

- ▸ Neutral

- ▸ Inaccessible

- ▸ Very Inaccessible

23. **Adaptation and Improvement:**

⊙ How responsive is your organisation to making changes based on feedback and evaluation results?

- ▸ Very Responsive

- ▸ Responsive

- ▸ Neutral

- ▸ Unresponsive

- ▸ Very Unresponsive

24. **Long-Term Commitment:**

- How committed is your organisation to maintaining and improving psychosocial safety in the long term?

  - Very Committed

  - Committed

  - Neutral

  - Uncommitted

  - Very Uncommitted

Section 7: DFV Awareness and Response

Introduction:

DFV can have significant impacts on both the victims and the workplace environment. This section of the questionnaire is designed to assess your organisation's awareness of DFV, the support systems in place, and the effectiveness of policies and procedures to address DFV in the workplace.

Understanding DFV and Its Impact:

25. **Awareness of DFV:**

- How aware are employees of the potential impacts of DFV on their colleagues and the workplace?

  - Very Aware

  - Aware

  - Neutral

  - Unaware

  - Very Unaware

26. **DFV Impact on Workplace:**

   ❯ How well does your organisation understand the impact that DFV can have on employee productivity, well-being, and overall workplace safety?

      ▸ Very Well

      ▸ Well

      ▸ Neutral

      ▸ Poorly

      ▸ Very Poorly

Policies and Support Systems:

27. **DFV Policies:**

   ❯ Does your organisation have specific policies in place to support employees affected by DFV?

      ▸ Yes, comprehensive DFV policies

      ▸ Yes, but they are limited

      ▸ No, but we are developing them

      ▸ No, we do not have any DFV policies

28. **Policy Communication:**

   ❯ How effectively are DFV-related policies communicated to employees?

      ▸ Very Effectively

      ▸ Effectively

- ▶ Neutral

- ▶ Ineffectively

- ▶ Very Ineffectively

29. **Support Mechanisms:**

❯ What level of support does your organisation provide to employees who may be experiencing DFV?

- ▶ Comprehensive support, including counselling, leave, and referral services

- ▶ Some support, but it is limited

- ▶ Minimal support

- ▶ No support currently

30. **Confidentiality for DFV:**

❯ How well does your organisation ensure confidentiality for employees who disclose experiencing DFV?

- ▶ Very Well

- ▶ Well

- ▶ Neutral

- ▶ Poorly

- ▶ Very Poorly

Training and Awareness:

31. **Employee Training on DFV:**

    ❯ Does your organisation provide training for employees on recognising the signs of DFV and understanding how to respond appropriately?

       ▸ Yes, regular and comprehensive training

       ▸ Yes, but it is infrequent

       ▸ No, but we are planning to offer it

       ▸ No, we do not provide this training

32. **Manager and Leader Training on DFV:**

    ❯ Are managers and leaders trained specifically on how to handle disclosures of DFV and support affected employees?

       ▸ Yes, comprehensive training

       ▸ Yes, but it is limited

       ▸ No, but we are planning to offer it

       ▸ No, we do not provide this training

33. **Awareness Campaigns:**

    ❯ How frequently does your organisation run awareness campaigns or provide information about DFV to employees?

       ▸ Regularly

       ▸ Occasionally

- ▸ Rarely

- ▸ Never

Response and Intervention:

34. **DFV Response Protocol:**

   ◉ Does your organisation have a clear protocol for responding to DFV disclosures, including referral to appropriate services?

   - ▸ Yes, a well-defined protocol

   - ▸ Yes, but it is not well-known

   - ▸ No, but we are developing one

   - ▸ No, we do not have a specific protocol

35. **Intervention Effectiveness:**

   ◉ How effective is your organisation in intervening and providing support when an employee discloses experiencing DFV?

   - ▸ Very Effective

   - ▸ Effective

   - ▸ Neutral

   - ▸ Ineffective

   - ▸ Very Ineffective

36. **Monitoring and Follow-Up:**

⟡ Does your organisation have a system for monitoring the well-being of employees who have disclosed DFV and providing ongoing support?

▸ Yes, a structured system is in place

▸ Yes, but it is informal

▸ No, but we are considering it

▸ No, we do not monitor or follow up

Creating a Safe Environment:

37. **Safe Spaces:**

⟡ How well does your organisation provide safe spaces for employees to discuss DFV concerns without fear of judgment or repercussions?

▸ Very Well

▸ Well

▸ Neutral

▸ Poorly

▸ Very Poorly

38. **Zero Tolerance for DFV-Related Harassment:**

⟡ Does your organisation enforce a zero-tolerance policy for any form of harassment or discrimination related to DFV?

▸ Yes, strictly enforced

▸ Yes, but enforcement is inconsistent

- No, we do not have a specific policy
- No, we have not considered it

39. **Supportive Work Environment:**

How would you rate the overall work environment in terms of supporting employees who may be affected by DFV?

- Very Supportive
- Supportive
- Neutral
- Unsupportive
- Very Unsupportive

Section 8: Identifying Service Needs

40. **Service Prioritisation:**

Which areas of psychosocial safety do you believe require the most attention in your organisation? (Select all that apply)

- Leadership and Culture
- Policies and Procedures
- Employee Well-Being and Support
- Workplace Relationships and Dynamics
- Training and Development
- Evaluation and Continuous Improvement

41. **Desired Services:**

> ❯ What types of services would you be most interested in to support your organisation's psychosocial safety? (Select all that apply)

    ▹ Comprehensive Psychosocial Safety Audit

    ▹ Policy and Procedure Development

    ▹ Leadership and Manager Training

    ▹ Employee Training and Awareness Programs

    ▹ DFV Support Training

    ▹ Conflict Resolution and Mediation Services

    ▹ Ongoing Support and Consultation

    ▹ Other: _____

Conclusion: Please review your responses to this questionnaire and consider the areas where your organisation could benefit from additional support. If you would like a detailed consultation or assistance in developing and implementing a psychosocial safety strategy, please contact us to discuss how we can help you achieve a safer, more inclusive workplace.

Sample Policies and Procedures

1. Policy on Psychosocial Safety

Objective: To provide a safe and supportive work environment that promotes the psychosocial well-being of all employees.

Scope: This policy applies to all employees, contractors, and visitors within the organisation.

Policy Statement:

- The organisation is committed to promoting a workplace environment that supports mental health and well-being.

- All employees are entitled to a work environment free from psychological hazards.

- Managers and leaders are responsible for implementing and maintaining this policy.

Procedures:

- Conduct regular assessments of psychosocial risks.

- Provide training for employees and managers on recognising and addressing psychosocial hazards.

- Establish clear reporting mechanisms for psychosocial safety concerns.

- Implement support systems, such as Employee Assistance Programs (EAPs).

2. DFV Support Policy

Objective: To provide a safe and supportive environment for employees experiencing domestic and family violence (DFV).

Scope: This policy applies to all employees within the organisation.

Policy Statement:

- The organisation is committed to supporting employees affected by DFV.

- Employees experiencing DFV will have access to confidential support and resources.

- The organisation will take appropriate steps to ensure the safety of affected employees in the workplace.

Procedures:

- Provide training for all employees on recognising and responding to DFV.

- Establish a confidential reporting system for DFV concerns.

- Offer flexible work arrangements and leave options for affected employees.

- Partner with external organisations to provide additional support and resources.

Training Materials and Resources

1. Psychosocial Safety Training Modules

Module 1: Introduction to Psychosocial Safety

- Definition and importance of psychosocial safety
- Key concepts and terminology

Module 2: Recognising Psychosocial Hazards

- Common psychosocial hazards in the workplace
- Signs and symptoms of psychosocial stress

Module 3: Strategies for Promoting Psychosocial Safety

- Best practices for creating a supportive work environment
- Techniques for stress management and resilience

Module 4: Responding to Psychosocial Safety Concerns

- Reporting and addressing psychosocial safety issues
- Providing support to affected employees

2. DFV Awareness and Response Training

Module 1: Understanding DFV

- Definition and types of domestic and family violence (DFV)
- Impact of DFV on employees and the workplace

Module 2: Recognising Signs of DFV

- Behavioural and physical indicators of DFV
- Communicating sensitively with affected employees

Module 3: Providing Support for DFV Survivors

- Creating a safe and supportive environment
- Internal and external resources for DFV support

Module 4: Confidentiality and Reporting Procedures

- Ensuring confidentiality and trust
- Steps for reporting DFV incidents

Resources for Organisations to Share

Implementing and sustaining psychosocial safety, addressing domestic and family violence (DFV), and promoting mental health and well-being in the workplace require ongoing effort and access to relevant resources. By leveraging the books, research articles, online resources, training programs, and support services listed below, organisations can create a safer, more supportive, and inclusive work environment for all employees.

These resources provide valuable support and information for promoting psychosocial safety, addressing DFV, and enhancing mental health and well-being initiatives in Australian workplaces.

By providing these comprehensive resources and references, organisations can further enhance their efforts in creating and maintaining psychosocially safe workplaces.

Books and Articles:

- *The fear-free organisation: Vital insights from neuroscience to transform your business culture* by Paul Brown, Joan Kingsley, and Sue Paterson

- *The psychologically safe workplace: Risk management strategies for mental health and well-being* by Dr. E. Kevin Kelloway, Dr. Karina Nielsen, and Dr. Jennifer K. Dimoff

- *Trauma-informed care in behavioural health services* by the Substance Abuse and Mental Health Services Administration (SAMSA)

- *Domestic Violence: Changing Culture Saving Lives* by Lisa McAdams

Research Papers:

- "Psychosocial risk factors and work-related stress" by the European Agency for Safety and Health at Work

- "The impact of workplace bullying on individual well-being: The moderating role of coping" by Ståle Einarsen and colleagues

- "Creating psychologically safe workplaces: The role of leadership and trust" by Amy Edmondson

Online Resources:

- Mental Health First Aid (www.mentalhealthfirstaid.org)

- National Institute for Occupational Safety and Health (NIOSH) – Workplace Safety and Health Topics (www.cdc.gov/niosh)

- Workplace Strategies for Mental Health (www.workplacestrategiesformentalhealth.com)

External Support Organisations:

- Employee Assistance Professionals Association (EAPA) (www.eapassn.org)

- National Domestic Violence Hotline (NDVH) (www.thehotline.org)

- International Association for Workplace Bullying and Harassment (www.iawbh.org)

Further Reading and Resources

Creating a psychosocially safe workplace and addressing issues such as domestic family violence (DFV) and mental health requires continuous learning and access to relevant resources. Below is a list of further reading materials and resources that can provide valuable insights and support for implementing and sustaining psychosocial safety initiatives in your organisation.

Books:

- *Domestic violence: Changing culture, Saving lives – A workplace guide for developing a culture of empathy and understanding* by Lisa McAdams

  - This comprehensive guide offers practical advice and strategies for creating a workplace culture that supports victims of DFV and fosters empathy and understanding.

- *The Fearless Organisation: Creating psychological safety in the workplace for learning, innovation, and growth* by Amy C. Edmondson

  - This book explores the concept of psychological safety and its importance in fostering a culture of innovation and learning within organisations.

- *Dare to lead: Brave work. Tough conversations. Whole hearts.* by Brené Brown

  - Brené Brown provides insights into how leaders can create a culture of courage and empathy, which are essential for psychosocial safety.

- *The bully-free workplace: Stop jerks, weasels, and snakes from killing your organisation* by Gary Namie and Ruth Namie

    - This book offers strategies for identifying and addressing workplace bullying, contributing to a safer and more respectful work environment.

Research Articles and Reports:

- "State of the American manager: Analytics and advice for leaders" by Gallup (2017)

    - This report provides data and insights into the impact of management on workplace culture and employee well-being.

- "Diversity wins: How inclusion matters" by McKinsey & Company (2020)

    - This report highlights the business case for diversity and inclusion, offering evidence on how inclusive cultures drive organisational success.

- "2021 WBI U.S. workplace bullying survey" by the Workplace Bullying Institute (WBI) (2021)

    - This survey provides statistics and insights into the prevalence and impact of workplace bullying in the United States.

Online Resources:

- Society for Human Resource Management (SHRM)

- SHRM offers a wealth of resources, including articles, toolkits, and webinars, on topics related to workplace culture, bullying, and harassment.

- Visit SHRM

- Workplace Bullying Institute (WBI)

  - WBI provides resources and support for individuals and organisations seeking to address workplace bullying and create healthier work environments.

  - Visit WBI

- Australian Human Rights Commission (AHRC)

  - AHRC offers resources and guidelines on workplace discrimination, harassment, and promoting a safe and inclusive work environment.

  - Visit AHRC

- Beyond Blue

  - Beyond Blue provides resources and support for mental health and well-being in the workplace, including training programs and toolkits.

  - Visit Beyond Blue

- Heads Up (an initiative of Beyond Blue to promote mentally healthy workplaces)

  - Visit Heads Up

- Black Dog Institute

  - Visit Black Dog Institute

- Safe Work Australia

  - Visit Safe Work Australia

- Australian Human Rights Commission (AHRC)

  - Visit the Australian Human Rights Commission

Training Programs and Workshops:

- Mental Health First Aid (MHFA)

  - MHFA offers training programs that teach participants how to identify, understand, and respond to signs of mental health issues in the workplace.

  - Visit MHFA

- Diversity Council Australia (DCA)

  - DCA provides training and resources on diversity and inclusion, helping organisations create more inclusive and equitable workplaces.

  - Visit DCA

- Safe Space Workplace

  - Safe Space Workplace offers customised training programs and consulting services to help organisations implement psychosocial safety and support systems for domestic family violence and mental health.

  - Visit Safe Space Workplace

Support Services:

- Lifeline Australia

  - Lifeline provides crisis support and suicide prevention services, offering immediate assistance and resources for individuals in distress.

  - Visit Lifeline

- 1800RESPECT

  - 1800RESPECT offers confidential information, counselling, and support services for people impacted by DFV.

  - Visit 1800RESPECT

- Employee Assistance Programs (EAPs)

  - Many organisations offer EAPs that provide confidential counselling and support services for employees dealing with personal or work-related issues.

Glossary of Key Terms and Concepts

A

⮞ **Absenteeism:** The frequent absence from work or other duty without good reason.

⮞ **Adaptation:** Adjustments made in response to changes in the work environment or new information.

B

⮞ **Bullying:** Repeated, unreasonable actions aimed at intimidating or undermining an individual or group.

C

⮞ **Conflict Resolution:** Methods and processes involved in facilitating the peaceful ending of conflict.

⮞ **Confidentiality:** Ensuring that information is accessible only to those authorised to have access.

D

⮞ **Domestic and Family Violence (DFV):** Patterns of behaviour used by one person to gain and maintain power and control over another in an intimate relationship.

⮞ **Disclosure:** The action of making new or secret information known.

E

❯ **Employee Well-Being:** The overall mental, physical, emotional, and economic health of employees.

❯ **Engagement:** The level of enthusiasm and dedication an employee feels toward their job.

F

❯ **Feedback:** Information provided as a response to a person's performance of a task, used as a basis for improvement.

G

❯ **Goals and Objectives:** Specific aims or intended outcomes set by an individual or organisation.

I

❯ **Inclusivity:** The practice or policy of including people who might otherwise be excluded or marginalised.

❯ **Intervention:** Actions taken to improve a situation, especially a medical disorder.

L

❯ **Leadership:** The action of leading a group of people or an organisation.

❯ **Legal Considerations:** The legal factors that must be taken into account in decision-making processes.

M

❯ **Mental Health:** A person's condition with regard to their psychological and emotional well-being.

- **Mediation:** Intervention in a dispute in order to resolve it.

O

- **Open Communication:** The free and open exchange of information within an organisation.

P

- **Performance:** The execution of an action or the ability to perform a task.

- **Policies:** A course or principle of action adopted or proposed by an organisation or individual.

- **Procedures:** An established or official way of doing something.

- **Psychosocial Safety:** Ensuring the psychological and social well-being of employees in the workplace.

R

- **Respect:** A feeling of deep admiration for someone or something elicited by their abilities, qualities, or achievements.

S

- **Safety:** The condition of being protected from or unlikely to cause danger, risk, or injury.

- **Stakeholders:** All the people or organisations that have an interest or investment in the success of a company or project.

- **Support Systems:** Networks of people who provide an individual with practical or emotional support.

T

⊙ **Teamwork:** The combined action of a group, especially when effective and efficient.

⊙ **Training:** The action of teaching a person a particular skill or type of behaviour.

⊙ **Turnover:** The rate at which employees leave a workforce and are replaced.

W

⊙ **Well-Being:** The state of being comfortable, healthy, or happy.

⊙ **Workplace Culture:** The character and personality of an organisation, including its values, beliefs, interactions, behaviours, and attitudes.

Index

D

- **Domestic and Family Violence (DFV):** Patterns of behaviour used by one person to gain and maintain power and control over another in an intimate relationship.

- **Disclosure:** The action of making new or secret information known.

E

- **Employee Engagement:** The level of enthusiasm and dedication an employee feels toward their job.

- **Employee Well-Being:** The overall mental, physical, emotional, and economic health of employees.

F

- **Feedback:** Information provided as a response to a person's performance of a task, used as a basis for improvement.

G

- **Goals and Objectives:** Specific aims or intended outcomes set by an individual or organisation.

H

- **Humour:** The quality of being amusing or comic, especially as expressed in literature or speech.

I

- **Inclusivity:** The practice or policy of including people who might otherwise be excluded or marginalised.

- **Intervention:** Actions taken to improve a situation, especially a medical disorder.

J

- **Job Satisfaction:** The level of contentment employees feel about their work, which can affect performance.

K

- **Key Concepts:** Essential ideas or principles that form the basis of understanding a subject.

- **Knowledge Sharing:** The exchange of information or understanding among individuals, teams, or organisations.

L

- **Leadership:** The action of leading a group of people or an organisation.

- **Legal Considerations:** The legal factors that must be taken into account in decision-making processes.

M

- **Mediation:** Intervention in a dispute in order to resolve it.

- **Mental Health:** A person's condition with regard to their psychological and emotional well-being.

- **Monitoring:** Regularly checking or tracking the performance or quality of something over time.

N

⬡ **Needs Assessment:** A systematic process for determining and addressing needs or gaps between current conditions and desired conditions.

O

⬡ **Objectives:** Specific, measurable steps that can be taken to meet a goal.

⬡ **Open Communication:** The free and open exchange of information within an organisation.

P

⬡ **Performance:** The execution of an action or the ability to perform a task.

⬡ **Policies:** A course or principle of action adopted or proposed by an organisation or individual.

⬡ **Presenteeism:** The practice of employees coming to work despite being unwell, distracted, or disengaged, which results in reduced productivity and performance.

⬡ **Procedures:** An established or official way of doing something.

⬡ **Psychosocial Hazards:** Aspects of work that have the potential to cause psychological or social harm.

⬡ **Psychosocial Safety:** Ensuring the psychological and social well-being of employees in the workplace.

Q

⬡ **Quality Assurance:** The maintenance of a desired level of quality in a service or product.

R

⊙ **Respect:** A feeling of deep admiration for someone or something elicited by their abilities, qualities, or achievements.

S

⊙ **Safety:** The condition of being protected from or unlikely to cause danger, risk, or injury.

⊙ **Stakeholders:** All the people or organisations that have an interest or investment in the success of a company or project.

⊙ **Support Systems:** Networks of people who provide an individual with practical or emotional support.

T

⊙ **Teamwork:** The combined action of a group, especially when effective and efficient.

⊙ **Training:** The action of teaching a person a particular skill or type of behaviour.

⊙ **Turnover:** The rate at which employees leave a workforce and are replaced.

U

⊙ **Understanding:** The ability to comprehend an issue, situation, or concept.

V

⊙ **Values:** The principles or standards of behaviour; one's judgement of what is important in life.

W

- **Well-Being:** The state of being comfortable, healthy, or happy.

- **Workplace Culture:** The character and personality of an organisation, including its values, beliefs, interactions, behaviours, and attitudes.

X

- **X-Factor:** A noteworthy special talent or quality.

Y

- **Yearly Review:** An annual assessment of progress, performance, or development.

Z

- **Zero Tolerance:** A policy of not allowing any violations of a rule or standard.

Reviews

In "Safe Spaces: Creating a Psychosocially Safe Workplace," Lisa tackles the complex and often misunderstood concept of psychological safety in the workplace. She distils these intricate issues into clear, actionable insights, making the book an essential read for anyone invested in fostering a healthier work environment.

Lisa emphasises that psychosocial safety is more than a legal and ethical obligation—it's vital for a thriving workplace culture. Her research is both robust and accessible, filled with real-world examples and case studies that connect theory to practice.

A standout feature is the psychosocial audit, a game changer for leaders and business owners. This tool, paired with a straightforward action plan, provides clear guidance for assessing and improving workplace culture. Lisa's exploration of coercive behaviours, particularly "micro" bullying tactics, is eye-opening. Her candid examination helps readers identify subtle issues that might otherwise go unnoticed.

Throughout the book, Lisa asserts that creating a psychologically safe workplace is not just aspirational; it's essential for driving sustainable financial results. Overall, "Safe Spaces" is a compelling guide rich with practical tools and insights, making it an invaluable resource for leaders and HR professionals aiming to create a thriving work environment. Highly recommended for anyone seeking to understand and implement psychosocial safety in their organisations.

Victoria Butt - Parity Consulting

Lisa McAdams' book, "Safe Spaces: Creating a Psychosocially Safe Workplace," provides a vital exploration of how inappropriate behaviours can undermine psychological safety in the workplace. Lisa emphasises that addressing these issues is essential for fostering a culture of respect, diversity, equity, inclusion, and empathy.

The book is well-structured, beginning with foundational concepts and moving into practical strategies for assessing and implementing psychosocial safety measures. Lisa effectively breaks down complex topics into accessible sections, making the material relevant for HR professionals and organisational leaders alike.

A significant strength of the book is its holistic approach to psychosocial safety. Lisa delves into both overt and subtle forms of workplace toxicity, including upward bullying—a critical issue that she addresses with depth. This chapter highlights how upward bullying can create a toxic environment, emphasising the need for open communication and support systems.

Real-world examples throughout the text illustrate key concepts, demonstrating both the consequences of neglecting psychosocial safety and the benefits of proactive measures. Lisa provides actionable advice for organisations to develop comprehensive safety plans, implement policies, and sustain a supportive workplace culture.

Overall, "Safe Spaces" is an important contribution to workplace psychology and management. Lisa has crafted a resource that not only informs but also empowers organisations to create environments where employees feel safe, valued, and supported. This book is essential reading for anyone committed to enhancing workplace culture and promoting psychological well-being.

Maureen Kyne – Upward Bullying Expert

In an era where the lines between work and home are increasingly blurred, this book offers a timely and essential guide to fostering psychosocially safe workplaces. As we navigate this new landscape, the role of the workplace has evolved dramatically, and the need for supportive, nurturing environments is more critical than ever.

Lisa McAdams highlights the importance of support, mentoring, and opportunities for learning and growth. Moreover, this book addresses the challenges of toxic workplaces, providing actionable insights on how to navigate and transform these environments. It empowers leaders and employees alike to recognize the signs of toxicity and take proactive steps toward change.

Overall, this book is a must-read for anyone looking to enhance their workplace environment. It offers valuable insights and strategies for creating a culture that prioritises people above all else, ensuring that employees feel valued, supported, and empowered to thrive.

Suzie Barnett – Two Good Co.

As the Founder of Mondo Search, having placed over 2800 leaders in business over 25 years and set up the Women's Resilience Centre, supporting women stepping out of domestic abuse and trauma in my experience the top reason employees leave organisations is a lack of support from their leadership team. This book is a "must-read" for all leaders who want to build a positively magnetic culture. In Safe Spaces: Creating a Psychosocially Safe Workplace, Lisa McAdams offers a timely and essential guide for leaders fostering significant and impactful best practice culture leadership in their organisations. McAdams outlines practical strategies and case studies addressing key challenges such as covert and overt unsafe behaviours, unresolved trauma, and toxic behaviours. Her insights and findings taught me new approaches and innovations.

Simone Allan – Women's Resilience Centre

What an important message you're raising awareness about. Your passion shines through your writing! I think the book is really informative, well-structured and allows the reader to learn from the case studies as well as reflect on their current culture.

Alison Flemming, Mirvac

Milton Keynes UK
Ingram Content Group UK Ltd.
UKHW020048271124
451585UK00012B/1120

9 780648 318521